AKERS'
Simple Library Cataloging

7th edition

Completely revised and rewritten

by

ARTHUR CURLEY

and

JANA VARLEJS

The Scarecrow Press, Inc.
Metuchen, N.J., & London
1984

All catalog cards in this volume, whether printed or typed,
are reproduced at 75 per cent of actual size.

Library of Congress Cataloging in Publication Data

Akers, Susan Grey, 1889–
    Akers' Simple library cataloging.

    Includes index.
    1. Cataloging. I. Curley, Arthur. II. Varlejs,
Jana. III. Title. IV. Title: Simple library
cataloging.
Z693.A52 1984   025.3   83–14423
ISBN 0–8108–1649–0

CONTENTS

iii

Appendices:

iv

ACKNOWLEDGMENTS

If Susan Grey Akers could read this, the seventh edition of her Simple Library Cataloging, we are not sure that she would recognize more than the occasional page or paragraph. It is our hope, however, that she would find the spirit of the book consistent with that of its predecessors, especially since she felt that small could be beautiful, and that even the littlest library could provide good access to its collection through the catalog. Concern for the library patron and for the usefulness of the catalog was her guiding principle for the first five editions of this work. We value the example she set, and have tried to follow it.

In preparing this edition, the authors have relied on the help and advice of many librarians. They owe a special debt, however, to two people. John Philip Mulvaney contributed to the revision of the classification and subject heading chapters while he was a student at the Rutgers Graduate School of Library and Information Studies (he is now in charge of technical services at Juniata College in Pennsylvania). Elizabeth Mikita, currently a cataloger at Thomas Jefferson University, was the indispensable assistant for much of the rest of the book, keeping us in line with AACR2, finding many of the new examples used, and revising the glossary.

We also wish to thank the various commercial cataloging services for their cooperation, especially Baker & Taylor, and Barbara Lee for compiling the index.

What is simple library cataloging? Is it watered down, com-
promisingly abridged, haphazard? Not at all. Just as a
"simple" explanation--simple in the sense that it is clear,
precise, and in terms understood by an intended audience--
can render a complex matter comprehensible, so simple library cataloging can be a system of organization that is clear,
precise, and suited to the needs of a specific institution and
its users.

Obviously, a small library with only three, four, or
even a dozen staff members would not wish to adopt the staff
organization chart of a very large institution with numerous
department heads, division coordinators, and deputy assistant
directors. Not only is such an organization pattern unnecessary in a small institution; its imposition would create chaos.
Similarly, most systems of cataloging and classification were
designed with the needs of large libraries in mind. Like the
organization chart, they need to be adapted and simplified to
be of maximum value to the smaller library. The objective
of simplification is certainly not compromise with the quality
of cataloging; rather, it is the improvement of library service through more efficient cataloging and processing procedures.

The small library may serve fewer users than its
larger counterparts, but the informational needs of any of
its patrons, taken individually, may be just as considerable
as the needs of those who belong to a larger community or
institution. Precisely because its resources are limited, the
small library must strive for excellence in providing access
to the materials it does possess. In fact, its very small-
ness may permit some forms of excellence which would be
unattainable in most larger institutions. Just as the small
library can give greater personal attention to its clientele,
so it can give greater attention to the precision and accuracy
with which its materials collections are organized. The manageable number of collections (of plays and short stories, for

1

example) and of multi-volume sets in such institutions often
makes possible close analysis of contents and other special
user services; even more so, since the small library can
usually forego the extensive bibliographic description required
by complex cataloging codes to identify uniqueness of edition.
And, of course, the small specialized library may be as
strong as many a large library in its own areas of concentration and contain materials in a greater variety of formats,
yet need the advantages of simplified cataloging procedures
since its staff is too small to include an extensive technical
services section.

Consistency in cataloging practice, involving adaptation to changes in classification and subject-heading authority
files, is often much more feasible in the small library than
in the large, where even minor changes in a new edition of
the Dewey Decimal Classification, for example, can affect so
many thousands of volumes cataloged by the rules of earlier
editions as to render retrospective adjustment virtually impossible. Moreover, since "simple" library cataloging reduces the degree of subdivision both in classification numbers
and in subject headings, it reduces even further the extent to
which changes in national cataloging practices threaten consistency in the collections and catalogs of small libraries
which do so simplify. When simplification is judiciously
applied, then frequently--in the words of Mies van der Rohe
--"less is more."

In developing a catalog for a particular library one
needs to consider the community or institution which is to be
served. Is it growing or shrinking? What is the present
size of the library? Its probable future size? Is it likely
to become part of a larger cooperative system in the near
future? In deciding upon what materials to acquire, what
records to keep, what methods to use, are there any special requirements that might affect them? For instance, in
a school or college library, what courses are offered? Does
a library have to submit reports to a central agency, such
as a state library, the city or county superintendent of
schools? Does a library receiving funds from a special
source have to keep an inventory of the disbursement of those
funds in a prescribed way? What information is required for
reports to these external agencies?

The use to be made of the materials and the best
ways of serving the library's clientele are the first considerations in deciding upon the type of cataloging. Costs and

time, however, must also be considered. It is not worthwhile to develop a plan which will require a larger staff and
involve higher costs than are available or likely to become
so, or which will absorb so much of the present staff's time
that other library services are neglected. Adopt the simplest
plan for control of material which will meet the needs of the
library's clientele now and in the foreseeable future. Materials should be prepared and put out for use as soon as
possible after they are received. For example, a book,
pamphlet, or map which would be of significant use in a
course if it is made available this week may be of little or
no value if it becomes available only after a delay of weeks
or months. Simplification or streamlining of cataloging procedures is essential in small or understaffed libraries. On
the other hand, a system which simplifies to the extent that
it does not distinguish clearly between materials, or one that
creates work which will have to be done over as the library
grows, is not a good system. Time and money saved in organizing materials in such a way that reference work is ob-
structed and users frustrated are not really an economy. A
good system for one library may not be a good system for
another library, because of different conditions. But the importance of cooperation among libraries and the value of
many centralized services are strong arguments for reasonable consistency in cataloging and classification practices.
Also, our patrons must sometimes use other libraries--par-
ticularly young patrons as they advance through school--and
their ability to do so effectively is enhanced if the libraries
are organized according to common rational patterns.

A catalog is a concise index to the varied materials
in a library. It answers such questions as: What books
have you by John Updike? Do you have a recording of Beethoven's ninth symphony? Have you material on the Navajo
Indians? The catalog can also answer questions about the
individual author or book; for instance: What is the most
recent book in the library by Kurt Vonnegut? Does Carl
Sagan's Cosmos include illustrations? Who published The
Next Whole Earth Catalog? Besides showing what authors'
works are represented in the library, whether or not the
library has material on a given subject or contains a particular book, whether or not a certain book has illustrations,
and so forth, the catalog may bring out portions of books;
for example, it may tell the patron that High Tor is to be
found in Barrett H. Clark's Nine Modern American Plays,
and that material on Halloween is included in J. Walker
McSpadden's The Book of Holidays. The catalog also tells
where in the library an item is located.

The catalog in most libraries consists of cards containing the information required to answer questions such as the ones in the examples above. (Book, computer output microform, and online catalogs are other ways of presenting the same information in different formats, but the cataloging principles are the same and the procedures followed, at least in the initial stages of preparing the catalog, are the same.) Each item owned by the library is represented in the catalog by several entries, so that whether a patron looks under Sagan, under <u>Cosmos</u>, or under astronomy, there will be a catalog record for Carl Sagan's book, <u>Cosmos.</u> In other words, the book has been "entered" under three "headings": author, title, and subject:

```
    Sagan, Carl.
      Cosmos / Carl Sagan. -- New York : Random
    House, c1980.
      365 p. : ill. ; 26 cm.
```

```
      Cosmos.
    Sagan, Carl.
      Cosmos / Carl Sagan. -- New York : Random
    House, c1980.
      365 p. : ill. ; 26 cm.
```

```
      ASTRONOMY.
    Sagan, Carl.
      Cosmos / Carl Sagan. -- New York : Random
    House, c1980.
      365 p. : ill. ; 26 cm.
```

A book may also be sought under the name of a series of which it is a part, under a joint author, under an illustrator, etc., and added entries for these or other headings under which a patron might look should be included in the catalog. In addition to the entries for specific books there are references referring the user from a form of the author's name under which he or she may look to the form used in the catalog:

```
            Mertz, Barbara

              see

        Michaels, Barbara
        Peters, Elizabeth
```

There are also entries referring the user from the term or terms under which he or she may search for material on a subject to the term or terms used in the catalog for that subject:

```
                    GUIDANCE

                      see

                    COUNSELING
```

All of these entries--author, title, subject, added entry, analytical, and reference--when interfiled in alphabetical order constitute a dictionary catalog.

In the fifth edition of this book, the last written by Susan Grey Akers, she explained that the book's purpose was "three-fold":

1) to give the librarian of the small public, school, college, or special library who lacks professional education and experience under expert guidance the necessary directions for classifying and cataloging a collection of printed and audiovisual materials, that they may be made accessible;
2) to serve as a textbook for short elementary courses in cataloging; and
3) to serve as collateral reading in the earlier parts of the basic cataloging courses

She went on to state:

Fundamental rules for classifying and directions for using the Dewey Decimal Classification tables are given. An effort has been made to state the

necesary cataloging rules as clearly, simply, and briefly as possible. No attempt has been made to suggest all the possible ways of cataloging a small library.[1]

The purpose of this seventh edition remains much the same. The book does not treat Library of Congress classification or subject headings (or other systems), nor does it attempt to explain how to search, edit, or input machine readable records in an online environment. The impact of computers on cataloging is discussed, however, and the reader is alerted to the effect that automation is having and will continue to have on even the smallest library catalogs.

The discussions of descriptive cataloging rules, classification, and subject headings, and most of the examples reflect the second edition of the Anglo-American Cataloguing Rules, the eleventh edition of Sears List of Subject Headings, and the eleventh edition of the Abridged Dewey Decimal Classification.

Occasionally, more detail is given than may be needed by most small libraries. The authors feel that it is important for catalogers to understand the AACR2 descriptive rules in order to be able to interpret the cataloging records provided by centralized services and to have a firm basis for decisions about choosing outside cataloging services or simplifying inhouse cataloging. Also, the librarian who understands the basic principles of how material is entered in a catalog will be better able to help patrons use the library's catalog. Increasingly, as multitype cooperatives are formed for the purpose of sharing automated library systems, small libraries have opportunities to participate. The more closely that their catalogs adhere to the standards used for bibliographic records nationally, the easier it will be for small libraries to enter into cooperative projects that will ultimately offer greater efficiency and better service to the user.

Reference

1. Susan Grey Akers, Simple Library Cataloging (Metuchen, N.J.: Scarecrow Press, 1969), pp. 6-7.

Chapter 1

The basic need for inventory control in any library requires some descriptive enumeration of the books, periodicals, films, sound recordings, manuscripts, or other items which the library acquires. Such a listing might take the form of a simple accession register, a file of inventory (shelf-list) cards, or even a microcomputer "floppy disk," and consist of little more than abbreviated indication of author and/or title plus, optimally, an inventory number. In even its briefest form a descriptive list of this nature would satisfy most dictionary definitions of a "catalog"; and, it might actually constitute the only catalog record necessary for a small collection intended for no more complicated function than that of browsing. Such an instrument would, of course, hardly serve the many bibliographic, research, and informational needs for which staff and clientele turn regularly to a library's catalog. Nonetheless, provision of descriptive information adequate to the identification of an item in a library's collections, and its differentiation from other items, is the first purpose of library cataloging.

This point may seem an obvious one, but it bears stressing. Most libraries will wish to provide much more information on a catalog card than simple inventory descriptors, but how much more and how precisely honed are important matters of policy meriting careful analysis of institutional mission, user needs, and relationships with other libraries, as well as budget and personnel resources available. The quality and the cost of access to information are too dependent on sound cataloging policies for the latter to be defined, de facto, either by haphazard practices or by slavish adherence to arcane details of a cataloging code--which may have been designed to meet the needs of a very different type of library--in the mistaken belief that cataloging is a mystical business of dogmatic "rights" and "wrongs."

On the other hand, few libraries should seriously

7

consider the practice of "original" cataloging for more than a small percentage of the collection in this age of readily and inexpensively available cataloging copy through cooperative or commercial sources. For reasons of both economy and quality, most libraries will seek whenever possible to "buy" rather than create catalog copy, and to avoid the prohibitive costs of wholesale revision will usually conclude that the advantages of general conformity to national standards outweigh the benefits of local autonomy in cataloging matters.

But even the library which regularly acquires Library of Congress catalog cards, or has access to an OCLC terminal, or belongs to a regional processing center, or dutifully copies "Cataloging in Publication" data from the title-page verso, will confront not only the need for informed scrutiny and judicious adaptation of cataloging copy thus received but, as well, an ever-mounting backlog of back-room items for which cataloging copy is simply not available, or else not appropriate. In the small yet highly specialized library, it is to be expected that many items will demand original cataloging; however, even the small general library will regularly acquire works for which existing catalog copy cannot be found, in such categories as local history, annual reports and corporate publications, archives of local government or a parent institution, some older materials obtained through gift or retrospective purchase, and an elusive host of others. In addition, precisely because its resources are slim, the service-conscious small library may well choose to supplement the regular collections by cataloging pamphlets and government documents on popular or important topics and by providing directly through the catalog access to portions of larger works, such as plays and short stories in anthologies. Then again, for reasons of speed and economy, some libraries may decide to create their own simplified catalog cards for fiction, popular biographies, paperback books, certain categories of children's books, or popular materials of short life-expectancy. If, for example, a library must provide (and constantly replace) numerous copies of a standard work which exists in several different publishers' editions, much time spent in filing, altering, and withdrawing catalog cards can be saved by having just one simplified descriptive entry to represent all copies; this is appropriate, of course, only if the need to be met is such (as is the case with many school reading assignments) that differentiation among editions is not important.

A sound knowledge of cataloging principles is important,

then, not just in order to perform cataloging functions, but to develop a framework of cataloging policies appropriate to a given library.

The way in which the body of information on a catalog card is organized is important for many reasons. Major arguments need hardly be mounted to suggest the inefficiency of reliance on memory or whim to determine what information to include and from what sources, choice of form and terminology, and order in which presented. Consistency, however, is not an end in itself (except, as Emerson said, for little minds); it is essential to the precision required for that purpose of cataloging already cited: identification of an item in a library's collections and its differentiation from other items. There is, also, a corollary purpose of the first importance: providing access to items in the collection. Since catalog entries, or "points of access," must be extracted from the assembled body of descriptive information, the form of a title or an author's name to be used should be based upon a consistent code of cataloging rules--if the catalog is to be an effective means of access.

Fortunately, the gargantuan task of creating such a code does not fall upon the individual library. Development of consistent cataloging principles has been for some time the focus of national, and international, efforts.

The latest product of these efforts, formally promulgated in 1978 but not implemented nationally until 1981, is the Anglo-American Cataloguing Rules, Second Edition, popularly and universally known as AACR2.[1] The principles and rules enunciated in this comprehensive document will influence profoundly, if not dictate, the cataloging practices of nearly every library. No, there is no law which requires any library to abide by its prescriptions; but, it has been adopted as the basic authority for descriptive cataloging as well as forms of entry by the Library of Congress and virtually every other major source of cataloging copy. In a truly massive computer project, OCLC converted seven million cataloging records to AACR2 format. Many major libraries simply "froze" their pre-AACR2 catalogs and began anew. Any library can--and in some instances should-- diverge in practice from this or that particular rule; nonetheless, AACR2 now constitutes an inescapable framework for cataloging practices throughout the English-speaking world.

The cataloger in a small library needs to understand

the basic principles of AACR2 (there is now also an abridged
edition [2]), and to treat its rules as a framework, not as
an inflexible set of commandments. While many AACR2 rules
are ideally suited to even the smallest library, some fundamental assumptions of the code reflect primarily the needs
of major research libraries in an age of computers and international cooperation. This is appropriate, even laudable, but
it does present the small library with certain challenges of
adaptation; and AACR2 does attempt to address that reality to
the extent that it permits different levels of description and
strives in some sections to be non-prescriptive.

In 1876, Charles Ami Cutter published a set of "Rules
for a Printed Dictionary Catalog, " [3] announcing as their
purpose:

1. To enable a person to find a book of which either
       the author,
       the title, or
       the subject is known.
2. To show what the library has
       by a given author,
       on a given subject, and
       in a given kind of literature.
3. To assist in the choice of a book
       as to its edition (bibliographically).
       as to its character (literary or topical).

The American Library Association's Catalog Rules:
Author and Title Entries [4] of 1908 differed little from the
essentials of Cutter's rules, which had been developed primarily with the book collections of public libraries in mind,
but subsequent editions revealed two different trends: increasing simplification, from the perspective of public access,
resulting from standardization of forms of entry and authority
control; but, also, increasing adaptation to the complex scope
of research library resources. The Paris Principles [5] of
1961, the product of a major multi-national conference of cataloging experts, contributed significant impetus to international standardization. But pressures to reflect traditional
national practices still remained sufficiently strong as to require separate British and North American texts in 1967 of
the first Anglo-American Cataloging Rules, [6] as well as
numerous options and alternatives within the rules themselves.
Even so, the Library of Congress (and therefore most other
American libraries) adopted AACR (1) with a major compromise, known as "superimposition, " whereby only newly estab-

lished headings would be affected by the new rules but already established headings would continue to be used. Considering the magnitude of changing a single entry such as "Great Britain" to "United Kingdom," one can well understand the resistance.

Internationalism would soon prevail, nonetheless. From the 1969 International Meeting of Cataloging Experts, in Copenhagen, there emerged the concept of an International Standard Bibliographic Description (ISBD) [7]; and by 1974, joint planning among the national libraries, as well as the national library associations, in Canada, Great Britain, and the United States had paved the way for agreement on development of a truly unified code of descriptive cataloging.

It is interesting to note that the Paris Principles of 1961 ascribe to the library catalog a purpose not strikingly different from that of 1876 vintage, cited above:

> The catalogue should be an efficient instrument for ascertaining
>
> 1. whether the library contains a particular book specified by
>   (a) its author and title, as printed in the book, or
>   (b) if no author is named in the book, its title alone, or
>   (c) if author and title are inappropriate for identification, some other significant characteristics;
> 2. which works by a particular author and which editions of a particular work are in the library.

This statement from the Paris Principles contains two subtle shifts of emphasis, however, which would assume major significance in AACR2: a movement away from the primacy of "authorship"; and a greater reliance on the physical item in hand, as the source of bibliographic data, rather than on external sources of standardization.

AACR2 represents a more radical break with past practice than did any previous code. That this should be so can be better understood if one considers the extent to which its objectives differed from those of previous codes. They include:

> a) reflect developments in machine processing of bibliographic records.

b) conform to the International Standard Bibliographic Description (ISBD) as a basis for the bibliographic description of monographs and to the principle of standardization in the bibliographic description of all types of materials.
c) maintain general conformity with the Paris Principles of 1961.
d) reconcile in a single text the North American and British texts of 1967.

Charles Ami Cutter and Susan Grey Akers would, indeed, be surprised. But librarians in small to medium-sized academic, public, school, and special libraries should not be surprised that a cataloging code which proceeded from such considerations does not, in all respects, reflect the needs of their libraries.

References

1. Anglo-American Cataloguing Rules; Second Edition. (Chicago: American Library Association, 1978).
2. Michael Gorman, The Concise AACR2. (Chicago: American Library Association, 1981).
3. Charles Ami Cutter, "Rules for a Printed Dictionary Catalogue," in Public Libraries in the United States of America: Their History, Condition, and Management. (Washington, D.C.: Government Printing Office, 1876).
4. American Library Association. Catalog Rules, Author and Title Entries. (Boston: A.L.A. Publishing Board, 1908).
5. Statement of Principles Adopted at the International Conference on Cataloguing Principles, Paris, October 1961; annotated edition. (London: IFLA Committee on Cataloguing, 1971).
6. Anglo-American Cataloging Rules; North American Text. (Chicago: American Library Association, 1967).
7. ISBD(M): International Standard Bibliographic Description for Monographic Publications. (London: IFLA Committee on Cataloguing, 1974).
   ISBD(G): General International Standard Bibliographic Description; annotated text. (London: IFLA International Office for UBC, 1977).

Chapter 2

<u>DESCRIPTIVE INFORMATION</u>

Descriptive cataloging consists of two major parts: 1) description of the book (or other item) as a physical object; 2) determination of "access points," or "headings" to be used in the catalog. A major change which AACR2 has wrought is reversal of the traditional order of treatment. The reasons put forward by the editors of AACR2 are worth noting:

> The order of the major parts of previous cataloguing rules (AA 1908 as well as AACR 1) showed that the cataloguing process was viewed in terms of the premachine cataloguing entry--that is, that the first task of the cataloguer was to establish the main entry heading and its consequent added entries and then make the description. That description was modified in light of the decisions made on headings (see, for example, the rules in both codes on statements of authorship and imprint). This produced an entry that was adapted to card or book catalogues based on the main entry principle but was largely unsuited to any newer forms, and completely unsuited to developed machine-readable records with their multiplicity of uses. The overall structure of AACR 2 is designed to recognize the multiple-use bibliographic record. The first task of the cataloguer is conceived of as establishing a standard and self-sufficient set of descriptive data relating to the physical object being catalogued (book, motion picture, sound recording, etc.). The second task is conceived of as providing name and title access points (headings and uniform titles) to permit retrieval of the standard description.[1]

The small library concerned with preparing a catalog card as quickly and efficiently as possible, rather than with developing a machine-readable multiple-use record, will most likely continue to establish author and/or title headings first

13

and then proceed in order down the card. But, the AACR2 order will be presented here in order that the principles may be better understood.

The description should include such information as is necessary to distinguish the book from all other books, even different editions of the same work, and should include its scope, contents, and bibliographic relationships. This data should be presented as simply and concisely as possible and in the same form and order for all books. The basis for this description is the title page of the book and what can be gained from an examination of the book itself. Stated more simply, the purpose of cataloging is to identify the book and to distinguish it from all other books and even other editions of the same work.

A decision about the extent of descriptive cataloging is not merely a matter of following established rules for such cataloging, but is a major administrative decision affecting costs and quality of library service. On the one hand, much information about the physical characteristics of a volume (essential in a rare book library) serves little purpose in the small school or public library. On the other hand, a small library with limited reference resources is very dependent on the catalog as a reference tool. A library lacking the complete Cumulative Book Index (CBI) as well as comprehensive indexes to plays, short stories, poems, etc. in collections will depend upon the catalog for information about "contents" of books to a far greater extent than will the larger library with an extensive collection of indexes and bibliographies. Also, where the shelves are open to the readers, many readers will spend little time at the catalog looking at the cards. However, even in the smallest library, the catalog may be called upon to answer some questions about a book which is out in circulation; and in looking for material on a subject the reader will sometimes examine all the cards before going to the shelves, considering the author, publisher, date and length of the books.

AACR2 provides for three different levels of description. Most small general libraries will find the first most appropriate, and will choose an even simpler level for some categories of materials. The second level has been adopted by the Library of Congress and is also reprinted here so that the organization of the typical LC catalog card may be better understood, and since small libraries with specialized collections or special bibliographic needs will require elements of

level two description. The third level provides for the most comprehensive descriptive information, required only by a major research or rare book collection.

Here are the first two AACR2 levels of description:

First level of description. For the first level of description, include at least the elements set out in this schematic illustration:

> Title proper / first statement of responsibility, if different from main entry heading in form or number or if there is no main entry heading. — Edition statement. — Material (or type of publication) specific details. — First publisher, etc., date of publication, etc. — Extent of item. — Note(s). — Standard number.

Second level of description. For the second level of description, include at least the elements set out in this schematic illustration:

> Title proper ₁general material designation₁ = parallel title : other title information / first statement of responsibility ; each subsequent statement of responsibility. — Edition statement / first statement of responsibility relating to the edition. — Material (or type of publication) specific details. — First place of publication, etc. : first publisher, etc., date of publication, etc. — Extent of item : other physical details ; dimensions. — (Title proper of series / statement of responsibility relating to series, ISSN of series ; numbering within the series. Title of subseries, ISSN of subseries ; numbering within subseries). — Note(s). — Standard number.

The first step in cataloging a book is to examine the title page, from which the librarian gets most of the information for the catalog entry. Besides the author and the title, the title page may give the author's degrees and other data, yet this information on the catalog card would not be of sufficient value to warrant the space it would take. The title page may also give a statement about the edition--as second edition or revised edition--and may specify how the book is illustrated. Then there is the imprint, that is, place of publication, publisher, and date of publication, given at the bottom of the title page. The librarian should examine not only the title page for the items mentioned but also the pages preceding the title page and the cover to see if the book belongs to a series, e.g., "The Rivers of America"; the back

JEFFERSON AND HIS TIME

VOLUME SIX

The Sage of
Monticello

BY DUMAS MALONE

With Illustrations

Boston

LITTLE, BROWN AND COMPANY

1981

of the title page (verso) for the copyright date; the colophon, if there is one, and the prefatory matter for further information regarding the edition; the table of contents for the list of works if the book includes a number of separate works, e. g. , plays; and the book itself: 1) for the extent of the item (formerly collation)--that is, the number of pages or volumes and illustrations, and 2) for bibliographies, appendices containing material of special value and other special features which should be brought out in the notes.

In some books, part of the title of the book, the author's name, or the place of publication or publisher's name spreads over two pages, facing each other. This is called a "double title page" or a "double-spread title page." The necessary information is taken from both pages, and no mention of this type of title page is needed in the catalog entry. Another kind of book it may be well to mention here is the book with more than one title page. In some instances there is an added title page for the series to which the book belongs, a special title page for a second volume, or a facsimile of the title page of an earlier edition. Catalog the book from the title page for the volume rather than the series, for the set rather than the volume; catalog from the printed title page if there is also an engraved one. If such information would be useful in the particular library, include a note about the other title page or pages.

If a necessary item of description is missing from the publication itself and must be supplied from an external source, it is enclosed in brackets. If a work is published without a title page, or without one which applies to the whole work, it is cataloged from some other part of the work (cover title, caption title, etc.), and the source of the information is indicated.

However, the great majority of books acquired by the small general library will pose no special problems for the cataloger. To take an example, here is the title page of a book [opposite].

The information thus gathered is sufficient to enable the cataloger to construct the descriptive portion of the catalog card, and then proceed to determination of main and added entries, subject headings, and classification symbol. The completed card might look like this:

```
B
JEF          Malone, Dumas.
                The sage of Monticello / by Dumas Malone. --
             Boston : Little, Brown, 1981.
                551 p. : ill. ; 23 cm. -- (Jefferson and his
             time ; v. 6)

                ISBN 0-316-54463-9

                1. Jefferson, Thomas, 1743-1826.  2. U.S.--
             History--War of 1812.  3. Presidents--U.S.--
             Biography.  I. Title.  II. Series: Malone,
             Dumas.  Jefferson and his time.
```

Card 1.   Main entry card.

Had the library had access to Library of Congress cataloging, it would look like this:

```
Malone, Dumas, 1892-
    The sage of Monticello / by Dumas Malone. — 1st ed. —
Boston : Little, Brown, 1981.
    xxiii, 551 p. : ill. ; 23 cm. — (Jefferson and his time ; v. 6)
    Bibliography: p. [521]-535.
    Includes index.
    ISBN 0-316-54463-9 : $17.50

    1. Jefferson, Thomas, 1743-1826.  2. University of Virginia—History.  3.
United States—History--War of 1812.  4. Presidents—United States—Biogra-
phy.   I. Title.  II. Series: Malone, Dumas, 1892-      Jefferson and his
time ; v. 6.
E332.M25  vol. 6              973.4'6'0924—dc19        81-5782
                                    [B]              AACR 2  MARC

Library of Congress
```

Card 2.   Library of Congress cataloging copy for book repre-
          sented by card 1.

While there is less detail in card 1, the essential information is presented in both examples, and follows the same
order, designed to conform to International Standard Bibliographic Description (ISBD) practice, which requires that ele-

ments of the description (i. e. , that portion of the card which begins with the title and ends with the ISBN and price) be grouped by areas and be separated by specific types of punctuation. The reason for this is to organize and standardize the data so that it can be readily interpreted by both people and computers across the world, and to allow enough information to be presented to suit the needs of large research libraries.

It should not be necessary for a small library to make its homemade cataloging reflect the LC format in all its details, but it is desirable that the basic information be given in the same sequence and that all entries in a given library's catalog be as uniform as possible in style, i. e. , in spelling, capitalization, punctuation, abbreviations, use of numerals, etc. Of course, if a library uses centralized cataloging for an appreciable part of its collection, the homemade cards should be consistent with the cards obtained from outside. Since most commercial services that supply simplified cards to small libraries now base their cataloging on that provided by the Library of Congress, the components of the cards and their order do largely conform to LC practice, but there is unfortunately no single standard that determines the degree of detail provided or the spacing, indention, and punctuation used (see chapter 11 for examples of printed cards). The style of the sample cards given in this manual usually reflects ISBD, but as suggested above, the particular guidelines and style chosen by the user of this manual must be determined by the policy which has been adopted by the individual library.

Organization of Information

The skeleton cards 3 and 4 below and card 5 illustrate the form used for most sample cards in this manual and show the relative locations of the various parts of an entry. Indention and spacing is intended to emphasize the different groups of information and to give prominence to certain words, such as the author's name, or whatever forms the main entry heading.

```
1234567890123456789
2
3Call
4No.      Author.
             Title : subtitle / first statement of
          responsibility ; each subsequent statement
          of responsibility. -- edition statement. --
          First place of publication, etc. : first
          publisher, etc., date of publication.
             Extent of item : other physical details ;
          dimensions. -- (Series)

             Note.
             Note-------------------------------------
          ----------------------.
             Standard number.

             Tracing----------------------------------
          --------------.
```

Card 3.   Skeleton card for simplified cataloging, author main
          entry.

```
             Title : subtitle / first statement of
          responsibility ; each subsequent statement
          of responsibility. -- edition statement.
          -- First place of publication, etc. :
          first publisher, etc., date of publication.
             Extent of item : other physical details ;
          dimensions. -- (Series)

             Note.
             Standard number.


             Tracing.
```

Card 4.   Skeleton card for simplified cataloging, title main
          entry.

Author main-entry heading

Call no. { Classification
           Author letters
Title
Edition

Physical description area

Notes

Tracing

Statement of responsibility
Publisher } Publication, distribution, etc., area
Date
Series statement

025.02
BLO
Bloomberg, Marty.
    Introduction to technical services for library
technicians / Marty Bloomberg, G. Edward Evans.
-- 4th ed. -- Littleton, Colo. : Libraries Unlimited, 1981.
    363 p. : ill. ; 24 cm. -- (Library science text
series)

    Bibliography: p. 343-354.
    Includes index.
    ISBN 0-87287-228-9

    1. Processing (Libraries)   I. Evans, G. Edward,
1937-   II. Title.   III. Series

Card 5.   Card with components labeled.

ISBD/AACR2 format groups the descriptive information into the following major areas: 1) Title and statement of responsibility; 2) edition; 3) material specific details [not used for printed monographs]; 4) publication (imprint); 5) physical description (collation); 6) series; 7) notes; 8) standard number (and price).

This method of organizing the description results in an entry which contains all the information needed to identify the work without reference to the heading, since the name of the author is repeated, as in card 6.

```
Robbins, Tom.
    Still life with Woodpecker / Tom Robbins.
 -- New York : Bantam Books, 1980.
    277 p. ; 24 cm.

    ISBN 0-553-01260-6




             I. Title
```

Card 6. Main entry card, ISBD format, repeating name of author in authorship statement.

Source of information for description. The information for the various descriptive parts of the catalog entry should be derived from the following sources, which are given in preferential order:

Area	Prescribed Sources of Information
Title and statement of responsibility	Title page
Edition	Title page, other preliminaries, and colophon

Area	Prescribed Sources of Information
Publication, distribution, etc.	Title page, other preliminaries, and colophon
Physical description	The whole publication
Series	The whole publication
Note	Any source
Standard number and terms of availability	Any source

The term "preliminaries" encompasses half title, verso of the title page, added title page, cover, and spine. If information has to be supplied from a place other than what is authorized in the table above, it is enclosed in brackets. The extent of item and notes are phrased by the cataloger using standard bibliographical terminology and quotations from the work itself or outside sources, as necessary.

The discussion of the parts of the catalog entry which follows below reflects ISBD and AACR2 rules, but also suggests how these rules may be simplified by small libraries.

Title. AACR2 distinguishes between title proper, alternative title, parallel title, and other title information. This can be confusing at first glance, and therefore some examples are offered at the outset (definitions are given in the Glossary).

Kurt Vonnegut's God Bless You, Mr. Rosewater, or Pearls before Swine is one of the few modern examples of an alternative title ("Pearls before Swine" being the alternative title). The AACR2 phrase, "other title information," usually refers to a subtitle, as in The Brethren: Inside the Supreme Court, or as in The West End Horror: A Posthumous Memoir of John H. Watson, M.D.. Both subtitles-- the phrases following the colons--give important information about the books. On the other hand, the subtitle of Peter Drucker's Management: Tasks, Responsibilities, Practices adds little to the information conveyed by the title proper, "Management."

A parallel title is generally a translation of the title proper into another language, e.g.:

Ein Sommernachtstraum = A midsummernight's dream

The title proper, as may be deduced from the above--
and as defined succinctly by Michael Gorman [2]--is the
"chief name" of an item, the essential element that may not
be omitted. Alternative titles are part of the title proper,
but sub- and parallel titles are not.

The distinction is emphasized in the punctuation separating the various kinds of titles (see card 7). The AACR2 dis-
section of titles into parts may appear to be needlessly complex, and it is true that the requirements of computers and
international cooperation--rather than those of small libraries
--have shaped these rules. On the other hand, once the dis-
tinctions are grasped, many decisions about what title information must be included and what may be omitted become
routinized for the small library, and that is all to the good.

Eastman, P. D. (Philip D.)
    ɾBig dog little dog. Spanish & Englishɟ
    Perro grande— perro pequeño : un cuento de las buenas
noches = Big dog— little dog : a bedtime story / P.D. Eastman
: translated into Spanish by Pilar de Cuenca and Inés Alvarez.
— New York : Random House, c1982
    ɾ32ɟ p. : col. ill. ; 21 cm — (A Random House picturebook)
    Summary: Two dogs are opposite in every way, but are the very best of
friends.
    ISBN 0 394-85142-0 (pbk.) . $1.25
    ɾ1. Dogs—Fiction. 2. Friendship—Fictionɟ I. Title. II. Title: Big dog—
little dog.
    PZ7.E1314 Bi   1982   ɾEɟ—dc19   81-12070
                                        AACR 2 MARC
    Library of Congress   AC

Card 7. Treatment of parallel and other title information.

The basic rule is to transcribe the title proper exactly
as it appears on the title page, except for necessary adjustments in punctuation and capitalization. In English, only the
first word of the title proper and proper names and adjectives
are capitalized. If the title proper is in another language,
the rules applicable to capitalization in that language are followed. The first word of a title within a title proper is capitalized, as is the first word in a parallel or alternative title.
For example:

Selections from The idylls of the king

Die Zauberflöte = The magic flute

God bless you, Mr. Rosewater, or Pearls before
swine

When the name of an author or publisher is part of the title
proper, it is included in the title statement, but not the statement of responsibility:

Eileen Ford's A more beautiful you in 21 days

Marlowe's plays

Larousse's French-English dictionary

Numerals should be transcribed as they appear in the chief
source of information:

16 greatest original bluegrass hits

The 4:50 from Paddington

As stated above, alternative titles are always included
as part of the title proper, but other title information and
parallel titles may be omitted in first level cataloging. For
example:

Management / Peter F. Drucker. --
New York : Harper & Row, 1974.

On the other hand, other title information may be
added if the title proper needs explanation:

Longfellow : [selections]

When the chief source of information does not provide
a title, the cataloger may take it from elsewhere in the item,
or from a reference source. If necessary, the cataloger may
devise a brief descriptive title (see card 121). Either way,
enclose the resulting title in brackets and indicate its source
in a note.

When an item shows a collective title and the titles
of the individual works in the chief source of information,
use the collective title as the title proper and give the individual titles in a note:

```
        Crime times three : three complete novels
    featuring Adam Dalgliesh of Scotland Yard /
    P. D. James. -- New York : Scribner, c1979.
        254, 224, 296 p. ; 22 cm.

        Contents:  Cover her face -- A mind to murder
    -- Shroud for a nightingale.
        ISBN 0-684-16065-X
```

In the case of collections without a collective title, and in which no single work predominates, list the individual titles in the order in which they appear in the chief source of information, including any linking words:

> Lord Macaulay's essays ; and, Lays of ancient Rome

> The Wapshot chronicle ; The Wapshot scandal

When the works contained in a single item are by different people, but no work predominates, use the following format:

> Unnatural death / Dorothy Sayers. Hare sitting up / Michael Innes.

In all the above cases, an alternative would be to make separate entries for each work, linked by a "with" note (see cards 92-93). If one of the works predominated, the title of the predominant work would be the title proper, and the others would be given in a note (see card 94).

Following the title proper, it is optional to add a "general material designation" to show the catalog user immediately the medium of the item:

> Hamlet [sound recording]

> Hamlet [motion picture]

AACR2 gives two lists of terms which may be used, the first to be used by British catalogers, and the second by North American catalogers:

List 1	List 2
cartographic material	$\left\{\begin{array}{l}\text{map} \\ \text{globe}\end{array}\right.$
graphic	$\left\{\begin{array}{l}\text{art original} \\ \text{chart} \\ \text{filmstrip} \\ \text{flash card} \\ \text{picture} \\ \text{slide} \\ \text{technical drawing} \\ \text{transparency}\end{array}\right.$
machine-readable data file	machine-readable data file
manuscript	manuscript
microform	microform
motion picture	motion picture
multimedia	kit
music	music
object	$\left\{\begin{array}{l}\text{diorama} \\ \text{game} \\ \text{microscope slide} \\ \text{model} \\ \text{realia}\end{array}\right.$
sound recording	sound recording
text	text
videorecording	videorecording

Every library must decide whether to use any or all of these general material designations (GMDs), basing the decision on what will be most helpful to the library's users. In libraries that containing more print materials than audiovisual materials, it is usually sensible to omit the GMD "text," but to adopt the use of other GMDs that apply, such as "sound recording," "microform," etc. The use of GMDs will be discussed at length in Chapter 9.

It should be noted here, however, that an item that is a reproduction of a work originally appearing in another medium
should be described under the rules applicable to the reproduction. A book in microfiche format would have the GMD
"microform," a map reproduced on a slide would have the
GMD "slide," etc., and would be described accordingly.

Statement of responsibility. Under AACR2 rules, the
title statement is followed by the statement of responsibility
which appear first in the chief source of information. If the
name of the author, publisher, etc., is part of the title,
however, it need not be repeated. Other statements which
are prominent in the chief source are recorded in the form
and order in which they appear, or make the most sense
(see cards 8 and 12).

```
      Crockett, James Underwood,
        [Flower garden]
        Crockett's Flower garden / by James Underwood
      Crockett ; with the assistance of Marjorie
      Waters ; photography by Russell Morash ; [draw-
      ings by George Ulrich]. -- 1st ed. -- Boston :
      Little, Brown, c1981.
        311 p. : ill (some col.) ; 27 cm.

        Includes index.
        ISBN 0-316-16132-2

        1. Flower gardening. I. Waters, Marjorie.
      II. Title. III. Title: Flower garden.
```

Card 8. LC cataloging, showing mixed responsibility.

```
      Crockett, James Underwood.
        Crockett's Flower garden. -- Boston : Little,
      Brown, c1981.
        311 p. : ill. ; 27 cm.

        ISBN 0-316-16132-2




        1. Flower gardening. II. Title. III. Title:
      Flower garden
```

Card 9. Simplified cataloging for book in Card 8.

The simplified record for the Crockett book rests on the cataloger's judgment that library users will not seek this book under Waters, and that the names of the illustrators are not essential to the identification of the book. Because the chief author's name is part of the title proper, it is not repeated in the statement of responsibility. Strictly speaking, the treatment of the statement of responsibility in the simplified Crockett example is incorrect, as the rule for First Level description says that the statement is given "if different from main entry heading in form or number or if there is no main entry heading." [1. 0D1]

In the examples, the explanatory words "translated by" and "photography by" are taken from the title page. If the information had been taken from another source and inserted by the cataloger in order to clarify the statement of responsibility, the words would be in brackets, as shown in card 8. It is not necessary to insert "by" when there is a single author and the relationship is perfectly clear.

When a single statement of responsibility includes more than three names (e.g., four editors, five joint authors), list only the first name, followed by the sign of omission "..." and "et al." in brackets, as in card 10. Note, however, that the names of the two editors are included in the statement of responsibility, and are traced.

```
Z694        Anglo-American cataloguing rules / prepared by the
.A5         American Library Association ... [et al.] ; edited by
1978        Michael Gorman and Paul W. Winkler. — 2d ed. — Chicago
            : ALA, 1978.

            xvii, 620 p. ; 26 cm.

            ISBN: 083893210X. 0838932118 pbk.

            1. Descriptive cataloging — Rules. I. Gorman,
            Michael, 1941- II. Winkler, Paul Walter. III. American
            Library Association.




            Z694 .A5 1978          025.3/2          78-13789
            Disk No. ALA001
            MINI MARC                                informatics
```

Card 10. Multiple authorship.

ANGLO-AMERICAN CATALOGUING RULES

SECOND EDITION

Prepared by

> THE AMERICAN LIBRARY ASSOCIATION
> THE BRITISH LIBRARY
> THE CANADIAN COMMITTEE ON CATALOGUING
> THE LIBRARY ASSOCIATION
> THE LIBRARY OF CONGRESS

Edited by

> MICHAEL GORMAN *and* PAUL W. WINKLER

AMERICAN LIBRARY ASSOCIATION / *Chicago*

CANADIAN LIBRARY ASSOCIATION / *Ottawa*

1978

While AACR2 simplifies things for the cataloger by calling for what is essentially a straightforward transcription of the information given in the chief source, some judgment must still be exercised. Names of persons or bodies with minor responsibility should be omitted from the statement of responsibility, although they may be included in notes. Performer credits for sound recordings, consultants, writers of prefaces, etc. are generally excluded from the statement of responsibility. The cataloger should not supply a statement of responsibility when there is none in the chief source, but ought to add a note when some explanation is needed to identify a work adequately.

Libraries that adopt the policy of using the first level of description (see p. 15) for most of the items they catalog may omit the statement of responsibility when it is exactly the same as the main entry.

Edition. Although AACR2 rules require that the number of the edition be given even in the case of a first edition, in simplified cataloging the absence of an edition number on the catalog card implies that the work is a first edition. An impression or printing statement is included only in the case of items having particular bibliographic importance. The cataloger should be aware of the lack of uniformity among publishers in the use of the terms edition, impression, and printing, and should study the information on the title page and other preliminaries carefully.

When it is known that a work has been published in various editions which have been revised, translated or illustrated by different people, the information about the reviser, translator, etc., follows the edition statement, rather than being a part of the author statement (see Card 11).

Publication, distribution, etc. Formerly called the "imprint," this area has been renamed under the AACR2 rules in recognition of the fact that not all items are "published" in the strict sense of the word. Sound discs are pressed, films are released, and so on. For books, it is still proper to refer to imprint, which consists of the place of publication, the name of the publisher, and the date of publication, which are recorded on the catalog entry in that order. The imprint serves to identify and to characterize the work and sometimes to indicate where it is available. Different editions are most commonly distinguished by the

```
Fowler, H. W.
    A dictionary of modern English usage. -- 2nd
ed. / rev. by Ernest Gowers. -- New York :
Oxford, c1965.
    725 p. : 19 cm.
```

Card 11. Statement of responsibility relating to edition.

differences in their imprints. The date is especially important, and can be an indication of the current usefulness of a
book to the patron searching the catalog. Imprint data derived
from a source other than the title page, preliminaries, or
colophon are enclosed in brackets. Publication/distribution
data for materials other than books may be derived from
additional sources, described in the relevant chapters.

    a. Choice of data. When it appears that a work was
published/distributed in several places by one or several
publishers/distributors, usually the first named place and
name are used in the entry. However, when a place or
name other than the first named are treated typographically
or in some other way in such a manner as to indicate their
primary responsibility, use these also. If the first named
place refers to a distributor, add the place and name of the
publisher, if one is given. If a city in the United States with
an American publisher is named in a secondary position in
a work containing a foreign imprint, it is included in addition to the foreign imprint (in contrast to the example in
card 11):

    London ; New York : Longmans, Green
    Paris : Gauthier-Villars ; Chicago : University of
        Chicago Press

If neither the place of publication nor the publisher is named in the work, but the place of printing and the printer are, the latter is used in the imprint. Similarly, if a distributor or manufacturer is shown, record the information.

b. Place of publication/distribution. The place of publication is the place in which the office of the publisher is located. If the place of publication is unknown, the location of an institution or society publishing the work may be given. If neither the place of publication nor printing/manufacture is known, indicate this by entering [s.l.] for sine loco.

The place of publication is followed by its country, state, or similar designation (in abbreviated form) when the place is obscure or might be confused with another of the same name. If a city name is abbreviated on the title page transcribe it as given, but give the complete name in brackets to clarify it when needed:

> Rio [de Janeiro]
> Mpls [i.e., Minneapolis]

c. Publisher/distributor, etc. The publisher statement should be abridged as much as possible without risking confusion. Unnecessary parts may be omitted and abbreviations may be used (see Appendix A). Names known to be forenames may be given as initials or omitted in the case of well known publishers. However, the following should not be omitted:

- Words or phrases indicating the function performed (other than solely publishing):

  > Distributed by New York Graphic Society
  > Printed by the G. Banta Pub. Co.
  > Planographed by Edwards Bros.

- Name of one of several bodies where the responsibility is divided, as in the case where one body has done editorial supervision and another the publishing or distribution

- Phrases indicating the official status of a government printer, or the official authorization of a private printer

> ● The statement that a work is privately printed, if a publisher or press is named in the imprint.

When the publisher is also the author of a work, the name may be abbreviated in the publishing statment, as long as the full name has been given in the title or author statement:

> Health today /issued by the World Health Organization. --Geneva : WHO, 1970

If the name of the publisher is unknown, enter [s. n.] for sine nomine. Occasionally, a library may want to include the address of a publisher that would otherwise be difficult to locate, as in card 12.

```
Fitzgerald, F. Scott (Francis Scott)
    Poems, 1911-1940 / F. Scott Fitzgerald ; edited
by Matthew J. Bruccoli ; foreword by James
Dickey. -- Bloomfield Hills, Mich. (1700 Lone
Pine, Bloomfield Hills 40013) : Bruccoli Clark,
1981.
    189 p. : ill. ; 23 cm.
```

Card 12.   Subsidiary authors; publisher's address

d.   Date.   Various kinds of dates may appear on the title page and verso--the date of the latest printing, the copyright date, the date of the first impression of the given book, etc.   The important point is to be able to identify the particular edition of the book at hand, which might vary from other editions of the same title.

The basic rule is to give the year of publication, distribution, etc. of the edition named in the edition area.   If there is no edition statement, use the first edition date.   For books, the date may be taken from the title page, preliminaries, or colophon; if it comes from another source, it is en-

closed in brackets. The date on the item is given as found, but qualified when it does not correspond with the date of publication:

> 1975 [i.e. 1957] (typographical error on title page, correct date discovered in preliminaries)

When the date of publication of an edition is not known, or is different from the copyright date, give the copyright date--by itself if no other date is available, or together with the printing date:

> c1980
> c1973 , 1979 printing

If there are dates related to both publication and distribution, both may be shown:

> London : Educational Records, 1973 ; New York : Edcorp [distributor], 1975

If the dates are the same, give the date after the last named publisher, distributor, etc.

If there are several copyright dates, the latest is used, unless it is only a renewal date or applies to a part of the work only. If the work is in more than one volume and the imprint dates of the individual volumes differ, the inclusive dates are given, e.g., 1971-1975. If the work is not complete, give the earliest date, followed by a hyphen and four spaces.

If no dates can be found on the title page, preliminaries, or colophon, the cataloger supplies an approximate date as follows:

[1892 or 1893]	one of two years certain
[1892?]	probable date
[ca.1892]	approximate date
[between 1906 and 1912]	not earlier nor later (use only for dates less than 20 years apart)
[189-]	decade certain
[189-?]	decade uncertain
[18--]	century certain
[18--?]	probable century

The small library should not be overly concerned with establishing the date of an edition or researching an approximate date, but should simply use the dates as they are given in the book. In the rare instances of undated material which are encountered in the small library, it is seldom a problem to approximate the decade, at least.

Physical description. This term has replaced "collation" previously used for the physical description of a book and includes the number of pages of a one-volume work, or the number of volumes and pages, information about the illustrations, size, accompanying materials if any, and series note, in that order. The small library does not need to follow all the rules prescribed by ISBD for the benefit of large research libraries. For example, the dimensions of a book can be omitted; illustrations need not be enumerated or described as to type or color; unnumbered pages need not be counted, and where a work consists of more than one volume, pagination may be ignored. The library should decide how much detail is reasonable and then follow that policy consistently.

Rules for describing nonprint materials are given in Chapter 9.

1. Pagination: The number of volumes and the number of pages are established through an examination of the book or set. In giving the number of pages, the last numbered page of each section is recorded. A section is either a separately numbered group or an unnumbered group which is long enough (20% of the total) to warrant special attention.

Gorman suggests the following simplification:

> For single-volume printed items - give the number of pages in the main numbered sequence of the volume ; if there is more than one main numbered sequence , give the number of pages in each sequence in turn. Ignore unnumbered sequences and minor sequences :
>
> 327 p. not [32] , 327 p.
> 119 p. not xii , 119 p.

If a work is in two or more volumes, and the library does not have all of them, give what it has in pencil so that

the changes may be made easily if other volumes are added, e. g. , v. 1, 3. When a book does not have its pages numbered, record it simply as 1v. If the number of bibliographical volumes or parts of a work differ from the number of physical volumes, give both, e. g. , 2 v. in 1.

2. Illustrations: The title page may include a statement as to the number and type of illustrations, or this information, like the paging, may be discovered only through an examination of the book. The abbreviation "ill. " may be used, regardless of the type of illustration, and even a single illustraticn puts a work in the illustrated category. Where the number of illustrations is easily determined, it may be given, and special types (maps, e. g.) may be indicated. When a work contains only illustrations or very little text, that fact is noted. If all illustrations are in color, use "col. ill. " If some are in color, "(some col.)" may be used.

3. Size: Size is given in centimeters, with the height first: 20 x 8 cm. Measure to the next whole centimeter up. Width is given only when it is less than half the height or greater than the height. Knowing the size of a book can help the user locate it on the shelves, or can be useful when requesting interlibrary loan or photocopying service. However, most small libraries will omit size unless it is particularly uncommon.

Unusual formats such as boxes, portfolios, or maps and illustrative material in pockets are best explained in a note. Accompanying material such as an answer booklet or sound recording which are intended to be used with the work should be noted in the physical description area, preceded by a plus sign. If the accompanying material has a title or author different from that of the main work, it may be best to treat it as a supplement.

Series. Many books belong to a series and it is sometimes important to include this information in the catalog entry. There are three kinds of series: author, subject, and publisher's (see p. 102 for a full definition). A Dance to the Music of Time by Anthony Powell, of which At Lady Molly's and Temporary Kings are two of the twelve volumes, is an example of an author series; "American Guide Series" and "Rivers of America" are examples of subject series; "Everyman's Library" is an example of a publisher's series. Of these, the last is generally of least importance to the library user, and therefore to the cataloger.

```
Holden, David.
  The house of Saud : the rise and rule of the
most powerful dynasty in the Arab world / by
David Holden, Richard Johns. -- New York : Holt,
Rinehart, and Winston, 1982, c1981.
  xiv, 569 p., [20] p. of plates : ill., maps,
ports. ; 25 cm.
```

Card 13.   Detailed description of extent of item; in simplified
cataloging, 569 p. would suffice.

        The name of the series is found at the top of the title
page, on the cover of the book, on one of the pages preceding the title page, or anywhere in the book. However, if it
appears only on the dust jacket, ignore it. A series statement gives the name of the series to which the book belongs.
If the name begins with an article, the second word as well
as the article begins with a capital letter. It is enclosed in
parentheses. If the series is not of sufficient importance for
an added entry, it is unnecessary for the small library to
include a series statement. In the example in card 14, most
libraries would drop the publisher's series, and some would
also drop the subject series.

        A statement of responsibility for a series may be
given if it is important to the identification of the item and
if it appears on it:

        Occasional papers / University of Illinois Graduate
        School of Library Science ...

        The series statement may include the number of the
volume if the series consists of consecutively numbered parts.
If a work belongs to more than one series, the second series
statement follows the first, in its own set of parentheses.
The series entered first is the more specialized or smaller
of the two (see card 14). However, if one is a subordinate
part of the other, the series and subseries are specified in
the same statement, within one set of parentheses.

```
Kishel, Gregory F.
  How to start, run, and stay in business / by
Gregory F. Kishel and Patricia Gunter Kishel.
-- New York : Wiley, c1981.
  200 p. : 23 cm. -- (Small business series,
0272-7811) (Wiley self-teaching guides)
```

Card 14. Two series, subject and publisher's.

Notes. Notes may be added to catalog entries when needed to explain the title or to correct any misunderstanding to which it might lead, or to give essential information or bibliographic details not included in the title and responsibility, edition, and publication statements, or in the physical description. They should be brief, clear, factual, and non-judgmental. The safest rule is not to add a note if there is doubt as to its value.

Information which is needed to identify a work or to distinguish one edition from another, or to aid in locating it on the shelves, but which cannot be fitted into the formal parts of the entry because of length or inappropriateness, should be given in a note. Notes relating to a reproduction should be given before notes pertaining to the original. Information needed for identification includes varying titles or individual titles in a multi-volume work, additional title pages, names of authors to whom the work has been attributed or other clarification of authorship, indication of the incomplete or imperfect nature of the work. Information needed to aid location might include the following: the work is bound with something else; it has a separate index or supplement.

Provision of other information in notes is optional. Contents notes, including indication of bibliographies and indexes, fall in this category, as do notes about bibliographical history and relationships to other works.

Each library must decide what kinds of notes are essential, what kinds are helpful, and what kinds dispensable, based on the needs of the library's users. Notes are generally given in the order outlined below. The use of notes for analytics will be discussed separately.

1. For serials, frequency is stated in the first note, unless it is made clear in the title. For sound recordings, the label number is given as the first note.

2. The nature, scope, or artistic form of the item is clarified in a short phrase, if the main description is inadequate or misleading:

```
        Deliverance / by James Dickey. -- Carbondale :
     Southern Illinois University Press, 1982,
     c. 1972
        157 p. : ill. ; 24 cm. -- (Screenplay library)

     Script of film based on his novel.
```

Card 15.   Note to clarify form of work, should user miss significance of series name.

3. If the language of the item is not clear from the main description, and if it is important for the library user to know, make a note (see card 16).

4. Works which are adaptations, abridgements, sequels, dramatizations, parodies, indexes, supplements, etc. are identified as such and the original work is cited:

Sequel to: Mutiny on the Bounty

Based on the short story by Shirley Jackson

```
Viridiana [motion picture] / [directed by] Luis
  Bunuel ; [produced by] R. Munoz Suay. --
  [Spain] : 1961 ; Minneapolis : Festival Films
  [distributor], 1983.
  2 film reels (90 min.) : sd., b&w. ; 16 mm.


In Spanish, with English subtitles.
```

Card 16.   Note indicates language.

5.   If the item has titles other than the title proper under which the user might search, give the information in a note, as in card 17.   Also, if the title has been provided by the cataloger, or taken from somewhere other than the prescribed source of information, indicate this in a note (see card 121).   Other examples are:

At head of title: They came from Ireland

Cover title: Biology seminars

Title varies slightly

Title from spine

6.   List credits and other statements of responsibility that will be helpful to library patrons, but that are not included in the main statement of responsibility (see cards 101-102).

7.   The edition and history note is especially important for serials which continue, or are continued by a different title.   It is also used to give information about the edition that cannot be fitted into the main description (see card 17).

8.   Important details about the publication, distribu-

Headstrom, Richard.
   Nature discoveries with a hand lens. -- Dover
ed. -- New York : Dover, 1981, c1968.
   412 p. : ill. ; 21 cm.

   Originally published under title: Nature in
miniature.

Card 17. Earlier title given in note.

tion, etc., which do not fit into the main description may
require a note:

     First released in 1969

     9. Details which do not fit into the physical descrip-
tion area, but which are important for the user to know, e.g.:

     For LaBelle projector

     In Bell and Howell autoload cartridge

     10. Accompanying material description that is awk-
ward to fit into the physical description can be given in a
note:

     Slides with every 7th issue

     11. In school library media centers, it may be use-
ful to include grade level:

     Intended audience: Grades 3-4

     12. If the library has the same item in two different
formats, this can be shown in the note:

     Also available in U-matic cassette

13.   A brief summary is often desirable, especially when the title is not self-explanatory and the item is in a format not easily examined, such as 16 mm film.

14.   Contents notes are often not necessary for collections of short stories, poetry, or plays on cards made locally if the library has copies of printed indexes to collections.

When a collection contains an author's complete works or more than 25 items, the contents are not listed. For a multi-volume work, however, contents should be given. When you wish to make an added entry for a part of a work, that part must be specified in a contents note, unless it is named elsewhere in the entry.   For example:

> Title page:
>   The Basic Training of Pavlo Hummel and
>   Sticks and Bones; Two Plays by David Rabe
> No contents note is necessary, even if title entries are wanted for both plays, because they are named in the title statement.

> But:

> Title page:
>   Six Modern American Plays.   Introduction by
>   Allan G. Halline
> If you wish to have an entry for each play, you should list all six in a contents note.

However, there is no rule that says you must make added entries whenever you give a contents note.

Many books contain bibliographies and similar matter which are often worth noting on the main entry card, even in small libraries.   A patron wishing more material on a subject than the library has available can be directed to books with bibliographies for suggestions of titles to request through interlibrary loan.   Indexes, discographies, filmographies, and appendices may also be noted, depending on the cataloger's judgment of their importance.   The following examples show the form in which notes are given:

> Bibliography: p. 331-345.
> "Chronological list of author's works": p. 242.

Includes bibliographies and index.
Appendices (p. 157-200): A. The Anglo-Japanese
  alliance -- B. The Russo-Japanese peace treaty
  -- C. The Japan-Korean agreement

The contents proper is given after all other notes,
forming a separate paragraph headed by the words "Contents"
or "Partial contents." The items are listed in the order in
which they appear in the work. Prefatory and similar material is not included, and introductions mentioned in the authorship statement are not repeated. Give the titles (followed
by statement of responsibility, if applicable) as they appear
at the head of each individual work within the whole. Separate by space, dash, space. The following examples show
the form in which contents notes are given:

Contents: An unfinished woman -- Pentimento
  Scoundrel time

Partial contents: Death of a salesman / Arthur Miller A streetcar named desire / Ten
nessee Williams -- Come back, little Sheba /
William Inge

Contents: v. 1. Plain tales from the hills
-- v. 2-3. Soldiers three ; and Military tales --
v. 4. In black and white -- v. 5. The phantom
'rickshaw, and other ghost stories -- v. 6. Under the deodars ; The story of the Gadsbys ; Wee
Willie Winkie -- v. 7....

15. The holdings note may be used to show that a
library's copy of an item is incomplete:

Library's set lacks v. 2

16. Whenever the cataloger decides to make separate
entries for distinct works which are contained in one physical
unit, such as a book or sound recording, but which have no
collective title, link the entries by a "with" note (see cards
92-93).

Standard number. If an item has an International
Standard Book Number (ISBN) or an International Standard
Serial Number (ISSN), give the number following the note
area:

ISBN 0-583-12321-X

ISSN 0002-9869

Books issued in both hard cover and paperback will have different ISBN numbers.   Also, a set may have an ISBN number
and its individual volumes may have separate numbers.   Give
only the number of the item that you are cataloging.

   Supplementary items.   Separately issued supplements,
indexes, concordances, etc. that are so closely related to
another work that they cannot be used independently may be
added to the entry for the original work as part of the physical description or as a note:

   5 v. : ill. ; 32 cm. + index

   Accompanied by revisions (23 loose-leaf p.) issued
   in 1982

If the related work has its own title and can be described
independently, it is linked to the original work by a name-
title added entry.

Simplified Entries for Fiction

Since the reader who wants fiction usually uses the catalog
only to find whether or not a certain book is in the library
or what books the library has by a certain author, cards for
fiction may be simpler than for nonfiction.   For this reason
most public libraries do not classify fiction nor assign a book
number, and describe it more simply than nonfiction when
they type the cards.   Some school and college libraries, however, prefer to classify their fiction as literature and to catalog it exactly as they do their nonfiction.

   The simplest form of entry may contain only the author's name and the title.   Some librarians find the copyright
date or the date of publication useful as the date answers the
reader's query as to which of the titles is the most recent.

   If more information regarding the book, e.g., the
publisher, is desired on the catalog entries, it is better to
catalog fiction and nonfiction alike.   But if this information
is available in trade catalogs and bibliographical tools which

are at hand, time may be saved by making simple catalog entries such as cards 18 and 19 and by referring to these printed aids for the occasional calls for additional information.

In short, one has reduced the descriptive information to include, essentially, only "access" elements (as described in the next chapter).

```
        Doctorow, E. L.
           Ragtime.   1975.




           I. Title.
```

Card 18.   Simplified main entry for fiction.

```
           Ragtime
        Doctorow, E. L.
```

Card 19.   Title card for fiction.

On the title card the information given on the author card is simply reversed, the title given on the top line, the author on the line below. As the reader frequently remembers the title rather than the author, title entries for fiction are important.

References

1. Michael Gorman, "The Anglo-American Cataloguing Rules," Library Resources & Technical Services 22: 211-12.
2. Michael Gorman, The Concise AACR2. (Chicago, American Library Association, 1981), p. 144.

Chapter 3

CHOICE OF ACCESS POINTS

Bibliographic accuracy is important in any library, but for the small library which does not contribute descriptive information to a shared data base the catalog is primarily a means of access to the resources of that library. So, from the body of descriptive information assembled by the procedures outlined in the previous chapter, it is important to extract those elements which, as "headings" in the catalog, will best enable the library user to find the appropriate book (or other library item). When it is a specific book that is sought, rather than information on a given subject, the logical "points of access" would be the name of the author and/or the title. In the majority of instances, the choice of entries will be relatively straightforward. But, who is the "author" of the "Report of the President's Commission on Civil Disobedience"; and, for that matter, under what "title" would one expect to find it in the catalog? In the case of biography, the name of the biographee is often a more useful point of access than author or title. A work may be the product of shared responsibility. A classic work may have appeared under varying titles. So, again, the need for rules to guide the cataloger is evident.

The term "access points," which has come into vogue with the publication of AACR2, is a reflection of the increasing importance of the computer as a bibliographic tool. In an electronic data base, there exists one standard descriptive entry for a work which can be retrieved instantly via online computer terminal by typing on its keyboard any of several words or phrases which have been coded in accordance with the computer's program to serve as "access points." The equivalent in the card catalog would be the words or phrases chosen to serve as "headings" for the several entries; but, since each card in the catalog is a discrete physical entity, the body of descriptive information which appears under one entry for a particular work may not be identical in all details to the information to be found under another

entry for the same work. One book may merit several entries in the catalog, but if the library must type each of these only one card need contain the complete body of descriptive information, tracings, etc. The heading chosen to appear at the top of that basic card, determining where it will file in the catalog, is called the main entry, and the card that begins with the main entry heading and includes all the bibliographic data about the work, together with the tracings (the list of subject and added entries under which it is also entered in the catalog), is a main entry card. The main entry also determines how a work is cited in bibliographies, union catalogs, etc., and is traditionally considered as constituting the formal identification of it. When duplicated, the main entry card constitutes a unit card to which other headings can be added in order to complete the set of cards for the work. When a library does not have duplicating facilities, cards for subject and added entries are typed in abbreviated form.

MAIN ENTRY

Personal author

Basic rule: Enter under author, or principal author, whenever possible; otherwise, enter under title.

By "author" is meant the person chiefly responsible for the creation of the intellectual or artistic content of a work. Thus composers, artists, photographers, etc. are the "authors" of the works they create; chess players are the authors of their recorded games, etc. The term author may also embrace an editor or compiler, but only if he or she has been primarily responsible for the contents of a work.

Corporate responsibility

A corporate body cannot truly be an "author," and works prepared by corporate officers or employees which are the result of scholarly investigation or scientific research should be entered under appropriate personal author. A work which emanates from a corporate body but which is not an expression of corporate thought or activity, and for which no personal author is indicated, should be entered under title. AACR2 permits main entry under corporate body only for works which fall into one of the following categories:

a) administrative works, dealing with the corporate body itself, such as annual reports;
b) legal and governmental publications such as laws, treaties, official communications, and administrative regulations;
c) collective thought of a body, such as commission or committee reports;
d) proceedings and similar reports of the collective activity of a conference, exhibition, expedition, or other special event;
e) sound recordings, films, and videorecordings for which a performing group has had responsibility beyond mere performance.

University of Chicago. Far Eastern Library.
    Author-title catalog of the Chinese collection : first supplement. -- Boston : G. K. Hall, 1981.
    4 v. ; 37 cm.

At head of title: Catalogs of the Far Eastern Library, University of Chicago.
ISBN 0-8161-0308-9

1. Chinese imprints--Catalogs. I. Title.

Card 20.   Corporate main entry; supplement cataloged separately.

Title

Main entry should be made under title for:

a) works of unknown, diffuse, or indeterminate authorship (card 21);
b) collections or works produced under editorial direction;
c) publications issued by corporate bodies which do not qualify for entry under corporate or personal headings (card 22);
d) sacred scriptures.

Recommendations for child play areas / Uriel
Cohen ... [et al.]. -- [Milwaukee] : School
of Architecture & Urban Planning. University
of Wisconsin-Milwaukee, [1980?]
vi, 808 leaves : ill. ; 28 cm.

Cover title.

1. Playgrounds--Planning. 2. Recreation
areas--Planning. 3. Play. I. Cohen, Uriel.

Card 21.   Title main entry--diffuse authorship.

More than just a cookbook / [edited by Lynn
Morgan]. -- Glendale, CA : Health Education
Dept. of Glendale Adventist Center, c1980.
1 v. : ill. ; 23 cm.

1. Low-calorie diet--Recipes. I. Morgan,
Lynn. II. Glendale Adventist Medical Center.
Health Education Dept.

Card 22.   Title main entry for work published by a corporate
body that does not qualify for main entry under a
corporate or personal name.

CHOICE OF ENTRIES

Joint authors, editors, compilers, etc.   When the wording or
typography indicates that one person or corporate body is

primarily responsible, enter under that name. Make added entries for the other names if there are not more than two, and always make an added entry for the first name listed on the title page, even when that is not the name of the principal author.

> Title page:
> Animal motivation; experimental studies on the albino rat, by C. J. Warden, with the collaboration of T. N. Jenkins, L. H. Warner, E. L. Hamilton and H. W. Nissen
> Enter under Warden; make no added author entries.

When the principal author is not indicated, but there are no more than three names, enter under the first and make added entries under the other two:

> Title page.
> Health for effective living; a basic health education text for college students, by Edward B. Johns, Wilfred C. Sutton, Lloyd E. Webster
> Enter under Johns, with added entries for Sutton and Webster.

> Title page:
> The correspondence between Benjamin Harrison and James G. Blaine, 1882-1893 ...
> Enter under Harrison, with an added entry for Blaine

If a work is in several volumes and the names of the authors are given in a different order in each, enter under the first name listed in the first volume:

> Title page, book 1:
> Child-life arithmetics.... Three book series, by Clifford Woody, Frederick S. Breed, James R. Overman

> Title page, book 2:
> ... by Frederick S. Breed, James R. Overman, Clifford Woody

> Title page, book 3:
> ... by James R. Overman, Clifford Woody, Frederick S. Breed
> Enter under Woody, with added entries for Breed and Overman.

When a new edition changes the order in which the authors
are listed, retain the first edition main entry unless the new
edition is radically different:

> Title page:
> Outline of sociology, by John Lewis Gillin and
> Frank W. Blackmar, 3d ed.
> ("A somewhat thorough rewriting." In earlier
> editions Blackmar's name appeared first on
> the title page)
> Enter under Gillin, with added entry for Blackmar.

Adaptations. Enter under the adapter when the literary style
or form of the original has been changed, i. e., when it has
been rewritten for children, dramatized, made into a novel
or verse:

> Title page:
> Sinclair Lewis' Dodsworth, dramatized by Sidney
> Howard
> Enter under Howard, with an author-title added entry
> for Lewis

> Title page:
> The boys' King Arthur, Sir Thomas Malory's His-
> tory of King Arthur and his knights of the Round
> Table; edited for boys by Sidney Lanier.
> Enter under Malory, with added entry for Lanier
> (it is edited, with an introduction, but not rewritten)

> Title page:
> The book of King Arthur and his noble knights;
> stories from Sir Thomas Malory's Morte D'Arthur
> by Mary Macleod
> Enter under Macleod, with an added entry under Mal-
> ory.

The Macleod work is similar to the one edited by Sidney
Lanier, but Macleod has selected certain stories from Malory
and reworded them to suit young readers. It is not Malory's
language and is therefore entered under the adapter's name.
Lamb's Tales from Shakespeare is cataloged in the same way:
the main entry under Lamb as adapter, with an added entry
under Shakespeare. Anonymous classics which are retold
are treated the same way, so that James Baldwin's Story of
Roland is entered under Baldwin, but has an added entry under

---

Eichenberg, Fritz, 1901-
    Poor troll : the story of Ruebezahl and the princess / adapted
and illustrated by Fritz Eichenberg. — Owings Mills, Md. :
Stemmer House Publishers, c1981.
        p.   cm.

Adaptation of: Rübezahl / J.K.A. Musäus.
Summary: The enchanted carrots Ruebezahl, the mighty prince of the trolls,
gives Princess Emma provides her with a way to escape his mountain palace.
ISBN 0-916144-94-1 : $9.95

  [1. Fairy tales. 2. Folklore—Germany. 3. Trolls—Fiction]   I. Musäus,
Johann Karl, August, 1735-1787. Rübezahl. II. Title.

PZ8.E35 Po   398.2'1'0943—dc19   82-795
                                            AACR 2 MARC CIP

Library of Congress   AC

Card 23.   Main entry under adapter.

the uniform title "Chanson de Roland." Likewise, Eleanor
Hull's Boys' Cuchulain; heroic legends of Ireland may be entered under Hull as in the Children's Catalog, but with an
added entry under Cuchulain.

    Another type of book which is sometimes puzzling is
that consisting of selections from an individual work of an
author. Hill's translation of a selection of The Canterbury
Tales is an example. In some titles, the term "selected"
is used in the sense that the selections included are taken
from all the works of an author rather than from a single
work. In either case, the treatment is the same. The main
entry is made under the author's name, and the editor's or
translator's name is given an added entry.

Revisions. Enter an edition that has been revised, enlarged,
updated, abridged, condensed, etc., under the heading for the
original if the person or body responsible for the original is
named in a statement of responsibility or in the title, or if
the wording of the chief source of information indicates that
that person or body is still considered to be responsible for
the work. Make an added entry under the heading for the
reviser, abridger, etc.

      Title page:
         Guide to the study and use of reference books by
         Alice Bertha Kroeger. --3rd ed. revised throughout
         and much enlarged by Isadore Gilbert Mudge

Enter under Kroeger, with an added entry under
Mudge.

But, if the wording of the chief source of information
indicates that the person or body responsible for the original
is no longer considered to be responsible for the work, enter
under the reviser, etc. Make a name-title added entry under
the heading for the original.

Title page:
Guide to reference books. --7th ed. by Constance
M. Winchell; based on the Guide to reference books,
6th ed. , by Isadore Gilbert Mudge
Enter under Winchell, with an added entry under Mudge
(author-title).

Related works. A concordance, index, supplement, or sequel
is a work which is related to another work (or body of work);
nonetheless, it is usually a separate creation and therefore
should be cataloged under its own heading. (See cards 20 and
53.) AACR2 does offer an "alternative rule" for librettos,
permitting entry under the musical work to which it is related. If a supplementary item cannot be used independently,
it may be treated as accompanying material to the original
work (see p. 109), especially if it is brief.

Collections. Poems, stories, essays, etc. , by different authors are frequently brought together by a compiler and published as a collection. When there is a collective title which
applies to the whole book, enter under the title, and make
author-title added entries for the works compiled if there are
no more than three (or unless you wish to enter all), and an
added entry for the compiler.

Title page:
... Regency poets; Byron, Shelley, Keats. Com-
piled by C. R. Bull
Enter under title with added entries under Byron,
Shelley, Keats and under Bull.

If no collective title is given, enter under whatever heading
would be used for the first work listed on the title page.
Make an added entry for the compiler or editor and author-
title entries for the other works if there are no more than
three (or unless you feel that entries for all would be worth
the time involved):

Title page:
> The vision of Sir Launfal, by James Russell Lowell;
> the courtship of Miles Standish, by Henry Wadsworth
> Longfellow; Snowbound, by John Greenleaf Whittier;
> edited with an introduction and notes by Charles
> Robert Gaston

Enter under Lowell, with added entries for Longfellow,
Whittier, and Gaston

Diffuse authorship. If there are more than three persons or
bodies named as being responsible for a work, but none is
singled out as being primarily responsible, enter under title,
but make an added entry for the first named person on the
title page:

Title page:
> The United Nations and economic and social coopera-
> tion, by Robert E. Asher, Walter M. Kotschnig,
> William Adams Brown, Jr., and associates.

Enter under title, with added entry for Asher

Unknown or uncertain authorship. Anonymous works or those
issued by a body that lacks a formal name should be entered
under title. If authorship has been attributed, but remains
uncertain, make appropriate added entries. However, enter
directly under a set of initials or other personal designation
("A Physician," e.g.) used to represent an author's name.

Title page:
> The secret expedition; a farce (in two acts) as it
> has been represented upon the political theatre of
> Europe.

Enter under title

Title page:
> A memorial to Congress against an increase of
> duties on importations, by citizens of Boston and
> vicinity.

Enter under title

But:

Title page:
> Indiscretions of Dr. Carstairs, by A. DeO.

Enter under A. DeO.

Official vs. personal authorship.   An official communication, such as a message to a legislature, issued by a chief of state or head of government should be entered under the corporate heading for the office which he holds:

>   Title page:
>   No retreat from tomorrow; President Lyndon B.
>   Johnson's 1967 message to the 90th Congress.
>   Enter under:
>   United States.   President (1963-1969 : Johnson)

However, other speeches and writings of a head of government are entered as works of personal authorship:

>   Title page:
>   The vantage point; perspectives of the Presidency,
>   1963-1969.   Lyndon Baines Johnson
>   Enter under:
>   Johnson, Lyndon Baines, 1908-1973.

Chapter 4

Having chosen from the descriptive information about a work those elements--personal author, corporate body, title--which will serve as access points, the cataloger must next determine the <u>form</u> in which those elements will appear as "headings": that is, the name, word, or phrase placed at the head of the catalog entry to provide an access point in the catalog. "Gulliver's travels, by Jonathan Swift" will file in a very different part of the catalog than would "Travels into several remote nations of the world, by Lemuel Gulliver." The same would be true for "Lorca, Federico García and "García Lorca, Federico"; or "Clemens" and "Twain"; or "United Kingdom. Arts Council" and "Arts Council of Great Britain."

Both AACR (1) and AACR2 have introduced major changes in the rules for form of heading. And even though many of the changes are ones which the small library should welcome, in principle (such as use of the name by which an author is generally known, in preference to an obscure legal name), reconciling old and new forms is a major--and costly --challenge. Many larger libraries have "frozen" their old catalogs and started new ones to accommodate AACR2 changes.

The small library has rather more flexibility in this matter, but policies should be carefully thought out and codified. It is usually wiser practice, and kinder to the next generation, to convert to the newer form than to cling to an outdated one, especially since the latter choice could severely restrict a library's ability to make effective use of available catalog copy from the Library of Congress or other sources. Ideally, new forms should be accepted and older cards altered to conform, particularly if the number of cards involved is small or the changes are minor and easily effected. This is not always practical, however. Interfiling new and old is sometimes a reasonable option for the small library, especially in cases such as "Lawrence, D. H." and "Lawrence,

David Herbert," since the user looking up either form is certain to find the now-combined file; in the large library, with many different entries under "Lawrence," this would not be an acceptable option.

For categories of change involving large numbers of cards--"Great Britain" to "United Kingdom," for example-- if the cost of altering all the old cards seems prohibitive, the library may simply use "see also" reference cards to connect the separate files or may move all the older cards to the newer location but preface the entire section with a raised "guide card" instead of changing the heading on every card; normal attrition will eventually reduce the number of older forms to manageable size, but only if sufficient notation of the policy is recorded that the now intentionally "misfiled" cards are withdrawn when a book with such an entry (main or added) is withdrawn from the collection. There would, of course, be a "see" reference card in the catalog directing users from the old to the new heading.

Libraries that obtain the bulk of their cataloging from a centralized service must keep up with the decisions about forms of entry made by the agency where the cataloging originates. For example, the Library of Congress has decided not to change the heading "Great Britain" to "United Kingdom," the term used in AACR2. Since most centralized and commercial cataloging in the United States is based on LC practice, a small library that buys its cards from a vendor is probably going to have to adopt whatever practice is followed by LC. On the rare occasions that the library would have to do original cataloging, it would be important to know where LC departs from AACR2 in order to maintain consistency.

Until the twelfth edition of Sears List of Subject Headings comes out, there will also be some discrepancies in forms of headings in the catalogs of libraries that use Sears for subject entries, but have adopted LC/AACR2. For example, Sears uses U.S.--HISTORY, etc., but the AACR2 form is United States.

PERSONAL NAMES

Even in cataloging the smallest collection, it will soon be discovered that all authors do not have simple names, such as George Bernard Shaw; and even if they have, they may publish one book as Bernard Shaw, another as George Bernard

Shaw, and a third as G. Bernard Shaw. In that case, the obvious thing to do in order that all entries for books by or about the same person may come together in the catalog is to find out how the person's name most frequently appears on the title pages of his or her works, and then to use that form. If other forms of the name are rather well known, a reference can be made from them, i.e., a card or cards giving other forms can direct the reader to the form of the name used; and, when appropriate, works published under different forms of name may be so entered in the catalog.

Many libraries--large, scholarly libraries, such as university libraries and the Library of Congress, as well as the smaller public and school libraries--have adopted the policy of using the form of the name usually found on the title page of the author's works. Such cataloging aids as the H. W. Wilson Standard Catalogs have done likewise.

Usage, as shown in biographical dictionaries, encyclopedias, publishers' catalogs, is important and should be considered when deciding upon the form of a name. Printed aids, as, for instance, the Standard Catalogs, may change the form of name used merely by changing it in the next published issue. But if a library decides to change the form of a name already used in its catalog, either a reference must be made from the form formerly used to the form to be used, or all the entries for that name must be changed. Women authors marry and may use their husbands' names for later works, while some authors use pseudonyms for some works but not for others.

For most of its books, the library will buy printed catalog cards, or it may now (or in the future) participate in a cooperative cataloging center which supplies the catalog cards along with the books, or it may subscribe for such service from a commercial firm. In these cases the library will want to use the form of name used on the printed cards. A very small number of changes to conform with local practice would be reasonable, but numerous changes would defeat the whole purpose and economy of using such valuable sources. Having considered these factors, the next question is what to do about the names for books to be cataloged locally.

An investigation of any miscellaneous group of books shows quite a variety of kinds of names, and librarians have sought to simplify the task of locating them in the catalog by formulating rules to cover the points most often met. The

basic authority is the <u>Anglo-American Cataloging Rules</u>, second edition, jointly prepared and kept up to date by the library associations of the United States, Canada, and Great Britain, the Library of Congress, and the British Library.

Basic Rules. According to AACR2 the title page or its substitute is the normal source used to determine how a name is to be entered in a catalog. Outside sources can be used if a work is published anonymously or if there is reason to distrust the statements in the work itself.

Choose, as the basis of the heading for a person, the name by which he or she is commonly known. This may be the person's real name, pseudonym, title of nobility, nickname, initials, or other appellation.

If a person's name consists of several parts, select as the entry element that part of the name under which the person would normally be listed in authoritative alphabetic lists in his or her language or country. Adoption of these rules represents a significant triumph of common sense in the evolution of library cataloging practice. Prior to the mid-1960s, extensive detective work was required to determine the true legal name of an author, in total disregard for the name he or she chose to use on the title page. The main result of all this expense and delay was that the library patron seeking, for example, a novel by Pearl Buck would find none of her books in the "B" section of the fiction shelves. If that patron had the patience to consult the catalog rather than simply leave the building in frustration, just possibly a cross reference would lead to the discovery that librarians, united against the world, had established "Sydenstricker, Mrs. Pearl" as the only proper place of entry for Pearl Buck's books.

Some authors are not commonly identified in their works by one particular name. If it is desirable to establish one form of entry, the name most familiar to the reading public is the logical choice. But if there is doubt, the following order of preference is suggested: 1) under the name most frequently found in the author's works; 2) under the name by which the author is generally identified in reference sources; 3) under the latest name used. For example, one would use Windsor, Edward, Duke of--not Edward VIII, King of Great Britain.

Unfortunately, even such simple and logical rules may not solve all problems. A case in point is the heading established by LC for Hans Christian Andersen:

H. C. Andersen (Hans Christian), 1805-1875.

This reflects the fact that the Library of Congress has a large enough collection of the author's works as published since his day to know that the name most frequently found is H. C. and not Hans Christian, as we tend to think of it today. If we wish to be consistent with the authority list of the major cataloging source in the United States, we must therefore accept H. C., and comfort ourselves with the thought that this heading and other surprises (e. g., Bernard Shaw, rather than George Bernard Shaw) are compensated for by the authority to use D. H. Lawrence rather than David Herbert, and T. S., rather than Thomas Stearns Eliot.

Pseudonyms. If all of an author's works appear under one pseudonym, use it. For example:

    Eliot, George
      Refer from: Cross, Mary Ann Evans

If the works of a person appear under several pseudonyms (or under the real name and one or more pseudonyms), choose one of those names if the person has come to be identified predominantly by that name in later editions of his or her works, in critical works, or in other reference sources (in that order of preference). Make references from the other names. For example, enter under Stendhal and refer from Beyle, Marie Henri and from Bombet, Louis Alexandre César. Although Stendhal is the name which most often appears on the title page of The Red and the Black or The Charterhouse of Parma, these works have been published in numerous editions, sometimes under the writer's real name, Beyle. Also, some of his lesser known novels bear only his real name. So, if each book is cataloged and shelved in strict conformity to the information on the title page--which is the rule to be followed in nearly all cases--Stendhal's books as well as his catalog entries would appear in two different places, and the student who knew only one of the names might find only some of the books. It is best in such cases to establish one form of entry and provide an appropriate cross reference in the catalog, e. g., for A. A. Fair and Charles J. Kenny, make references to Erle Stanley Gardner. In fact,

since many borrowers go straight to the shelves, especially
for fiction, the library wishing to give the best service to its
patrons will use book dummies or other shelf marking devices
to refer users to the correct section for Stendhal, Twain, O.
Henry, Lewis Carroll, and other major writers whose works
are frequently sought.

On the other hand, the mystery writer John Creasey
has written over 500 books under half a dozen or more pseudonyms. The time and cost involved should prohibit changing
the lettering on the spine of each of his books so as to shelve
them together. Moreover, this would not be a very helpful
service to the library's patrons, who will inevitably look under the name by which the book is advertised, that is, the
name on the title page. Even the usual cross references in
the catalog are unnecessary in cases of this sort, although
one general guide card under Creasey might point out that
"this author has also used the names Ashe, Gordon; Halli-
day, Michael; ..." etc. Similarly, Ellery Queen is a well
known joint pseudonym for Frederic Dannay and Manfred Lee.
But Queen is the name under which virtually all library users
will look, and references from the real names are unnecessary. While general rules of cataloging are extremely helpful and enable the cataloger to make books quickly available
instead of having to worry at length about the "right" form
of entry, the rules are only guidelines, and should not be
followed so slavishly that the catalog becomes filled with unnecessary, redundant, and confusing entries. Every rule of
cataloging must pass this test: will it really help the library
user?

Fullness of Name. If the forms of name appearing in the
works of an author vary in fullness, the form most commonly found should be used. James Fenimore Cooper should
not be reduced to James Cooper, but Joseph Hilaire Pierre
Belloc will be found without difficulty if only Hilaire Belloc,
the name by which he is primarily known, is used. Refer
from the full name if anyone is likely to look under it, especially if the first name has been omitted.

Names represented by initials may be spelled out, in
parentheses following the form of name chosen as heading,
if necessary to distinguish two or more persons:

> Milne, A. A. (Alan Alexander)
> H. D. (Hilda Doolittle)

Dates of birth and death may also be added for purposes of differentiation:

Adams, Charles Francis, 1807-1886
Adams, Charles Francis, 1835-1915
Adams, Charles Francis, 1866-1954

Some libraries find it generally useful to have authors' dates of birth and death included in the heading on the catalog card:

Cather, Willa Sibert, 1876-1947
Bennett, Arnold, 1876-1931

Where bibliographical tools are few, it can be convenient for both students and librarians to have these dates on the catalog cards. The librarian, in looking up the forms of the name for the heading in the catalog, may note the dates and include them in the heading. If the dates are not readily found, they may be omitted and added later. However, dates are essential only for the identification of different persons whose names are the same.

Compound Surnames. Use the form by which the person prefers to be known. If in doubt, use the form in which the name is listed in reference sources:

Lloyd George, David
Refer from: George, David Lloyd

If the elements of the surname are hyphenated, even occasionally, enter under the first:

Day-Lewis, C. (Cecil)
Refer from: Lewis, Cecil Day

In other cases of names known to be compound surnames the entry element is determined by normal usage in the language of the person involved:

García Lorca, Federico
Refer from: Lorca, Federico García

References should be made from the other part if it is at all likely that anyone would look under it.

Surnames with Prefixes.   The practice most common in the person's own language should determine the form of entry. Standard reference works are the best sources for examples, but the following are some of the most frequently encountered:

Dutch and Flemish: Enter under the part of the name following the prefix, except when the prefix is ver:

> Ver Boven, Daisy
> Gogh, Vincent Van

English: Enter under the prefix:

> De Quincey, Thomas
> De Voto, Bernard
> La Farge, Oliver
> Du Maurier, Daphne
> Van Buren, Martin

French: If the prefix consists of an article or of a contraction of an article and a preposition, enter under the prefix:

> Du Chaillu, Paul
> Le Rouge, Gustave

If the prefix consists of a preposition or of a preposition followed by an article, enter under the part of the name following the preposition:

> La Fontaine, Jean de
> Musset, Alfred de

German: If the prefix consists of an article or of a contraction of a preposition and an article, enter under the prefix:

> Vom Ende, Erich

If the prefix consists of a preposition or a preposition followed by an article, enter under the part of the name following the prefix:

> Goethe, Johann Wolfgang von
> Mühll, Peter von der

Italian: In general, enter under the prefix:

> Da Ponte, Lorenzo

However, in the case of medieval and early modern Italian names, de, de', degli, dei, and de li are rarely construed as prefixes:

> Medici, Lorenzo de'

Portuguese: Enter under the part of the name following the prefix:

> Fonseca, Martinho Augusto da

Scandinavian: Enter under the part of the name following the prefix:

> Linné, Carl von

Spanish: Enter under the part of the name following the prefix, except when the prefix consists only of an article:

> Cervantes Saavedra, Miguel de
> Gama, Vasco da
> Las Heras, Manuel Antonio

References may be made under the various prefixes explaining how names with such prefixes are entered in the catalog.

Titles of Nobility, Honor, Address, etc. The practice of adding titles of rank and honor to authors' names is a painless one if cards are purchased. But for the small library the task of establishing correct titles can be a difficult and an unnecessary one. Admittedly, an author's claim to title may be the sole basis for any public interest in a book by or about her or him, in which case it may be a valid public service for the catalog to point out that this is Lady Beverley Blowser, so that readers may know at once that this is the eccentric heiress who rents out her servants for laboratory experiments and not just some common Beverley Blowser. But unless the noble person uses his or her "title" on the title page, or would be confused with others of like name, the small library can spare itself the trouble of determining whether so-and-so is now an earl or still a lowly baron.

Forename Entries. Sometimes a title of nobility or similar

descriptive is necessary, as in the case of a person whose name does not include a surname, such as King Alfred or Pope Innocent. A person whose name does not include a surname and who is not primarily identified by a title of nobility should be entered under the part of the name by which he or she is primarily identified in reference sources. Include any secondary name acquired informally, e.g., John, the Baptist. But, add after the name any identifying word or phrase that is commonly associated with the name, but which cannot be regarded as an integral part of it:

Joseph, Nez Percé chief.
Clovis, King of the Franks
Gustav I Vasa, King of Sweden
Mary, consort of George V. King of Great Britain
Constantine I, Emperor of Rome
 Refer from: Constantine, Saint
Francis, of Assisi, Saint
Augustine, Saint, Bp
Gregory I, Pope
 Refer from: Gregory, Saint, Pope Gregory I
      Gregory the Great, Pope
Clement VIII, Antipope
Bessarion, Cardinal
Newman, John Henry, Cardinal
Dositheos, Patriarch of Jerusalem
Gregorius, Abp of Corinth

Occasionally people who do have surnames (or their equivalents) are generally referred to by their first names by both the public and many reference sources, e.g., Michelangelo Buonarroti. That better-known form of name is the one to use.

 Pre-AACR practice required entry under Buonarroti; and matters became even more complicated after AACR (1) permitted use of the more generally known form of name, Michelangelo, but the Library of Congress continued to use "Buonarroti," in keeping with the practice of superimposition, whereby only newly established name forms would reflect the new rules but already established names would continue to be used. The dilemma which this posed for libraries ended, fortunately, on January 2, 1981 (referred to at the time as "Day One"), when the Library of Congress abandoned the practice of superimposition simultaneous with adoption of AACR2.

<u>Classical Names</u>. Enter under the form of name most commonly used in reference sources, e.g.:

> Cicero, Marcus Tullius
> Horace
> Homer

CORPORATE NAMES

Just as personal names upon closer observation group themselves into certain classes--simple surnames, compound surnames, names with prefixes, etc., so corporate names may be grouped as subordinate and related bodies; governments, government bodies and officials; conferences, congresses, meetings, etc.; religious bodies and officials; radio and television stations.

In determining the proper entry for corporate bodies, several factors must be considered. For instance, is the work of a subordinate unit to be entered directly under the specific unit or under the parent body? What is the proper entry for legislative decrees of the chief executive as opposed to legislative enactments; for a constitution of a state; for texts of a religious observance?

Cataloging the publications of corporate bodies can be very difficult and time-consuming. Of course, in comparison with clearcut works of personal authorship, institutional publications will account for only a small percentage of a general library's acquisitions. On the other hand, these are precisely the kinds of materials for which printed cards or other cataloging aids are frequently found to be unavailable. In the back rooms of small libraries--and even some not so small ones--one can often discover numbers of annual reports, government documents, and other elusive corporate publications which have been waiting so long for someone to figure out what to do with them that they have become rather out of date.

Since many of these publications arrive as unsolicited gifts, the first question to be asked is whether the library really has any particular need for such-and-such an item. A "free" publication does not long remain so if several dollars in staff time are spent in researching the proper way to catalog it. The next question to be asked is whether a publication which seems worth keeping really needs to be cataloged.

Many reports of institutions and government agencies are better suited to the pamphlet file. If the library has a business section, annual reports filed alphabetically in pamphlet boxes or displayed like periodicals may be of even greater use than if they are fully cataloged. If either topic or format suggests a short life-span, then such alternatives to full cataloging should certainly be considered. For publications of corporate origin which must be cataloged locally, guidelines adapted from AACR2 are offered in this chapter. However, a library with a collection devoted to a special subject such as law or religion is more likely to encounter large numbers of corporate publications than is the small general library, and therefore even the smallest special library will find these guidelines insufficient and will need to use the complete AACR2.

Forms of Entry. A corporate body may be entered directly under its name, as a subheading of the higher body of which it is a part, or as a subheading of the government of which it is an agency, which is usually the name of the place in which it is located. Whether the entry is to be direct or indirect depends upon how easily the name of the body provides unique identification, and on its relationship, if any, with other bodies. The most important consideration must be the form under which library users will most readily find the entry. As in the case of personal names, the form by which the corporate body is predominantly known should be given priority.

The rules for corporate entry, as outlined here, are condensed considerably from the detail in which they are presented in AACR2, yet even so their application in the small library can be a complicated and time-consuming business, since corporate publications are very much the exception for most small libraries and so established precedents and bases of comparison are relatively lacking. Just remember: enter directly under the best-known (or predominant) form of name which conveys distinct identity.

Basic rules:

1) enter a corporate body directly under the name by which it is predominately identified;

2) enter even a subordinate body, other than a government agency, directly under its own name, unless that name:

a) implies relationship to a parent body (dept., division, branch, etc.)

        b) implies administrative subordination (committee, e.g.) and requires reference to the parent body for identification;

        c) denotes a unit likely to belong to more than one parent body;

        d) is that of a university unit representing a particular field of study;

        e) includes the entire name of the parent body;

    3) enter a dependent subordinate body (as in 2 a-e above) as a subheading of the lowest element in the corporate hierarchy that is entered under its own name;

    4) add descriptive designators or place names as necessary for identification or clarity.

> Bodleian Library
> > Refer from: Oxford University. Bodleian Library
>
> but:
> Colorado State University, Cooperative Extension Service.

> Title page:
> > Media programs: district and school. Prepared by the American Association of School Librarians, ALA
>
> Enter under:
> American Association of School Librarians
>
> Harvard Law School
>
> Yale University. Library
>
> Bell Telephone Laboratories. Technical Information Library
>
> School of Hard Knocks. Class of 1982
>
> Democratic Party (Ohio)
>
> Emil Verban Society
>
> Carnegie Library of Pittsburgh
>
> Jackals (Fraternal order)
>
> AFL-CIO
>
> International Sackbut Symposium (1981:Ulm)

The rules for some categories of corporate publications, such as those of government bodies, are especially complicated, and these are dealt with below in greater detail as are other aspects of corporate name entries which will be of interest to small libraries with special collections or policies of cataloging many items which are relegated to the vertical files in other libraries.

Government Bodies and Officials. As students of cataloging should be aware, in considering the basic rules for corporate bodies, the editors of AACR2 have launched a major attack on traditional concepts of corporate "authorship. " The very notion is now considered artificial, and personal author or title entries are often preferred when available. Complexity and uncertainty persist, however, largely because of differences between "authorship" and "responsibility. " It is true that a corporate body cannot actually be an "author"; but it is often equally true that "responsibility" for a publication emanating from a corporate body can be appropriately attributed only to the corporate body itself. In the case of government bodies, the "corporate" nature of responsibility is even stronger.

The new rules of direct entry under conventional name represent an important improvement over the cumbersome artificiality produced by traditional reverence for details of hierarchical structure. Should the library user be expected to understand the complex hierarchy of federal government agencies? For instance, even a reasonably well-informed person interested in a boating chart of Lake Erie might expect such a document to be issued by the Department of the Interior. Wrong! Responsibility expressed hierarchically would be: "United States. Department of Commerce. National Oceanic and Atmospheric Administration. National Ocean Survey. Lake Survey Center. " But even though the new rules permit elimination of unnecessary elements in the hierarchy, the need to ascribe "responsibility" in the case of government publications will seldom produce access points of much use to the small-library user. A reasonable compromise for the small library might be primary reliance on subject entries or even general "subject guide-cards" in the catalog referring users to pamphlet files or a special government documents section. In any case, the small library should consider user needs from a cost/benefit perspective in formulating policies for cataloging government publications.

The conventional name of a country, province, state,

county, municipality, or other political jurisdiction is used as the heading for its government, unless the official name of the government is more familiar:

>   Massachusetts.
>   not Commonwealth of Massachusetts

a) Distinct entities: Corporate bodies created or controlled by a government but which have distinct identities of their own should be entered directly under their own names. Cultural organizations, parks, authorities, and similar institutions fall in this category:

>   National Science Foundation
>   National Agricultural Library
>   Veterans Administration Hospital, Durham, N.C.
>   Mather Air Force Base
>   Grand Teton National Park
>   Houston Independent School District
>   Library of Congress
>   Minneapolis-St. Paul Sanitary District
>   National Coal Board
>   Tennessee Valley Authority
>   Canadian National Railways
>   Federal Reserve Bank of Richmond
>   Church of England
>   Smithsonian Institution

b) Basic agencies: Agencies through which the basic legislative, executive, and judicial functions of government are exercised should be entered as subheadings of the heading for the government:

>   United States. Supreme Court
>   United Kingdom. Air Ministry

In addition to those agencies whose very names imply subordination, legislative bodies, courts, armed services, chief executives (acting officially), and embassies are entered subordinately.

c) Officials: The heading for a sovereign, president, other chief of state, or governor, consists of the title of office followed by the inclusive years of reign or incumbency

and, by name in brief form--all as a subheading under the
name of the government. If the title varies with the incumbent (e. g. , King and Queen) use a common designation of the
office (e. g. , Sovereign):

> United Kingdom. Sovereign (1936-1952 : George VI)
> United States. President (1946-1952 : Truman)

If, in addition to the heading for a chief of state, a heading
is established for him as a person, make explanatory references under each heading:

> George VI, King of the United Kingdom

Here are entered private communications, public speeches,
and collections that include both private and official communications. For publications constituting official acts of
the sovereign (e. g. , messages to Parliament, proclamations,
etc. ,) see entries under

> United Kingdom. Sovereign (1936-1952 : George VI)

When the heading applies to more than one incumbent, omit
dates and names from the heading:

> North Carolina. Governor

The heading for a head of government who is not also
a chief of state consists of the title as a subheading under
the government; dates and names are not included:

> United Kingdom. Prime Minister
> Detroit. Mayor

The heading for any other government official is that
of the minstry or agency represented:

> United States. General Accounting Office
>   Refer from: United States. Comptroller General

d) Legislative bodies: If a legislature has more than
one chamber, enter each as a subheading under the legislature:

> United States. Congress. Senate
>   Refer from: United States. Senate

Enter committees and other subordinate units as subheadings under the legislature or of a particular chamber, as appropriate:

> United States. Congress. Joint Committee on the
> Library
> United States. Congress. House. Select Committee
> on Government Organization

Add the number and year for successive legislatures which are numbered consecutively, when the heading is for the body or chamber as a whole:

> United States. Congress (89th, 2d session : 1966)

e) Courts: Enter a court as a subheading under country, state, or other jurisdiction. Add the appropriate regional jurisdiction in parentheses when necessary:

> North Carolina. Supreme Court
> Vermont. Court of Chancery
> United States. District Court (North Carolina :
> Eastern District)
> (Name: United States District Court for the
> Eastern District of North Carolina)

f) Armed forces: Enter each service as a direct subheading under the name of the government. Enter a component branch as a subheading under the service, unless its name begins with the name of the service or with an adjective derived from that name:

> United States. Army. General Staff
> United States. Marine Corps
> United States. Navy. Fleet, 7th
> United States. Naval Air Transport Service
> United States. Marine Corps. Division, 2nd (Name:
> 2nd Marine Division)
> Canada. Army. Royal Canadian Army Medical Corps
> United States. Army. Army, Fifth
> United States. Army. Corps, II
> United States. Army. Engineer Combat Battalion,
> 2nd
> New York (State), Militia
> New York (State), National Guard

g) Embassies, legations, etc.: Enter a continuing office representing the government of one country in another as a subheading under the name of the country represented. If the heading is for an embassy or legation, add, within parentheses, the name of the country to which it is accredited; if it is for a consulate or other local office, add the name of the city in which it is located:

> United States. Legation (Bulgaria)
> United Kingdom. Consulate, Cairo
> Australia. High Commissioner in London
> United States. Mission to the United Nations

Religious bodies. Although the rules for entering religious bodies are generally consistent with those for other types of corporate entities, there are some special provisions, and it is helpful to consider the most frequently used ones as a group. Religious bodies, including local ones, are entered directly under their names, in accordance with the general rules.

a) Church councils: While ecumenical, interdenominational, and Early Christian councils should be entered directly under their names a general or regional council of a corporate denominational body should be entered as a subheading under the corporate body:

> Methodist Church (United States) General Conference
> Society of Friends. Philadelphia Yearly Meeting
> Catholic Church. Province of Baltimore. Provincial
>   Council (10th : 1869)

b) Dioceses: Enter these and other subordinate units as subheadings under the parent body:

> Protestant Episcopal Church in the U.S.A. Diocese
>   of Southern Virginia
> Catholic Church. Archdiocese of Santiago de Cuba

but:

> Greek Archdiocese of North and South America
>   (an autonomous entity)

c) Ecclesiastical officials: The heading for a bishop, patriarch, etc., in an official capacity, consists of title as

a subheading under the diocese, order, etc., followed by the inclusive years of incumbency and, in parentheses, by the name in brief form:

> Church of England. Diocese of Winchester. Bishop (1367-1404 : William of Wykeham)
> Dominicans. Master General (1486 : Barnabas Sassone)
> Catholic Church. Pope (1958-63 : John XXIII)

d) Religious orders and societies: Enter under the name by which best known:

> Franciscans
> Refer from: Order of St. Francis
> Jesuits
> Refer from: Society of Jesus

e) Local churches: A local church, monastery, convent, mosque, temple, etc. is entered directly under its own name, with additions as necessary for more precise identification:

> Third English Lutheran Church (Baltimore)
> St. Paul's Cathedral (London)
> Tenafly Presbyterian Church
> San Gabriel Mission
> Tintern Abbey
> Westover Church, Charles City County, Va.

If the headings for two or more churches are so similar that they are likely to be confused, the denomination or a more precise location may be added:

> St. James Church (Manhattan : Catholic)
> St. James Church (Bronx)
> St. James Church (Manhattan : Episcopal)

Variant forms: As in the case of personal authors, corporate names do not always appear in the same form on title pages. Similarly, two bodies may have identical names, and need to be distinguished in some way.

If different forms of the corporate name are found, choose the name as it appears at the head of the title. Also,

choose the briefest form that provides adequate identification
for cataloging purposes.

> Unesco
>> Refer from: United Nations Educational, Scien-
>> tific and Cultural Organization

In the locality or even in the region, references from the
full name may be unnecessary; e. g., in California or on the
West Coast, no reference may be necessary from Henry E.
Huntington Library and Art Gallery.   However, if changes have
occurred in the official name of a corporate body, establish
headings under each name for cataloging publications appearing under this name.   Make appropriate cross references
between the headings under which publications of the body appear in the catalog.   An explanatory reference should be filed
under each of the names, for example:

> Pennsylvania State University

>> The name of the Farmers' High School was
>> changed in 1862 to Agricultural College of
>> Pennsylvania; in 1874 to Pennsylvania State
>> College; in 1953 to Pennsylvania State University.
>> Works by this body are entered under the name
>> used at the time of publication.

Conventional name: When a corporate body is frequently
identified by a conventional form of name in reference sources,
prefer the conventional to the official name.   Also, when the
name of a body of ancient origin or one that is international
in character has become firmly established under an English
form, enter it under this form, regardless of the forms
which may appear on its publications.   Instances of conventional names of this type are especially prevalent among religious bodies, fraternal and knightly orders, and diplomatic
conferences.

> Catholic Church
> Benedictines
>> Refer from: Order of St. Benedict
> European Economic Community
> Free Masons
> Westminster Abbey
> Yalta Conference

Additions and modifications.   Place names, dates, and other descriptors may be added in order that corporate names may be properly identified.   An atlas or gazetteer is the best source for determining the correct form of a geographical name.

1.   Add the name of the place in which the body is located if the same name has been used by another body in a different location:

> Union College (Lincoln, Neb.)
> Union College (Schenectady, NY)

2.   Prefer the name of an institution to the name of the place in which a body is located when it provides better identification:

> Quadrangle Club (University of Chicago)

3.   Add the name of the country, state, province, etc., in parentheses, instead of the local name if the name has been used by different bodies that have a character that is national, state, provincial, etc.:

> Labour Party (United Kingdom)
> Labour Party (New Zealand)

4.   If a local place name that is part of a corporate name is insufficient to differentiate two or more bodies, add in parentheses the name of the state, province, or country:

> Washington County Historical Society (Ark.)
> Washington County Historical Society (Md.)

5.   If the name of a given place might be confused with another of the same name, add the name of the larger geographic entity in which it is located, such as country, constituent state, island group, etc.; state or province may be used with U.S. or Canadian local place names:

> Victoria (Australia)
> Palma (Majorca)
> St. Aubin (Jersey)
> Winnipeg (Manitoba)

6.   Omit the term indicating type of governmental administration unless it is required to distinguish the place from another place of the same name:

Meath <u>not</u> County Meath

<u>but</u>:

District of Columbia

7. Distinguish political or governmental jurisdictions with the same name by adding in parentheses the type of jurisdiction or other appropriate designation:

New York (N.Y.)
New York (U.S. : State)
Berlin (Germany : West)

8. Omit initial articles unless required for reasons of clarity or grammar:

Library Association
<u>not</u>: The Library Association
<u>Club</u> (London)

9. Omit terms such as incorporated or limited, unless they are needed to make clear that the name is that of a corporate body:

Bell Telephone Laboratories

<u>but</u>:

Films Incorporated

10. When the corporate name begins with initials, enter in that form but refer from the surname.

G. Schirmer
A.K. Smiley Public Library

11. A conference, symposium, or other meeting should be identified by number, date, and place--in that order:

Pi Iota Gamma Society, Constitutional Convention
(3rd, 1974 : Atlantic City)

12. If the name of a corporate body leaves any doubt as to its identification, add in parentheses a word or phrase to clarify the meaning of the heading:

Bounty (Ship)

WNCN-FM (Radio Station : New York, N.Y.)
Friedrich Witte (Firm)

UNIFORM TITLES

For some works to be entered in a library catalog it will not
be possible to identify either a personal author or a responsible corporate body. In these cases, the title becomes the
most important means of identifying the work. Usually it is
simply transcribed as given on the title page, but there are
some instances where special rules for title entry must be
followed. Even when the author is known, certain other types
of works also need to be entered according to these rules.

When a work has appeared through the centuries in a
great variety of editions, versions and translations, a uniform
title enables the cataloger to bring together in the catalog all
entries for a given work, be it a poem, epic, romance, tale,
play, chronicle, or religious scripture, regardless of the
varying titles under which the various editions have been published. The following types of works are generally identified
by uniform titles:

> Sacred scriptures
> Creeds and confessions
> Liturgical works
> Anonymous works without titles
> Early anonymous chronicles and literary works
> Early collections entered under title
> Early anonymous compilations of ancient laws and
>   customs
> Peace treaties and international conventions

Music and laws are also usually given uniform titles in order
that differing editions might be brought together under the
same heading in the catalog. For a brief discussion of uniform titles for music, see pages 197 to 206.

General rule. When different editions, versions, translations,
etc., of a work appear under various titles, one title should
be selected as the uniform title under which all will be cataloged. References should be made to the uniform title from
the different titles or variants of the title under which a work
has been published or cited in reference sources:

Song of the Nibelungs
see Nibelungenlied

Fielding, Henry
[Joseph Andrews]
The history of the adventures of Joseph Andrews
and his friend Mr. Abraham Adams.

While uniform titles are required most often to bring
together editions of classics such as the above, more recent
works sometimes also may be given a uniform title, as in
the case of the Headstrom book illustrated in card 24 (in a
simplified form also in card 17).

```
          Headstrom, Richard.
            [Nature in miniature]
            Nature discoveries with a hand lens / Richard
          Headstrom. -- Dover ed. -- New York : Dover
          Publications, 1981, c1968.
            412 p. : ill. ; 21 cm.

            Originally published under title: Nature in
          miniature: 1st ed. New York : Knopf, 1968.
            ISBN 0-486-24077-0




            1. Zoology.   2. Botany.   I. Title
```

Card 24.   Uniform title for work first published under dif-
            ferent title.

If the 1981 edition had been changed significantly, in addition
to having been titled differently, the entry would be under the
new title.   Other examples are Jane Fonda's Workout Book
and Crockett's Flower Garden (see cards 34 and 8), where
[Workout book] and [Flower garden] have been established as
the uniform titles.   A third type of uniform heading that is
now seen quite frequently is made when a work originally issued under one title is brought out in another country under
a different title (see card 54).

There has been a great increase in the use of uniform

titles since AACR2, primarily because of the advances in universal bibliographic control. While the small library in this country may find it adequate to identify Plaidy's book only by its American title and Headstrom's book by its new title, large bibliographic data bases abhor the confusion caused by two names for the same work. Using a uniform title allows the records to file together alphabetically, regardless of edition.

The small library that does its own cataloging should set a policy to guide the cataloger in the use of uniform titles in such cases as those discussed above. Most likely, it will want to use a uniform title for a work such as <u>Joseph Andrews</u>, and added entries for the short title forms for the Fonda and Crockett books. In the case of the Plaidy book, no action at all may be required, unless the library happens to own both the British and American editions. If the Headstrom book is not entered under uniform title, it would be wise to make an added entry for the earlier title.

<u>Works written before 1501.</u> Use the title in the original language by which it has come to be identified in reference sources and in most modern editions:

> Beowulf
> Chanson de Roland

However, prefer a well established English title for a classical Greek work:

> Aristophanes
>   Birds
> Homer
>   Iliad
> Plato
>   Republic

<u>Anonymous classics.</u> For an early anonymous work originally written in a language using an alphabet other than the Roman alphabet, use the English title. The following list, based on various codes and aids, gives some headings commonly used:

Arabian nights	El Cid Campeador	Kalevala
Beowulf	Cuchulain	Mabinogion
Chanson de Roland	Grail	Mother Goose

Nibelungenlied   Reynard the Fox   Seven sages
Njals saga   Robin Hood

```
Mother Goose.
   If wishes were horses, and other rhymes /
illustrated by Susan Jeffers. -- New York :
Dutton, 1979.
   1 v. : ill.

   ISBN 0-525-32531-X




   1. Nursery rhymes.  I. Jeffers, Susan.
```

Card 25. Entry under uniform title. Note that uniform title
is not bracketed when it is main entry.

Separately published parts. When a part (or parts)
of a work to which a uniform title has been assigned is published separately, it may be cataloged under the title of the
part, but a reference should be made from the uniform title
of the main work:

> Arabian nights
>   For separately published stories from this work
>   see
> Ali Baba
> Sinbad the Sailor

Collections. The uniform titles Works, Selections,
Plays, etc. may be used to bring together different editions
of an author's works:

> Ibsen, Henrik
>   [Plays]
>   Six dramatic works.

Sacred scriptures. Special rules appear in AACR2 for

cataloging biblical literature, and a special library of religious
literature, no matter how small, needs to consult those rules.
The following is intended only as a guide for a small general
library.

For parts of the Bible, use the uniform title, followed
by Old or New Testament (O.T. or N.T.), followed by the
specific book or commonly used group name. For a complete
Bible, note the version as a subheading, and the language, if
other than English:

> Bible. N.T. Luke
> Bible. O.T. Ezra
> Bible. N.T. Epistles.
> Bible. O.T. Pentateuch.
> Bible. Authorized.
> Bible. Latin. Vulgate.

If the library feels that it has enough material to warrant it, references from the titles of individual books, variant names of books, and group names may be made.

The sacred literature of any other religion is entered
in a similar way under a uniform heading:

> Talmud
> Koran
> Vedas

Laws. The uniform title, Laws, etc., should be
used as a subheading under the name of the appropriate jurisdiction for collections of legislative enactments or administrative regulations other than those on a particular subject.
Citation or other distinctive title should be used for subject
compilations or single laws.

> Providence
>   [Laws, etc.]
>   Revised ordinances of 1974.

> but:
> United States
>   Civil Rights Act of 1964.

Treaties. Most treaties are entered directly under
their names, as discussed under the section on direct entry.

A bilateral or trilateral treaty is entered according to the following order of preference: under the home country if it is a signatory; under the party on one side of a bilateral treaty if it is the only party on that side and there are two or more parties on the other; under the party whose catalog heading is the first in alphabetical order. Add the subheading Treaties, etc. after the name of the country. If the treaty is bilateral and there is only one party on the other side, also add the name of that party. The date of signing always forms the last part of the heading. Added entries are made under the other parties to the treaty.

> Title page:
> > Loan agreement between the United States of America and the European Coal and Steel Community, signed April 23, 1954.
> Enter under:
> > European Coal and Steel Community
> > > [Treaties, etc. United States, 1954 Apr. 23]
> > > Loan agreement....

Chapter 5

ADDED ENTRIES

If every library user could be expected to know precisely which books he or she needed, and could also be expected to know the exact heading under which librarians would choose to catalog each book, there would need to be only one catalog card for each book in the library. But as every librarian knows, library patrons frequently know only the title of a book, or need information on some subject. So, after the cataloger has decided on the main entry for a book, it is necessary to consider additional entries which will enable the card catalog to provide maximum access to the collection.

An added entry is a secondary entry; i.e., it is any other than the main entry. There may be added entries for editor, translator, title, variant title, subjects, series, etc. An added entry card is basically a duplicate of the main entry card, with the addition of a special heading. In the small library, however, whether the added entry is an exact and complete duplicate of the main entry (plus special heading) will depend on whether the library already has in hand a set of several duplicate cards for the book being cataloged, or whether it must prepare and type each one. In most cases the library will have already purchased printed cards, or it may have the facilities to make duplicates itself from the main entry card. Some commercial sources of printed cards can even provide sets with headings already added. But when prepared card sets are not available for an item to be cataloged, the librarian should consider whether all the descriptive information on the main entry card is really needed on every other entry. The minimum information required for most added entry cards is the heading, the call number, the author, title, publisher, and date (with subtitle omitted). An even shorter form is permissible for fiction title entries, as explained in previous chapters. Libraries which regularly include extensive contents notes on the main entry card may simply stamp "See main entry for contents" on appropriate added entry cards.

Names

Added entries should be made for persons or corporate bodies
connected with a publication under which a catalog user is likely
to search. This is especially important when the main entry
for a work is under a title or corporate body (see card 26).

```
         Rogers, JoAnn V.
027.62   Libraries and young adults : media, service and
         librarianship / edited by JoAnn V. Rogers. --
         Littleton, Colo. : Libraries Unlimited, 1979.
         238 p. ; 24 cm.

         ISBN 0-87287-195-9




         1. Libraries, young adults.  I. Rogers, JoAnn V.
```

Card 26.   Added entry for editor of work entered under title.

        Added entries may be made for joint authors (up to
three), for a compiler, editor, illustrator, translator, or
even for the person who writes the introduction to the book
of another, provided these added entries are likely to be
useful. If there are more than three joint authors or editors, an entry is made only for the first one (see card 10).
An added entry under Woodward would be useful for Bernstein and Woodward's All the President's Men, because some
readers will look under Bernstein and some under Woodward.
The Boys' King Arthur, mentioned on page 53, needs an added
entry for Lanier, since the book is often spoken of as Lanier's King Arthur.   Also, while the main entry for Macleod's
The Book of King Arthur and His Noble Knights is under Macleod, an entry is needed for Malory for the reader who is
interested in everything in the library relating to Malory.

        When the main entry is under author, an added entry
is made for an editor if he or she has added significant material or if the work has been issued in many editions with

different editors, e. g. Shakespeare's plays; under a translator if the translation is in verse or if the work has been
translated into English by many different translators; under
an illustrator if the artist's contribution is significant. If a
writer like Ezra Pound or Richard Wilbur translates another's
work, an added entry enables the student to consider not only
their original writings but their translations as well. The
student interested in The Iliad is likely to wish to see both
Pope's and Lattimore's translations, and to look in the catalog under the translators' names, though knowing it is Homer's
Iliad. Occasionally an added entry is necessary for a compiler or an editor for the same reason. If the library is
likely to have a call for illustrations by a well-known artist,
e. g. Sir John Tenniel, an added entry under his name would
make it possible to find examples of his illustrations. If the
library has a copy, and it should have, of The H. W. Wilson
Company's Children's Catalog, it may be used to locate books
with illustrations by a particular artist and no added entry
need be made under illustrator. It must be remembered,
however, that reliance on this type of index presupposes the
availability of a librarian who can help the patron who has
failed to find the entry in the card catalog.

To make added entries, the name in its best-known
form (with dates, if the library uses them), is written on
the line above the main entry. Begin at the second indention, so that the main entry heading may remain in a prominent position. If the added heading occupies more than one
line, succeeding lines begin at the third indention.

The function of the person for whom the added entry
is made--e. g., illustrator, compiler, editor, translator,
etc.--does not need to be indicated after the name if unit
cards are used which spell out the full statement of responsibility. If the library types abbreviated cards for added entries, then some explanation is necessary (compare cards 28
and 29). The rules permit abbreviated designations of function only in the following cases:

> compiler--comp.
> editor--ed.
> illustrator--ill.
> translator--tr.

Another type of name added entry is for the author of
a work related to the one being cataloged. Usually, this takes

```
            Woodward, Bob.
364.1       Bernstein, Carl.
BER             All the President's men / by Carl Bernstein
            and Bob Woodward. -- New York : Simon and
            Schuster, 1974.
                349 p. : ports. ; 24 cm.




                1. Watergate affair, 1972-    2. The Washington
            Post.  I. Woodward, Bob.  II. Title.
```

Card 27. Added entry for joint author, unit card.

```
            Wilbur, Richard, 1921-
842.4       Molière, 1622-1673.
MOL             [Selections. English. 1982]
                Four comedies / Molière ; translated by Richard
            Wilbur. -- New York : Harcourt Brace Jovanovich,
            [1982], c1978.
                634 p. : ill. ; 21 cm.

                Contents:  The school for wives -- The mis-
            anthrope -- Tartuffe -- The learned ladies.

                ISBN 0-151-61781-3

                1. Molière, 1622-1673--Translations, English.
            I. Wilbur, Richard, 1921-    II. Title.
```

Card 28. Added entry for translator, unit card.

the form of a name/title added entry, with the name of the author and the title of the original work added above the unit card main entry at the second and third indentions, respectively (see card 30). Another example of the name/title added entry is given in card 96, showing the use of a uniform title.

```
            Wilbur, Richard, tr.
  842.4   Molière.
  MOL        Four comedies. -- New York : Harcourt Brace
            Jovanovich, 1982.
```

Card 29.   Added entry, no unit card.

```
            Kesey, Ken.
  812         One flew over the cuckoo's nest
            Wasserman, Dale.
              One flew over the cuckoo's nest : a play in
            two acts / by Dale Wasserman from the novel
            by Ken Kesey. -- New York : Samuel French,
            1974.
              83 p.
```

Card 30.   Added entry for the author and title of a work
           dramatized by another writer.

Titles

Title entries are made for all books of fiction and for most
nonfiction. Consider Cyril Bentham Falls' The Second World
War, a Short History and Wilbur Morrison's Fortress Without

a Roof. The former title is neither striking nor distinctive and may be used for many histories of the war. Undoubtedly many readers, however, will remember the latter and look for it in the catalog.

Title entries need not be made for the following: works with common titles that are incomplete or meaningless without the author's name, such as "Collected works," "Autobiography," "Letters," "Memoirs," "Bulletin," "Report," "Proceedings," etc.; works with introductory words commonly used in titles, e.g., "Introduction to," "The principles of," "A story of"; works with titles that are essentially the same as the main entry heading; works consisting solely of the name of a real person, unless fictionalized; works with titles that are the same as a subject heading under which they are entered. Fenton and Fenton's Mountains illustrates the last point. The title of this book is Mountains and the subject treated is mountains, so the subject heading would be MOUNTAINS. It is unnecessary to have the same book entered in the catalog twice under the same word; but if only a title card is made it will file at the end of all the cards for material about mountains even though the author's name begins with F; hence the rule, if the first word or words of the title and the subject are the same, do not make a title card. In the case of catalogs that are divided by name, title, and subject, one would still need both subject and title added entries.

Title entries should be made for all works published anonymously but whose authors have been identified and used as main entries. Alternate titles, cover titles or other titles by which a work might be known should be given added entries.

As discussed above, there are two possible forms for title entries, namely the short form and the unit card form. The short form title card has the call number, title, and author. Title cards may be just like the main entry, however, with the brief title added above the heading of the unit card. This form is in accordance with the statement made above, that an added entry is a duplicate of a main entry, with the addition of a special heading. If a unit card is used, the reader need not refer to the main entry card.

In some cases, a partial title entry may be needed in addition to a title-proper added entry. For example, J. George Frederick's A Primer of "New Deal" Economics

```
                  Fortress without a roof
    940.54  Morrison, Wilbur H.
    MOR
```

Card 31.   Added entry for title, short form.

```
                  Fortress without a root
    940.54  Morrison, Wilbur H., 1915-
                Fortress without a roof : the Allied bombing
            of the Third Reich / Wilbur H. Morrison. --
            New York, N. Y. : St. Martin's Press, c1982.
                288 p. : ill. ; 21 cm.

                ISBN 0-312-29981-8

                1. World War, 1939-1945--Aerial operations.
            2. World War, 1939-1945--Campaigns--Germany.
            3. Germany--History--1933-1945.   I. Title.
```

Card 32.   Added entry for title, unit card.

would have an entry for the full title and for the partial title, "New Deal" Economics.   Another example is illustrated by card 33.   While some patrons might look under Barron's, others will search under "How to prepare for...."

```
              How to prepare for the graduate record
                examination
     378      Brownstein, Samuel C.
                Barron's how to prepare for the graduate record
              examination : GRE / Samuel C. Brownstein and
              Mitchel Weiner ; author of special chapter on
              mathematics, Stephen Hilbert. -- 5th ed. --
              Woodbury, NY : Barron's, c1981.
                vi, 601 p. : ill. ; 28 cm.

              ISBN 0-8120-2346-3

              1. Graduate record examination--Study guides.
              I. Weiner, Mitchel.  II. Hilbert, Stephen.
              III. Title.  IV. Title: How to prepare for the
              graduate record examination.
```

Card 33.   Added entry, partial title.

When the title begins with a name which is the same
as the main entry, it is also helpful to have an added entry
for the partial title as well as the title proper (see card 34).
In the Jane Fonda example, the partial title has been established as a uniform title.   Similarly, when a classic work
is entered under its uniform title, e.g., "Arabian nights,"
an added entry is made for the title proper, e.g., "The thousand and one nights."

```
              Jane Fonda's workout book
     613.7    Fonda, Jane.
                [Workout book]
                Jane Fonda's workout book / by Jane Fonda ;
              photographs by Steve Schapiro. -- New York :
              Simon and Schuster, c1981.
                254 p. : ill. ; 28 cm.

              Bibliography: p. 252.
              ISBN 0-671-43217-0

              1. Exercise for women.  I. Schapiro, Steve.
              II. Title.  III. Title: Workout book.
```

Card 34.   Added entry, title proper.

Also, a title proper added entry is made for works entered under a name and uniform title, as in card 35. If a library has several editions of a work that requires the same added entry, it saves time and space to make one reference card (see card 36).

```
              The life and strange surprising adventures of
                 Robinson Crusoe of York
           Defoe, Daniel.
              [Robinson Crusoe]
              The life and strange surprising adventures of
           Robinson Crusoe of York / by Daniel Defoe. --
           London : Basilisk Press, 1979.
              180 p. : ill., facsim. ; 33 cm.
```

Card 35.   Added entry for title proper.

```
              Robinson Crusoe
           Defoe, Daniel

              Editions of this work will be found under
           the author's name.
```

Card 36.   Reference card for title of work available in many editions.

Subjects

There are usually more inquiries for material on a subject
than there are for books by a specific author or with a particular title.   The most used cards in the catalog are the
subject cards; that is, the cards which indicate on the top
line the subject of which the book treats.   For this reason,
a subject entry should be made for every book which deals
with a definite subject.   Sometimes a book covers several
different topics and requires two, three, or even more subject entries.   Subject entries are not necessary for books
containing a single poem or a single play, or for a collection of all or part of the works of an individual author.   Chapter 7 deals with the question of ascertaining what a book is
about and what subject headings best express its contents.
There is also the possibility of making general subject references for entire groups of books, e.g., books on birds, air-
planes, etc., or for all books of a certain form, e.g., books
of American poetry.   On card 37, note that the classification
number is given in the same position as on main entry cards
and the subject heading in the same position as added entry
headings on the cards shown in this chapter.   A line is skipped and a paragraph, beginning on the second line below the
heading, tells where books on the given subject may be found.
Another line is skipped and the second paragraph about the
use of the shelf list is given.

```
551.2    VOLCANOES

              Books about volcanoes will be found on the
         shelves under 551.2.

              For a complete author list of the books in
         the library on volcanoes, consult the shelf list
         under 551.2.
```

Card 37.   General subject entry for all books in a subject
          class.

A unit card with an added subject heading is given below in order to show the position of the heading. Subdivisions of a main heading may be separated from it by a space, dash, space or other punctuation marks agreed upon locally, as a long dash (e.g., U.S.--HISTORY). This heading is given in full capitals in order to distinguish it from title or other added entry headings. Some libraries use red ink in typing subject headings, in which case they are not capitalized.

```
           WORLD WAR, 1939-1945--AERIAL OPERATIONS
 940.54  Morrison, Wilbur H.
           Fortress without a roof : the Allied bombing
         of the Third Reich / Wilbur H. Morrison. --
         New York : St. Martin's Press, c1982.
           288 p. : ill. ; 21 cm.

           ISBN 0-312-29981-8




           1. World War, 1939-1945--Aerial operations.
         2. World War, 1939-1945--Campaigns--Germany.
         3. Germany--History--1933-1945.  I. Title.
```

Card 38. Added entry for subject.

Series

A series added entry is made for each separately cataloged work which might be sought as part of a series. The importance of the series determines whether or not an added entry is made, as discussed in chapter 6. If the parts of a series are numbered, the number is usually included in the heading. Added entries are rarely made for series with titles that include the name of the trade publisher or have nothing in common except their format. Ideally, the cataloger should have a sense of what type of series added entries will prove useful to the patron. AACR2 rules say, however, "in case of doubt, make a series added entry."

Cards 39 and 40 are examples of added entry cards

for two titles which are part of the kind of series that a library might wish to collocate in the catalog. Unless the library plans to acquire every book in the series, no real purpose is served by inclusion of the volume number in the heading. Patrons who wish to know what titles there are in a
series in addition to the ones owned by the library may be
referred to reference tools such as Books in Series or Cumulative Book Index. When the library does have all the
parts of a numbered series, such as The Reference Shelf,
the numbering should be included in the added entry heading,
so that the order of the entries in the catalog provides a
"table of contents" of the series (see card 48).

```
            The Canadians
  289.9   Austin, Alvyn.
            Aimee Semple McPherson / Alvyn Austin. --
          Don Mills, Ont. : Fitzhenry & Whiteside, 1980.
            63 p. ; 22 cm. -- (The Canadians)

            ISBN 0-88902-657-2




            1. McPherson, Aimee Semple.   2. Evangelists--
          Canada--Biography.   I. Title.   II. Series.
```

Card 39.   Series added entry.

Analytic

An analytical entry is an entry for a part of a work. It may
be for a complete work in itself which is published in a collection, or it may be for only a few pages inadequately described (either from the author or subject approach) by the
catalog entry for the work as a whole.

       Some books are made up of two or more separate
works of an author, or of different authors; or they may
treat several distinct subjects or phases of a subject. For
example, the two-volume edition of De la Mare's Collected
Poems contains his well-known poems for children, published
under the title Peacock Pie. In this collection the library

```
              The Canadians
941.082 Hayes, William A.
              Beaverbrook / William A. Hayes. -- Don Mills,
         Ont. : Fitzhenry & Whiteside, 1978.
              63 p. : ill. ; 22 cm. -- (The Canadians ; 46)
```

Card 40   Series added entry.

has the work, Peacock Pie, whether or not it has the separately bound edition. How can this be shown in the catalog?
By making author and title analytical entries for it. Law's
Science in Literature contains an essay by Madame Curie on
her discovery of radium. This material on radium is as important as any that will be found in many libraries. It can
be brought out by means of a subject analytical entry, i. e.,
a subject entry for a part of a book. Small collections and
special libraries need to have their material analyzed freely,
since the analytical entry may represent the only work by
the author, the only copy of the essay, play, etc., or the
only material on the subject. Frequently the analytical entry is used to call attention to an extra copy of popular material already available in another form.

It should be emphasized again that advantage should
be taken of work already done. The H. W. Wilson Company's
Children's Catalog, 14th edition, includes 11, 259 analytical
entries; their Senior High School Library Catalog, 12th edition, includes 15, 532 analytical entries. Printed indexes
such as Short Story Index, Play Index and others, although
they may seem expensive, would be more economical in the
long run than preparing analytical cards for collections of
short stories and plays.

Analytics can be provided in one of several ways.
One is similar to the name/title added entry discussed above

(see card 30). Another way is to make an "In" entry, which consists of a description of the part analyzed and a citation of the whole of which it is a part. Both ways of analyzing a part of a work are shown in cards 41 and 42. For a third way, see page 209.

```
              Aristotle.
                On metaphysics
    108.2     Classics in logic ; readings in epistemology,
                theory of knowledge and dialectics / edited
                by Dagobert D. Runes. -- New York : Philo-
                sophical Library, c1962.
                xiv, 818 p. ; 22 cm.




              Contents: Obscurity as sources of error /
              Peter Abailard -- On the nature of the intellect
              / Albertus Magnus -- On concepts / Al-Farabi --
              On metaphysics / Aristotle
                              (Continued on next card)
```

Card 41.   Analytical added entry, name/title.

```
    812       Williams, Tennessee
                A streetcar named desire.
                p. 49-93 ; 24 cm.
                In Best American plays : third series, 1945-
              1951 / edited with an introduction by John
              Gassner. -- New York : Crown, c1952, 1966
              printing.








              I. Title.
```

Card 42.   "In" entry.

```
812        Best American plays : third series, 1945-1951 /
              edited with an introduction by John Gassner.
              -- New York : Crown, c1952, 1966 printing.
              xxviii, 707 p. ; 24 cm.

              Contains 17 plays.




              1. American drama--Collections.  1. Gassner,
           John.
                                                     ANALS
```

Card 43.   Main entry for book referred to in card 42, indicating that analytics have been made.

```
           Peacock pie.
821        De la Mare, Walter.
D33           Collected poems, 1901-1918 / Walter De la Mare.
           -- New York : Holt, c1920.
              2 v. ; 20 cm.

              Contents: v. 1. Poems, 1906. The Listeners.
           Motley, 1919 -- v. 2. Songs of childhood, 1901.
           Peacock pie, 1913.




              I. Title: Songs of childhood.  II. Title:
           Peacock pie.
```

Card 44.   Selective title analytics for collection.

The decision to use the added name/title entry for analytics as opposed to the "In" format depends on the number of parts to be analyzed. In order to use the added entry method, the name/title must appear in the record for the work being ana-

lyzed, as in card 41. When there are more than three or four parts that you wish to bring out, it is easier to use the "In" method. While the rules call for a full citation of the title, statement of responsibility, and publication details for the collection being analyzed through the "In" method, the small library might take the liberty of omitting all but the call number and title in a case such as that shown in card 41. The user needs only the information that will lead to the book.

If it seems desirable to bring out titles of particular parts of a collection of works by one author, the easiest way to do so is to make title added entries, as in card 44.

Subject analytics for parts of books are most easily made by simply giving all appropriate subject headings in the tracing, relying on the patron to find the appropriate section of the book to which the subject heading refers.

Chapter 6

SERIES, OTHER RELATED WORKS, AND SERIALS

It is sometimes difficult to distinguish between sets, series, and serials, and therefore it may be helpful to discuss the differences at the beginning of this chapter.

The AACR2 glossary defines "series" as:

> 1. A group of separate items related to one another by the fact that each item bears, in addition to its own title proper, a collective title applying to the group as a whole. The individual items may or may not be numbered.
> 2. Each of two or more volumes of essays, lectures, articles, or other writings, similar in character and issued in sequence, e.g., Lowell's Among my books, second series.
> 3. A separately numbered sequence of volumes within a series or serial, e.g., Notes and queries, 1st series, 2nd series, etc.

The most familiar kinds of series are publisher's series such as Random House's Modern Library, or the Beginner Books. The small library will seldom need to include this type of series in the body of the catalog entry. Subject series are another matter, as library users are quite likely to be interested in locating the different titles in the series (see, for example, cards 39 and 40).

A third type of series is the author series, such as John Jakes' Kent Family Chronicles of The American Bicentennial series. Occasionally, one encounters a nonfiction series that is unified both by subject and by author, such as Robert Coles' Children of Crisis.

Until AACR2, "set" was another term used for distinguishing between series, serials, and other related works.

What used to be referred to as a set is now defined as a "multipart item," "a monograph complete, or intended to be completed, in a finite number of separate parts." The most familiar kind of set is the multivolume encyclopedia, published under a single title, with the volumes usually designated by volume numbers or letters of the alphabet (see card 45).

```
Compton's encyclopedia and fact-index. -- 1981
    ed. -- [Chicago] : F. E. Compton Co., c1981.
    26 v. : ill. (some col.) ; 27 cm.

    ISBN 0-85229-380-1 (set)




    1. Encyclopedias.  I. F.E. Compton Company.
```

Card 45.   Entry for set.

Another example of a set is Machlup's Information through the Printed Word: The Dissemination of Scholarly, Scientific, and Intellectual Knowledge (see card 46). This is a set or "multipart item," rather than a series, even though it has distinct titles for each volume. The difference between the Machlup monograph and the Coles series is that Machlup knew at the outset the scope and contents of the final work, whereas Coles did not envision a fifth volume until he actually wrote it, twenty years after the initial one. It was not possible for a cataloger to treat Coles' Children of Crisis as anything other than individual titles linked by the series name, whereas the Machlup work could be cataloged as a single entity at the appearance of the first volume.

A serial is defined as:

> A publication in any medium issued in successive parts bearing numerical or chronological designations and intended to be continued indefinitely. Serials include periodicals; newspapers; annuals (reports,

```
Machlup, Fritz.
   Information through the printed word : the
dissemination of scholarly, scientific, and
intellectual knowledge / Fritz Machlup, Kenneth
Leeson, and associates. -- New York : Prager,
1978-1980.
   4 v. : ill. ; 24 cm.

   Contents: v.1 Book publishing -- v.2 Journals
-- v.3 Libraries -- v.4 Books, journals, and
bibliographic services
   ISBN 0-03-047401-9 (v. 1)

   1. Publishers and publishing. 2. Book industries
and trade. 3. Periodicals. 4. Libraries.
I. Leeson, Kenneth. II. Title
```

Card 46.   Entry for set with individually titled volumes.

```
Coles, Robert.
   Privileged ones : the well-off and the rich
in America / Robert Coles. -- Boston : Little,
Brown, 1978, c1977.
   583 p. : col. ill. ; 22 cm. -- (His The
Children of crisis ; v. 5)

   ISBN 0-316-15149-1




   1. Children in the U.S.  I. Title.  II. Series:
Coles, Robert. Children of crisis ; v. 5.
```

Card 47.   Entry for one volume in a series.

yearbooks, etc.); the journals, memoirs, proceedings, transactions, etc., of societies; and numbered
monographic series.

Except for the last part of that definition, the distinction

between a serial and a series or set is quite clear. An example of a numbered monographic series which has the characteristics of a serial is H. W. Wilson's The Reference Shelf, which is indeed a series of monographs that could be cataloged individually. However, each is numbered, six are issued every year, the intention is to continue the series indefinitely, and one may subscribe to it, just like any serial. A tipoff to the cataloger encountering one of The Reference Shelf publications for the first time is the fact that each book bears its own ISBN number. From the point of view of the user, separate entries for each title are much more useful, because appropriate subject headings can be assigned to the individual numbers. Therefore, the preferred way of handling The Reference Shelf is to make individual entries, treating it as a series (see card 48). A similar example is Library Trends, which is a serial, but covers a different topic in each of its issues. Therefore, some libraries enter the various numbers individually, in order to provide subject access. Others make an entry under the serial heading, listing the separate numbers and their titles as they are received by the library.

```
        Saving social security / edited by Jason Berger.
        -- New York : H. W. Wilson, 1982.
        158 p. : ill. ; 19 cm. -- (Reference Shelf ;
        v. 54, no. 4)

        ISBN 0-8242-0688-1




        1. Social security--U.S.   I. Berger, Jason.
    II. Series.
```

Card 48.   Entry for issue in a "serial series".

In addition to series, serials, and multipart items, there are a number of other related works which need to be recognized by the cataloger. There are the "bound withs"; there are works which have no common title or formal series

title, but are related in that they are about the same characters or continue a narrative; there are works that are adaptations of other works; there are indexes, supplements, concordances, librettos, and similar categories; and there are editions of a work under different titles, in revised form, or in translation, etc.

Series

As discussed above, the main complication offered by series is their distinction from sets and serials. Once the cataloger has established that the item in hand is indeed a part of a series, the title proper of the series is recorded in parentheses, following the physical·description, if the nature of the series warrants it. Small libraries using the first level of description will usually omit a series statement, unless there is good reason to believe that patrons will search under the series title. One would certainly want a series entry for The Children of Crisis, for The Canadians (see cards 39 and 40), and for The Kent Chronicles (see card 49).

```
        Jakes, John W.
          The warriors / John Jakes. -- [Book club ed.].
        -- Garden City, N.Y. : N. Doubleday, c1977.
          492 p. : geneal. table ; 22 cm. -- (His The
        Kent family chronicles ; v. 6) (The American
        Bicentennial series ; v. 6)




          1 Title.  II. Series: Jakes, John W. The Kent
        family chronicles ; v. 6.  III. Series:  Jakes,
        John W. The American Bicentennial series ; v. 6.
```

Card 49.   Entry for title in an author series.

The Jakes series is rather unusual in that there are two names for the series. The first volume made no mention of Kent Family Chronicles, and it is not until the penultimate volume where that denomination appears on the title page.   It

is clear that The American Bicentennial Series, the name
originally chosen by the author and publisher, gave way to
the readers' choice of Kent Family Chronicles. Therefore,
it seems best to twist the rules very slightly and to give all
eight books both series designations, especially since one
may use any part of the item in hand as the source of information for a series name. Notice that the more specific series is given first.

Occasionally, one will encounter an item that is a
part of a series within a series. In such cases, the main
series, followed by the subseries are given in the same set
of parentheses:

(Music for today. Series 2 ; no. 8)
(Viewmaster science series. 4, Physics)

Multipart Items

Multipart items may or may not have titles for the individual
parts that are independent of the monograph title. If the titles
of the parts are independent and might be sought by the patron,
analytical entries should be made (see card 44). If the
volume titles are not likely to be sought by the patron, as
in the example in card 50, no analytics are made. Note
that the titles of the volumes are given in a contents note,
but are not traced, because they are not titles that are distinctive and likely to be searched for by the library user.

```
     The New book of popular science. -- [Danbury,
        Conn.] : Grolier, c1981.
        6 v. : ill. (some col.) ; 26 cm.

        Includes bibliographies and index.
        Contents: v. 1. Astronomy & space science. Com-
     puters & mathematics -- v. 2. Earth sciences.
     Energy. Environmental sciences -- v. 3. Physical
     sciences. General biology -- v. 4. Plant life.
     Animal life -- v. 5. Mammals. Human sciences --
     v. 6. Technology.
        ISBN 0-7172-1211-4 (set)

        1. Science--Popular works.  2. Technology--
     Popular works.  3. Natural history--Popular works.
```

Card 50.   Entry for set; parts not traced.

When all the projected parts of a multipart item are not issued at the time when the work is first cataloged, the information is presented as in card 51.

```
Woolf, Virginia.
    The letters of Virginia Woolf / editor, Nigel
Nicolson ; assistant editor, Joanne Trautmann.
-- New York : Harcourt Brace Jovanovich, 1975-
    v. : ill. ; 24 cm.

    First published under title: The flight of the
mind.
    Contents: v. 1. 1882-1912 (Virginia Woolf) --
v. 2. The question of things happening, 1912-1922
-- v. 3. A change of perspective -- v. 4. A re-
flection of the other person (1929-1931)

    1. Woolf, Virginia--Correspondence.  I. Nicol-
son, Nigel.  II. Trautmann, Joanne.  III. Title.
```

Card 51.   Open entry for multipart work.

At the time that the set was known to be complete, the cataloger would complete the entry by filling in the blanks for the publication dates and volume numbers, as well as adding the appropriate part titles to the contents note.

A multipart item may be composed of different media or may have parts that do not arrive in the library in the form of one to a volume. One may have a book with a cassette, a filmstrip with a pamphlet, a collection of pamphlets intended to be bound and treated as a volume, etc. The test should always be whether the collection of parts was intended to be used as a "monograph complete ... in a finite number of separate parts." An easy way to deal with subsidiary items that do not neatly fit the pattern of one title in five volumes is to treat them as "accompanying material," particularly in the case of mixed media. Chapter 9 has many examples of this approach.

If the multipart item is composed of pamphlets bound together, parts not equivalent to volume numbers, or a main set with supplements in pamphlet form, simple solutions can

usually be found through careful use of the physical description area:

> 12 pamphlets in portfolio.
> 8 v. in 5.
> 575 p. + annual paper supplements.

Other Relationships

There are a number of ways to indicate relationships between separately cataloged works in addition to a series statement. A uniform title may signal immediately a different edition of a work. A note may alert the catalog user to the fact that a work is an adaptation or revision of another work. In the case of indexes, concordances, and supplements, the relationship is usually expressed in the title of the work. Except in those cases where the work remains essentially the same --different edition, revision, or translation--it is entered separately under its own heading, and an added entry is made for the related work.

For example, An index to the Columbia edition of the works of John Milton by Patterson has a main entry under Patterson. A note on the catalog entry for the Milton work could alert the reader to the existence of an index, although the rules do not demand this. However, the rules do require a name-title added entry for the Milton work. Even if the link is only one way (from Patterson to Milton), the library can assure that the index volumes will be shelved with the set to which they relate by assigning the same call number.

Supplements, like indexes, receive separate main entries, with added entries for the original work. As discussed on page 55, brief supplements such as the annual paper additions to the H. W. Wilson Standard Catalogs may be treated as accompanying material, rather than entered separately. In the case of sequels, added entries are not made if the author does not change. Therefore, the R. F. Delderfield trilogy which begins with God Is an Englishman would not be linked by added entries. Since readers usually want to read sequels, a library may choose to add notes to each of the entries. Theirs Was the Kingdom would have as a note: "A sequel to God is an Englishman. Followed by Give us this day." Give Us this Day would have as a note: "A sequel to God is an Englishman, Theirs was the kingdom."

Delderfield, R. F.
  God is an Englishman. -- New York : Simon &
Schuster, c1970.
  687 p.

  The first volume of a trilogy. Followed by
Theirs was the kingdom, Give us this day.

When a sequel is not by the writer of the original work, however, main entry is under the name of the author of the sequel, and an added name-title entry is made for the original.

It is not always easy to decide how to enter revisions of works when the revision is done by someone other than the original author. AACR2 says that the cataloger must decide if the "modified" work is substantially changed from the original in its nature and content, or if the medium of expression has changed. It is quite easy to tell a change in medium, as when a stage play is rewritten as a novel or as a film script. In such cases, main entry would be under the name of the adapter, and an added name-title entry would be made for the original work (see card 30). When the medium of expression is not different, however, the work is treated as a new, but related work only when it is clear that the original has been rewritten to the point that it is no longer correct to attribute it to the original author. A typical example would be an adaptation for children of an adult classic. Usually, the title page will make it clear that the work has been "rewritten" or "retold" and there is no difficulty in deciding to enter under adapter, with a name-title added entry to link the works.

Usually, a work that has been abridged, enlarged or updated by someone other than the original author is still entered the same way. However, when the wording on the title page shows that the reviser is now considered to be primarily responsible for the work, a new main entry is made under the name of the reviser, and the relationship to the old edition

is established through a name-title added entry. The difference should be clear from the examples in cards 52 and 53.

Godin, Alfred J.
  Wild mammals of New England / by Alfred J.
Godin ; with drawings by the author. -- Field
guide ed. / adapted by Harry Vanderweide. --
Yarmouth, Me. : DeLorme Pub. Co., c1981.
  207 p. : ill., maps ; 22 cm.

  Includes index.

  1. Mammals--New England. I. Vanderweide,
Harry. II. Title.

Card 52.   Revision entered under original author.

Perkins, Flossie L.
  Book and non-book media : annotated guide to
selection aids for educational materials /
Flossie L. Perkins. -- Urbana, Ill. : National
Council of Teachers of English, c1972.
  298 p. ; 21 cm.

  Revision of: Book selection media / Ralph
Perkins. 1967.
  ISBN 0-8141-48086

  1. Children's literature--Bibliography.
I. Perkins, Ralph. Book selection media.
II. Title.

Card 53.   Revision entered under new author; works linked
        through name-title added entry.

When a work is published under different titles, but
is otherwise the same, The Library of Congress practice is

to enter it under a uniform title, which is usually the earliest. As can be seen from the example in card 54, this results in entries under both titles.

```
Plaidy, Jean.
  [Edward Longshanks]
  Hammer of the Scots / Jean Plaidy. -- 1st
American ed. -- New York : Putnam, 1981, c1979.
  318 p. ; 23 cm. -- (Her The Plantagenet
saga)

  London ed. has title: Edward Longshanks.
  ISBN 0-399-12641-4


  1. Edward I, King of England, 1239-1307--
Fiction. I. Title. II. Series: Plaidy, Jean.
Plantagenet saga.
```

Card 54.   Uniform title used for work published under different titles.

```
Flanagan, Hallie.
  Arena, the history of the Federal Theatre /
by Hallie Flanagan. -- Reprint ed. -- New York :
Arno Press, 1980, c1940.
  475 p., [16] p. of plates : ill. ; 24 cm.

  Reprint. Originally published: New York :
Duell, Sloan and Pearce, 1940.
  Bibliography: p. 439-447.
  ISBN 0-405-08521-4


  1. Federal Theatre Project (U.S.). 2. American
drama--20th century--History and criticism.
I. Title.
```

Card 55.   Reprint.

Facsimiles and reprints are linked to their originals through notes. Works bound together may be given separate entries, linked by "with" notes (see card 57), or may be

treated in a single entry with appropriate added entries (see card 56).

```
Gardner, Erle Stanley.
    Up for grabs / by A.A. Fair.  The hospitality
of the house / by Doris Miles Disney.  Teacher's
blood / by Ivan T. Ross. -- Roslyn, N.Y. : Pub-
lished for the Detective Book Club by W.J. Black,
[1964?].
    144, 154, 174 p. ; 24 cm.




    I. Disney, Doris Miles. The hospitality of the
house.  II. Ross, Ivan T. Teacher's blood.
III. Title.  IV. Title: The hospitality of the
house. V. Title: Teacher's blood.
```

Card 56.   Entry for works bound together. [Taken from A Manual of AACR2 Examples, compiled by the Minnesota AACR2 Trainers (Lake Crystal, Minn.: Soldier Creek Press, 1980), p. 10.]

Serials

As discussed above, serials include periodicals, newspapers, annuals, proceedings, etc. , of societies, and monographic numbered series. Small libraries usually do not catalog periodicals and newspapers, but will have entries in the catalog for serials such as The World Almanac and Who's Who in America. These are similar to those for monographs, with a few exceptions, as evident in the example in card 58.

The description of serials follows the same rules as for monographs, but there are several variations required by the nature of serials. The most conspicuous of these is the material (or type of publication) specific details area, which appears between the edition and publication areas for only two types of materials: cartographic and serial. Other aspects of cataloging peculiar to serials will be noted in the following summary of the rules.

The chief source of information for a printed serial is the first title page available, whether or not the library

```
Disney, Doris Miles.
  The hospitality of the house. -- Roslyn, N.Y. :
Published for the Detective Book Club by W.J.
Black, [1964?].
  154 p.

  With:  Up for grabs / A.A. Fair.  Teacher's
blood / Ivan T. Ross.




  I. Title.
```

Card 57. Separate entry for work bound with others.

```
Yearbook of special education. -- 1st ed.
  (1975 1976)      .      Chicago : Marquis Academic
Media, 1975-
  v. ; 29 cm.

Annual.
Library has: 1978/79-



  1. Handicapped children--Education--Yearbooks.
2. Exceptional children--Education--Yearbooks.
```

Card 58. Main entry for an annual.

has the original issue. This is in contrast to AACR1, where the latest volume determined the description. The change in this rule reflects the effort to standardize bibliographic records, so that the only variation from library to library would be in the holdings note.

While annuals and similar serials usually have a

standard title page, periodicals often do not. Therefore, the
rules permit substitution of the cover, caption, masthead,
editorial pages, colophon, and other pages--in that order--
for the chief source of information.

Choice of main entry follows the same rules as for
monographs. A serial issued by a corporate body is entered
under the name of that body only when it is of an administrative nature and is confined to its policies, staff, membership,
possessions, etc. Thus The ALA Handbook of Organization
is entered under the American Library Association, but
American Libraries is entered under title. Committee reports, regulations, conference proceedings, and similar items
would also be entered under the corporate body. Personal
authorship of serials is very rare, but does occur. Lasser's
annual income tax guides, for example, are entered under
his name.

The title proper is recorded as usual. If a name of
a corporate body (or its initials) is consistently used as part
of the title both in the serial itself and in indexes, etc., include the name as part of the title (e.g., UN Monthly Chronicle, FDA Consumer, ALA Yearbook).

Serials which include a date or number in the title
which vary with every issue are entered with the numerical
designation omitted from the title:

> Title page: 3rd Annual Report
> Title entered: Annual Report

Changes in title are a notoriously troublesome aspect
of serials cataloging. For a serial with main entry under
title, a new main entry is created whenever the title changes,
and the entries are linked by notes, as in cards 59 and 60.
When main entry is under a corporate name, and a change
in the name of the corporate body occurs, a new entry is
made, even if the name of the serial and its numbering remain the same. The reasoning is that a change in the issuing
body is likely to result in a different focus or emphasis in
the contents and scope of the serial.

When there are changes in the parallel or other title
information, a new entry is not made, but a note to the effect that "subtitle varies," or the actual wording, with dates,
should be given.

Society. -- v. 9, no. 4-   = No. 74-   (Feb.
1972)-   . -- New Brunswick, NJ : Transaction,
1972-
    v. : ill. ; 23 cm.

Monthly (except July/Aug. and Nov./Dec.)
Continues: Trans-action
ISSN 0147-2011

1. Social sciences--Periodicals.

Card 59.   New main entry for serial with changed title.

Trans-action : social science and the community /
a publication of the Community Leadership Project of Washington University. --Vol, 1, no, 1
(Nov. 1963)-v. 9, no. 3 = no.73 (Jan. 1972).
--St. Louis, Mo. : Washington University, 1963-
1972.
9 v. : ill. ; 23 cm.

Bimonthly.
Subtitle varies.
Continued by: Society.

1. Social sciences--Periodicals.   I. Community
Leadership Project (Washington University).

Card 60.   Closed entry.

The statement of responsibility is recorded if there
is one, except when it is also a part of the title proper, as
in British Library news or The ALA yearbook.   A major difference in serial cataloging is the omission of editorial responsibility.   This makes a great deal of sense, as editors
of serials tend to change frequently.   If a serial is closely
associated with an editor, and the cataloger thinks that the

patron would find an added entry for the editor useful, the name may be given in a note.

Edition statements will seldom be necessary, as the kind of information that would appear there is given in the numeric area for serials. An example of an exception might be a statement indicating a local, reprint, braille, or other special edition.

The numeric area gives the number of the first issue of a serial as it appears in that issue. Usually that will be Vol. 1, no. 1, followed by a hyphen and four spaces in order to leave room to fill in the number of the last issue, should the serial cease publication or change in a manner requiring a new entry. If the number of the issue is tied to a specific date, the date is given in parentheses (see card 59). This is done even when the library does not own the first issue, a fact which can be brought out in the notes. The point is to describe the serial as it exists historically, rather than incidentally in one library's collection, in order to facilitate machine-assisted exchange of information.

```
National Federation of State High School
   Associations.
   Field hockey rules. -- National Federation ed.
   --                 -- Kansas City, Mo. : National
      Federation of State High School Associations.
         v. : ill. ; 18 cm.

   Description based on: 1980-81.
   Cover title: Field hockey rule book.
   ISSN 0275-5394 = Field hockey rules. National
Federation ed.
      1. Field hockey--Rules. I. Title. II. Title:
Field hockey rule book.
```

Card 61.   Entry for serial for which information on first issue is lacking.

The publication/distribution area follows the pattern for monographs, except that the date of initial publication is

followed by a hyphen and four spaces to allow for the date of cessation.

The physical description area varies from that for monographs only in the omission of a number indicating the total volumes, in those cases where the serial is still "alive." Three spaces are left blank in front of "v." or whatever the appropriate designation is.

The note area is especially important for serials, as it provides the only opportunity for the library to let the patron know what the library actually owns. Frequency is another key item of information that may appear only in the note area, as it may not be clear from the body of the entry. The fact that the entry represents a title change in the serial is also brought out in the note area.

The order for typical notes for serials is as follows:

●Frequency: monthly, quarterly, etc., whenever this is not clear already
●Additional information about the language or title, such as "subtitle varies"
●Clarification of the statement of responsibility; name of the editor, if considered to be important
●Relationship to other serials, using phrases such as "continued by," "continuation," "merger of," "supplement to," etc.
●Irregularities in numbering, or temporary suspension
●The library's holdings, if the set is not complete

The International Standard Serial Number (ISSN) is usually the last item in the record.

Access points for serials are the same as for monographs. The typical periodical or newspaper will have a main entry under title, as authorship is almost always multiple. I. F. Stone's Weekly is one of the rare instances of personal authorship of a serial. Main entry under corporate body is not uncommon for serials such as annual reports, directories, conference proceedings, etc. One of the headaches of serials cataloging is the need to keep a close eye on name changes of corporate bodies that issue serials. A new main entry has to be made for the serial when the name of the corporate body (or personal name) under which the serial is entered changes, even when the title remains the same. If one recalls all the serials with generic titles such as

"directory," "annual report," etc., this rule makes sense:
the patron is going to look under the latest name of the organization, rather than the old name or title.

Special numbers of serials are cataloged as separate
works, with the relationship to regular issues clarified in the
notes. If they are to be shelved with the regular numbers
and are not particularly important, no special adjustment in
cataloging is needed.

As stated at the beginning of this section, most small
libraries will not catalog magazines and newspapers. These
publications are usually kept together in one area of the library, organized in alphabetical order by title, and chronologically under title. They are thus easy to locate without
reference to a catalog. Moreover, their contents are accessed through periodical indexes such as Readers' Guide
rather than through the catalog.

```
           Small computers in libraries : a newsletter.
           -- Vol. 1, no. 1 (Apr. 1981)-    . -- Tucson,
           Ariz. : Graduate Library School, University
           of Arizona, 1981-
              v. ; 28 cm.

           Monthly.
           Vol. 1 has 9 issues; vol.2, no.1 is dated
           Jan. 1982.
              ISSN 0275-6722


           1. Microcomputers--Periodicals.  I. University
           of Arizona.  Graduate Library School.
```

Card 62.   Note shows irregular numbering.

Whether or not periodicals are cataloged, a shelf list
record is needed and a concise listing of a library's magazine
and newspaper holdings and their location is very helpful to
the public. This may be simply a typed list, or in the form
of a visible strip-file, which is easily updated by inserting

additional strips in their alphabetical place as new material is added or a change in title or frequency occurs. The information given would be short title, frequency (perhaps), the date and/or number of the earliest volume owned, and location (e.g., Children's Room, on microfilm, etc.). If periodicals are not cataloged, the other details can be recorded on the shelf list card or the check-in forms used to record the receipt of periodicals can act as a substitute for shelf list cards.

SUBJECT HEADINGS

While a book can have only one classification number and be
shelved in only one place, it is quite possible that a specific
book contains important material about several topics, or information about some subject which is too specialized to merit
its own classification number. To compensate for this limitation of the classification scheme, library catalogs contain
entries under subject--sometimes several for a single title.

This chapter deals with the problem of determining
the subject of a book, and the topic or topics under which
it should be listed in the catalog. It is usually found that
more library users look for material on some subject than
for a specific author or title. Entering material in the catalog under subjects involves a knowledge of the terms people
use, and selection of as specific a term as the material warrants.

For geographic headings, e.g., Madagascar versus
Malagasy Republic, which term do the newspapers use? the
radio and TV programs? the magazines? Differences in the
vocabularies of people in different sections of the country
are important in certain fields. With reference to geographic
subdivisions, e.g., BIRDS--U.S., consider these questions:
does the library have anything on birds in countries other
than the United States? Is it likely to have? When readers
ask for a book on birds, though they do not say so, do they
not mean birds in the United States? Then use the general
subject heading, BIRDS. Use simple, modern subject headings; avoid cumbersome phrases and unnecessary subdivisions.

Some libraries find that subject entries for certain
types of fiction serve a real purpose and improve service,
especially for children. If mystery stories, to take a ubi-
quitous example, are entered in the catalog under the heading MYSTERY AND DETECTIVE STORIES as well as under

121

author and title, time will be saved for both readers and library staff, although the time saved by the staff in serving the public may possibly be counterbalanced by the time spent in assigning headings and making the extra cards. Most libraries will find the analytical indexes in standard bibliographic guides adequate substitutes for fiction subject headings in the library's own catalog. The H. W. Wilson Company's Standard Catalogs include subject headings for fiction, and Irwin's A Guide to Historical Fiction is only one of a number of available indexes to special categories of fiction.

For example, the young reader who wants a story about the American Revolution can be guided to Forbes' Johnny Tremain by consulting the index to the Junior High School Library Catalog. Similarly, someone who wants fiction about the Puerto Rican experience in America can be directed to Mohr's Felita through the Children's Catalog. The main entry gives not only the citation and an annotation, but also suggested subject headings under which the book can be entered in the catalog: PUERTO RICANS IN THE U.S. and CITY LIFE--Fiction.

If the library buys LC cards or other prepared cataloging, the cards for children's and young adult fiction will quite often include subject headings. However, if the library does its own cataloging, it is more economical to restrict subject headings for fiction as much as possible and to rely on the Standard Catalogs and other bibliographic aids. In any case, a subject card should be made only when a book, whether fiction or nonfiction, gives substantial information on that particular subject.

Determining the Subject

To determine the subject of a book for which cataloging information cannot be found requires a careful examination of its contents. For this reason, subject headings should be determined and assigned at the same time as the classification number; otherwise examining the book and determining what it is about have to be done twice. The two topics are separated in this manual because both are difficult and it is better to take them up separately until each is clearly understood.

Read the title page, look over the table of contents carefully, scan the preface or introduction, and dip into the

book itself in several places. This scrutiny will show what the book is about and what the author's purpose was in writing it. Such an examination may bring out the fact that the book treats of one subject, of several distinct phases of a subject, or of two or more subjects. No matter how many subjects a book covers, it can be given only one classification number and can stand on the shelves in only one place; but it may be entered in the catalog under as many subject headings as are necessary. If the book treats of one subject it requires only one subject entry, e. g., Alistair Cooke's America would be entered in the catalog only under the general heading UNITED STATES--HISTORY.

On the other hand, Toynbee's Half the World; the History and Culture of China and Japan needs to be entered under two subjects, CHINA--CIVILIZATION and JAPAN--CIVILIZATION. Similarly, Edwin H. Colbert's Wandering Lands and Animals should be represented in the catalog by two subject cards, one under FOSSILS and one under CONTINENTAL DRIFT. Another type of book has one general topic but includes a number of specific topics, as for example, Patricia Lauber's This Restless Earth. The general subject is geology, and a card will be made for the catalog with that word as a heading (see card 63). But the book will be much more

```
551      GEOLOGY
LAU      Lauber, Patricia
              This restless earth.  Ill. by John Polgreen.
         Random House, 1970.
              129 p.  ill.
```

Card 63.   Subject entry for a book.

useful in the children's library if it is also entered in the

catalog under the special topics with which it deals, e.g., pages 21-42 are on earthquakes, pages 45-67 on volcanoes, pages 76-81 on mountains, pages 82-96 on oceans. Subject analytical cards may be made for each of these topics, or as many of them as the library is likely to have calls for. This depends upon the other material available on the subject and the special interests of the library's users. A subject analytical entry is a subject card for a part of a book, with the specific pages in which the subject is covered cited as part of the heading (see card 64).

```
551        EARTHQUAKES, p. 21-41:
LAU        Lauber, Patricia
               This restless earth.  Ill. by John Polgreen.
           Random House, 1970.
               129 p.  ill.
```

Card 64.   Analytical subject entry for part of a book.

        Thus the book is examined, its subject determined, and one or more subject cards are made for the catalog. Whether these cards are general subject entries or subject analytical entries for a particular portion of the book depends upon whether two or more subjects are discussed together throughout the book or each subject is discussed separately.

Selecting Subject Headings

When deciding upon the heading for a subject entry, choose that heading which most truly represents the contents of the book or a certain part of the book; that is, the most specific subject or subjects possible. For example, if a book is about trees--how to identify them or their uses of ornamentation--select the specific term TREES. The subject heading BOTANY includes the subject TREES, but it obviously includes

a great deal more, and this book tells of no other plant than the tree. The subject heading FORESTS AND FORESTRY would be used for a book which treats of trees as they grow in forests, how to care for and preserve forests, but not for a book which treats trees as individual varieties, trees as an ornament for lawns and streets, and the like. It would not, therefore, be a suitable heading for this book. Likewise, Fabre's The Life of the Fly would have the specific heading FLIES, and not the general one INSECTS. Of two equally correct and specific headings, such as BIRDS and ORNITHOLOGY, the choice depends upon the type of library, and a reference may be made, directing the reader from the term not chosen to the heading used in the catalog. In a public or school library, choose the heading BIRDS as the term commonly used by the readers. In a special ornithological library, use the heading ORNITHOLOGY, for the users of such a library are quite familiar with the scientific term.

Consider opposite terms such as tolerance and intolerance. A book on one of these subjects necessarily includes material on the other. Choose one, e.g., TOLERATION, and put all the material under it, referring from the other term.

Select as many subject headings as are necessary to cover the contents of the book, but do not multiply them needlessly. Test each heading by asking whether or not a patron would be glad to find the book or books listed under the given heading if he or she were looking for material on that topic. It would be an unusual book which would need more than three subject headings, and one or two will cover most books. In the Children's Catalog, Life's The World's Great Religions has the subject heading RELIGIONS, and several subject analytical entries are given in the index, e.g., JUDAISM, pp. 97-118; Hinduism, pp. 13-34; etc. But it is not desirable to analyze books already indexed in other books available in the library. The usefulness of such books as Cutts' Scenes and Characters of the Middle Ages, which is not analyzed in any of the Wilson Standard Catalogs, would be greatly increased, however, by having subject analytical entries made for each of the groups described, e.g., KNIGHTS AND KNIGHTHOOD, PILGRIMS AND PILGRIMAGES.

Another example of the kind and number of subject headings may be illustrated by Louis Auchincloss' Pioneers and Caretakers: a Study of Nine American Women Novelists, which is about American fiction and American authors. The

Public Library Catalog lists this book and suggests as subject headings: AMERICAN FICTION; WOMEN AUTHORS--HISTORY AND CRITICISM; NOVELISTS, AMERICAN. In addition, nine analytical entries are made for the women discussed. If the library owns this catalog, the cataloger will not need to make these nine analytics, since the reader can be referred to the printed index to find references on individual authors.

Subject entries still need to be made, however. When the suggested headings are checked against a standard list such as Sears, AMERICAN FICTION, WOMEN AUTHORS, and NOVELISTS, AMERICAN are all found to be legitimate. The form subheading HISTORY AND CRITICISM is included in the list of subdivisions to be used in the fields of literature and music, and thus may be added to any of these headings.

In checking the headings against Sears, the cataloger would see that under NOVELISTS, AMERICAN appears the following:

> x   American novelists (which means: do not use, refer from)

Therefore, a reference card should be made, reading:

```
 _____

              AMERICAN NOVELISTS

                     see

              NOVELISTS, AMERICAN




 _____
```

Card 65.   See reference card.

Why use the terms AMERICAN FICTION, AMERICAN LITERATURE, etc., but NOVELISTS, AMERICAN; POETS,

AMERICAN; AUTHORS, AMERICAN? The answer has more
to do with custom than with logic, but the aids and the lists
agree that it is important to bring all material in the catalog
together under AUTHORS, AMERICAN; AUTHORS, ENGLISH;
while with the terms literature, poetry, fiction, etc., it is
more useful to put the national adjective first and bring together everything on the literature of one country, as AMER-
ICAN DRAMA, AMERICAN FICTION, AMERICAN LITERA-
TURE. Among these headings in the catalog will be the reference from AMERICAN NOVELISTS.

Besides subject entries for books and parts of books,
subject cards may be made to call attention to an entire group
of books. One method is to prepare one subject card for all
the books on a general subject, by simply referring the reader
to the books on the shelves by classification number, and to
the shelf list to find the books which may be temporarily out
of the library. This practice is particularly useful in very
small libraries where the patrons frequently choose their
books directly from the shelves and use the catalog primarily to see whether there are any books on a subject and where
they are. Also, the librarian's time is saved and space is
saved in the catalog.

```
551.2    VOLCANOES

             Books about volcanoes will be found on the
         shelves under 551.2

             For a complete author list of the books in
         the library on volcanoes, consult the shelf
         list under 551.2.
```

Card 66. General subject entry for all books in a subject
class.

If the library has books with chapters on a subject,
e.g. volcanoes, not indexed in the Wilson Standard Catalogs,
or if the library does not have these aids, subject analytical

cards for the catalog should be made for this material. If
there is a general subject entry in the catalog already, it
should be amended to include a third paragraph: "For parts
of books on volcanoes, see the cards following this one."

   Subdivisions. Some subjects need to be subdivided to
be exact. Most subjects can be divided by either phase, form,
geographical area, or period of time. For instance, the subject heading BIRDS would be used for a general book on that
subject. But if a book is limited to the protection of birds
or to migration, the general heading BIRDS can be limited
by adding a phase subdivision, e.g., BIRDS--PROTECTION,
or BIRDS--MIGRATION. If, however, the book is not a book
about birds but a list of books about birds, the form subdivision BIBLIOGRAPHY should be added and the heading becomes BIRDS--BIBLIOGRAPHY. Or the book may be on
birds of a specific place, and the heading may be limited
by a geographical area subdivision, e.g., BIRDS--BRAZIL.

   For some subjects, notably history, next in importance
to the geographical area is the period of time covered. For
a general history in which there is no geographical limitation,
the period of time covered is the significant factor. For a
book such as William H. McNeill's A World History, which
covers all countries and all periods up to the present, the
subject headings would be CIVILIZATION--HISTORY, and
WORLD HISTORY. But a history which, though including
all lands, ends at the beginning of the Middle Ages would
have the subject heading HISTORY, ANCIENT. A general
history of the United States, however, would have the subject heading U.S.--HISTORY. A time subhead may be added,
e.g. U.S.--HISTORY--REVOLUTION, or U.S.--HISTORY--
1898-1919. The use of subheads depends upon whether or
not the book is limited to one phase, period of time, etc.,
and the amount of material on that subject which the library
has or expects to have.

   If the collection contains only a few books treating
United States history, they may as well all have the same
subject heading, namely, U.S.--HISTORY. A slightly larger
library may have a dozen or so books and expect to add
more. If it has six general works covering the history of
the United States from the Revolution to the present time,
three books dealing exclusively with the Revolution, four on
the Civil War period, five on the history of the period 1898
to 1919, etc., it would be well to group them in the catalog
under headings such as U.S.--HISTORY; U.S.--HISTORY--

REVOLUTION; U.S.--HISTORY--CIVIL WAR; U.S.--HISTORY
--1898-1919.

A subject heading, as noted before, is the word or
words used to describe the content of the book; thus Peter-
son's How to Know the Birds will have the subject heading
BIRDS. Novels do not usually have a definite subject and
are read for their style; characterization, etc., rather than
for information. This is also true of poems and plays. They
have author and title entries in the catalog but seldom subject
entries. The heading POETRY is not used for a book of
poems, but for a work on the appreciation and philosophy of
poetry, and POETICS is used for works on the art and technique of poetry, so that a book like Robert Hillyer's In Pur-
suit of Poetry requires two subject headings, POETICS and
POETRY. If the library has much material on poetry, it
may subdivide the heading; i.e., POETRY--HISTORY AND
CRITICISM. The literary works of an individual are represented in the catalog only under the writer's name and under
the title if distinctive. Whoever wishes to read T. S. Eliot's
The Waste Land will look under Eliot or under Waste Land.
Eliot's collected poems will be found only under his name,
not under POETRY. It is, however, worthwhile and practical
to bring together in the catalog collections of poems, essays,
or dramas of three or more authors. This is done by adding a form subdivision to the heading. The heading POETRY
or AMERICAN POETRY is used for books about poetry, while
the headings POETRY--COLLECTIONS or AMERICAN POETRY
--COLLECTIONS are used for such works as Untermeyer's
Modern American Poetry. These latter headings, POETRY--
COLLECTIONS and AMERICAN POETRY--COLLECTIONS are
called form headings, as they refer to the form in which the
material is written, not to its content.

Form cards similar to card 67 might take the place
of the form heading POETRY--COLLECTIONS and AMERICAN
POETRY--COLLECTIONS and direct the reader to the books
on the shelves. If this practice is adopted, similar cards
would be made for ENGLISH POETRY--COLLECTIONS;
AMERICAN DRAMA--COLLECTIONS; ENGLISH DRAMA--
COLLECTIONS, etc.

To sum up this matter of the choice of subject headings: use the term (or terms) which most clearly describes
the contents of a book and is most likely to be familiar to
the users of the library, remembering that readers use different libraries if not simultaneously at least over a period

of time.   When choosing between synonymous headings, prefer the one that is most familiar to the people who use the
library, is most used in other catalogs, has the fewest mean-
ings other than the one intended, or brings the subject into
conjunction with related subjects.   But keep subject headings
simple and do not subdivide extensively unless the library
has considerable material on each subdivision.

```
AMERICAN POETRY--COLLECTIONS

    Books of poetry by individual American poets
will be found on the shelves under 811.  Col-
lections of poetry by several American poets
will be found under 811.008.

    For a complete list of books in the library
of poetry by individual American poets, consult
the shelf list under 811; for collections,
811.008.
```

Card 67.   General subject entry for all books in one or more
classes.

Lists of Subject Headings

Next in importance to choosing the right subject heading for
a given book is to use the same wording for all the subject
headings for books or parts of books on the same subject,
so that they may be brought together in the catalog.   To do
this it is essential to have a carefully worked out list of
headings from which to choose and to check it to show which
headings have been used.

        The list most widely adopted by small public and
school libraries is Sears List of Subject Headings.[1]   The
list used by most larger libraries is the LC list of subject
headings.[2]   LC cards give headings from this list, but
other cards which use Sears subject headings are available
for purchase (see chapter 11).   In general, libraries with

fewer than 50,000 volumes prefer the Sears list, while larger libraries or special libraries with subject concentration need the greater comprehensiveness of the LC list. Although there are some major differences in use of terms (ORNI-THOLOGY versus BIRDS, for example), it is the degree of specificity and cross-referencing which chiefly distinguishes the two lists, as demonstrated by the parallel excerpts on the following page.

If the library is served by a regional cataloging and/ or processing center, it must perforce adopt the same list of subject headings as is used by the center, for the savings afforded by cooperation will be negated if many of the headings have to be changed to conform to the local list. For-tunately, much of the disadvantage of LC headings for small libraries was alleviated when LC adopted a list of Subject Headings for Children's Literature.[3] This is, in effect, a list of exceptions to the master LC list, and brings headings into much closer alignment with Sears usage. The ALA Committee on Cataloging Children's Materials recommended the adoption of the LC list in the interests of standardization, and the tenth edition of Sears incorporated many of the LC children's literature headings. In the eleventh edition of Sears, this practice was continued, and the ninth edition and supplements of the Library of Congress list all include "An-notated Card Program Subject Headings for Children's Lit-erature." Libraries that do not subscribe to the entire LC list may order Working List of Subject Headings for Chil-dren's Literature, which LC describes as follows:

> A working list of all the alternate juvenile subject headings which have appeared in brackets on LC's annotated cards from 1968 through May 1982. This working list, last revised in May 1982, consists of an alphabetically arranged computer produced list without cross-references, scope notes, or in-structions on usage of any kind. It is used for ready reference by the Children's Literature Section, Subject Cataloging Division to determine which head-ings have been used before and which headings need correction. In order to determine correct usage and scope of each heading the Working List must be used in conjunction with LCSH 9 and its supple-ments.[4]

Despite the fact that the "Working List" is not supposed to be used without reference to the full LC list, it is a useful

LC

Beauty
  See Aesthetics
    Art—Philosophy
    Beauty, Personal
Beauty, Personal *(RA778)*
  sa Beauty contestants
    Beauty contests
    Beauty culture
    Beauty shops
    Body-marking
    Charm
    Clothing and dress
    Cosmetics
    Costume
    Dentistry—Aesthetics
    Hair
    Hairdressing
    Hand
    Manicuring
    Perfumes
    Skin
    Teeth
  x Beauty
    Complexion
    Grooming, Personal
    Grooming for women
    Personal beauty
    Toilet (Grooming)
  xx Beauty culture
    Beauty shops
    Cosmetics
    Face
    Hygiene
    Women—Health and hygiene
Beauty, Personal, in literature
Beauty contestants *(Indirect)*
  x Beauty queens
    Contestants, Beauty
  xx Beauty, Personal
    Beauty contests
    Women

Beauty contests *(Indirect)*
  sa Beauty contestants
  xx Beauty, Personal
Beauty culture *(Indirect)* *(TT950-979)*
  sa Beauty, Personal
    Beauty operators
    Beauty shops
    Cosmetics
    Hairdressing
    Mortuary cosmetology
  x Cosmetology
  xx Beauty, Personal
    Beauty shops
    Cosmetics
  — Equipment and supplies
    See Beauty shops—Equipment and
      supplies
  — Law and legislation
    See Beauty shops—Law and
      legislation
Beauty operators *(Indirect)*
  sa Collective labor agreements—
    Hairdressing
    Wages—Beauty operators
  x Beauticians
    Cosmetologists
    Hairdressers
  xx Beauty culture
    Beauty shops
Beauty queens
  See Beauty contestants
Beauty shops *(Indirect)*
  sa Beauty, Personal
    Beauty culture
    Beauty operators
    Cosmetics
  xx Beauty, Personal
    Beauty culture
  — Equipment and supplies
    x Beauty culture—Equipment and
      supplies

Sears

Beauty. *See* **Esthetics**
Beauty shops **646.7**
  See also **Cosmetics**

aid for catalogers of children's materials who use Sears.
Because the LC list is updated more frequently than Sears,
reasonably correct headings for new subjects may be established without waiting for a new edition of Sears.

School libraries and public library children's departments should not dismiss automatically the idea of using LC
subject headings, but should examine the options carefully.
Sears is shorter and therefore cheaper and easier to use.
It is not updated as often as the LC list, however, and it
does not take special cognizance of subject access from the
children's/young adult services perspective.

How to use lists of subject headings. Determine what
the book is about; then look in the list of subject headings
adopted by the library for a suitable heading which expresses
the content of the book. On examining the Sears List, an ex-
cerpt from which is reproduced below, note that the headings
are listed in alphabetical order and that some are in boldface
type. Those in boldface, e.g. BUYING, are to be used as
subject headings.

> **Busing (School integration)** (May subdiv.
> geog. state or city)
>   *x* Racial balance in schools; School busing;
>   School integration
>   *xx* **Segregation in education**
> **Butter**
>   *See also* **Margarine**
>   *xx* **Dairy products; Dairying; Milk**
> Butter, Artificial. *See* **Margarine**
> **Butterflies**
>   *See also* **Caterpillars; Moths**
>   *x* Cocoons; Lepidoptera
>   *xx* **Caterpillars; Insects; Moths**
> **Buttons**
>   *xx* **Clothing and dress**
> Buyers' guides. *See* **Consumer education;**
>   **Shopping**
> **Buying**
>   Use for works on buying by government
>   agencies and commercial and industrial
>   enterprises. Works on buying by the
>   consumer are entered under **Consumer**
>   **education; Shopping.** See notes under
>   these headings
>   *See also* **Consumer education; Instalment**
>   **plan; Shopping**
>   *x* Purchasing
>   *xx* **Consumer education; Industrial man-**
>   **agement; Shopping**

Note that just below the heading BUYING is a paragraph beginning "Use for ..." This type of explanatory note
is given below some of the headings to explain for what kind
of material they are to be used. Following this note the
words see also introduce one or more suggested headings
that may be better for the book in hand than the first subject
heading looked up. If that is the case, turn to such headings
as CONSUMER EDUCATION and SHOPPING in their alphabetical places in the list. But if BUYING is the better term,
use it. Note that the next line begins with x. This means
that the term or terms following the x should not be used as
headings, and that a see reference should be made from the
term or terms not used to the one that is chosen for the
heading. Thus a see reference should be made from PUR-
CHASING to BUYING.

Below x Purchasing is a line beginning with an xx.
This is to suggest related terms, which if also used as subject headings in the catalog should have references made from
them to BUYING, so that attention may be called to all related subjects. Such a reference from one heading that is
used to another that is used is called a see also reference.
Sunset's Garden and Patio Building would have subject entries in the catalog under GREENHOUSES; LANDSCAPE GAR-
DENING; and PATIOS. There would be see also references
from related headings; for instance, LANDSCAPE ARCHITEC-
TURE, see also LANDSCAPE GARDENING, if there were
other books in the catalog under LANDSCAPE ARCHITECTURE.

Proper names are generally not included in subject
heading lists. Names of persons and of organizations are
the subject headings for material about the person or organization. The form of the name to be used for the subject
heading is determined from the rules in chapter 4. For
instance, Hesketh Pearson's Dizzy, the Life and Person-
ality of Benjamin Disraeli would have as its subject heading
DISRAELI, BENJAMIN; and a history of Yale University would
have as its subject heading YALE UNIVERSITY. While this
type of heading is not found in printed lists, Sears does include JESUS CHRIST because of the unique subdivisions required, and SHAKESPEARE in order to provide a model for
subdivisions which can be used for similarly prolific and important authors. Names of places are also omitted from
most printed lists, with the exception of a few which are included for the purpose of serving as examples for subdivisions
under geographic names.

There are several other broad classes of headings within which the cataloger is permitted to supply the specific name. When using Sears, battles, birds, fish, etc. are examples of such categories. Thus, although the term SHARKS does not appear in Sears, it--rather than FISHES--should be used as the subject heading for a book about sharks. Whatever printed list is adopted by a library, the cataloger must study the prefatory material and directions very carefully before beginning to use the list.

Subject Cross References

In deciding upon subject headings, as explained before, sometimes it is found that there are two or more different terms that might be used for the same subject. For example, which is better, AVIATION or AERONAUTICS? MARIONETTES or PUPPETS? COUNSELING or GUIDANCE? Unless there is some very good reason for not doing so, one should always use the heading given in the subject heading list adopted by the library. If one looks up these groups of terms in Sears, the choices will be AERONAUTICS, COUNSELING, PUPPETS AND PUPPET PLAYS. However, some persons who will use the catalog will undoubtedly look under the terms AVIATION, GUIDANCE, and MARIONETTES. When they find nothing, will they think of the other terms? They may not. Therefore, adopt one of these terms and refer from the other; e. g. use COUNSELING and refer from GUIDANCE. The lists of subject headings not only suggest headings to be used but list synonymous and related terms from which it is wise to refer.

Some librarians do not consider see also references necessary for the small library's catalog and do not make them. Other librarians feel that they are needed especially in the small catalog, since the collection is limited, and that all material on related subjects should be brought to the inquirer's attention. The choice must take into account the budget for technical services versus that for reference services and the sophistication of the library's clientele. The optimum balance between user satisfaction and economy has to determine the cataloging policies of any given library. If a library chooses to make the minimum number of cross references, a copy of its subject heading list should be kept at the card catalog for consultation.

Most see references are made at the time that the subject heading to which they refer is first used, since they

are synonyms for the heading decided upon.   One should avoid
making too many references for the small catalog.   It is not
desirable to make see references from terms not in the vo-
cabulary of the public; for example, one would not refer from
CHASE, THE or GUNNING to HUNTING, or from HABITA-
TION, HUMAN to HOUSES, even though they are suggested
in Sears, unless the public using the library in question might
be likely to look under chase or gunning or habitations.   One
need not make a card DUNGEONS see PRISONS if the book
to be entered under PRISONS has nothing in it on dungeons.

        Before making see also's one should consider the fol-
lowing questions:

- Does the catalog have material under the term referred from?
- Is the term suggested for a reference one which anyone is likely to use?
- Is there material in the book on the topic that this
  reference term suggests?   For example, does the
  book on pantomimes have anything on the ballet?   If
  it has, make a reference from BALLET.

```
                        AVIATORS

                          see

                        AIR PILOTS
```

Card 68.   See reference card.

        It is true that after a reference is once made from
one subject to another, there is no way of telling which of
the books actually covers that phase of the subject except by
examining the books.   To revert to the example above, if

there is a card in the catalog which reads BALLET, see also
PANTOMIMES, the reader turns to PANTOMIMES and there,
among several books on the subject, finds upon examination
one or more which contains something on the ballet, and is
satisfied. But if, on the other hand, the user turns to the
subject PANTOMIMES and finds a few books, none of which
has the slightest reference to ballet, he or she may lose faith
in the catalog.

```
                    JUSTICE, ADMINISTRATION OF

                    see also

                    COURTS
                    CRIME AND CRIMINALS
                    GOVERNMENTAL INVESTIGATIONS
                    IMPEACHMENTS
```

Card 69. See also reference card.

        Thus a catalog may be made much more useful by the
wise and restricted use of see and see also references, since
the first subject the reader thinks of may not be exactly the
same as the term used for a heading for that subject in the
catalog. References, especially see also references, should
be made sparingly, as it is annoying to turn card after card
and find only see so and so, or see also so and so.

        Another and a slightly different kind of reference is
the so-called general reference card (see card 70). In Sears,
in the list of see also's under MANNERS and CUSTOMS is
found: "... also names of ethnic groups, countries, cities,
etc., with the subdivision SOCIAL LIFE AND CUSTOMS, e.g.,
INDIANS OF NORTH AMERICA--SOCIAL LIFE AND CUSTOMS;
JEWS--SOCIAL LIFE AND CUSTOMS; U.S.--SOCIAL LIFE
AND CUSTOMS, etc." This sort of reference is very useful
in a catalog and saves much duplication, as otherwise it

would be necessary to list on a reference card a heading for each individual country with the subdivision SOCIAL LIFE AND CUSTOMS.

MANNERS AND CUSTOMS

see also

names of ethnic groups, countries, cities, etc. with the subdivision SOCIAL LIFE AND CUSTOMS, e.g.

U.S. - SOCIAL LIFE AND CUSTOMS

Card 70.   General reference card.

Keep down the number of cross references. Be sure that no reference leads to a heading not in the catalog.   Do not make a see also reference from a subject on which there is no material, but wait until there is material on that subject.   On the other hand, one may make temporary see references.   For example, in order that the reader may find the small amount of material on the ballet that is included in the book on pantomime, one may make a temporary card, BALLET see PANTOMIMES.   Later, if there is a card with the heading BALLET, the reference card may be changed to read "see also."

Other Aids for Subject Headings

Small special libraries devoted to a single field will find general lists such as Sears and even LC insufficiently detailed. Indexing and abstracting services covering the field may sometimes serve their needs, or the pertinent professional associations or other libraries with similar collections may have prepared and published a list that can be purchased.   One should not start one's own list from scratch, except as a last resort after a careful search for alternatives.

Even small public and school libraries will have material on subjects not included in general lists nor authorized by them. This is especially true of new subjects which are constantly developing, such as genetic engineering, disco, Dungeons and Dragons. Established subjects may expand rapidly into new aspects, e. g., personal computers, or long unused headings may suddenly become current again (e. g., midwifery). The subject headings used in general and special periodical indexes, bibliographies of special subjects, and the terms in general and special encyclopedias will be found very helpful in determining the wording for such headings. First be sure that no term in the regular list meets the need, then look in the authorities mentioned for the best possible term.

Great care should be taken in the use of indexes coming out at regular intervals, e. g. The Booklist, the supplements to the Wilson Standard Catalogs, the various periodical indexes, since these lists can best serve their purpose by changing their headings to suit the latest development of the subjects. If a heading in a catalog is changed, all the cards with that heading should be changed.

To illustrate how the various aids may vary, take the subject of Watergate. Readers' Guide in 1972 introduced the headings WATERGATE INCIDENT, 1972 and WATERGATE TRIAL, but the cumulative 1973/74 issue used WATERGATE CASE. A cataloger who used Sears would not have found any heading in that list at the time, and would have had to make a decision about what form to use, in the hope that the choice would coincide with that of the editors of the next Sears edition. Since the trend for some time has been for Sears to follow LC usage, the cataloger would have been correct to select the LC form, WATERGATE AFFAIR, 1972-, which has indeed become the heading in Sears.

A more recent problem might have been presented by the disco craze in all its manifestations--music, dancing, rollerskating, etc. Sears is no help, but the annual supplements to LCSH have a number of headings, including ROLLER DISCO. A phone call to a nearby larger library which uses LC is a quick and economical way to find out what the LC wording is.

Checking Lists of Subject
Headings for Tracing

When a heading is decided upon for the first time, it is

checked in the list of subject headings to show that it has been adopted for entry. Note the check mark (✔) before WATERWAYS in the section from Sears reproduced below. In this way the librarian can tell which subject headings have been used without referring to the catalog. This is a great convenience, and care should be taken that each subject heading is checked the first time it is used. In cases where there is no suitable heading in the adopted list and a heading is selected from some other source, this heading is written in the printed list of subject headings in its alphabetical place. The sample from Sears tenth edition shows the subject heading WATERGATE AFFAIR, 1972- written in.

Water sports
    See also Boats and boating; Canoes and canoeing; Diving; Fishing; Rowing; Sailing; Skin diving; Surfing; Swimming; Yachts and Yachting; and names of other water sports
    x Aquatic sports
    xx Sports
✔ Water supply
    See also Aqueducts; Dams; Forest influences; Irrigation; Reservoirs; Water — Pollution; Water — Purification; Water conservation; Wells; also names of cities with the subdivision *Water supply,* e.g. Chicago—Water supply; etc.
    x Waterworks
    xx Civil engineering; Municipal engineering; Natural resources; Public health; Public utilities; Reservoirs; Sanitary engineering; Sanitation; Water—Pollution; Water conservation; Water resources development; Wells
Water supply engineering
    See also Boring; Hydraulic engineering
    xx Engineering; Hydraulic engineering
Watering places. *See* Health resorts, spas, etc.
✔ Waterways
    Use for general works on rivers, lakes, canals as highways for transportation or commerce
    See also Canals; Inland navigation; Lakes; Rivers

Handwritten in right margin:
✓ Watergate affair, 1972-
✓ xx Presidents - U.S.
    Election
✓ xx Corruption (in politics)

As subject headings used for the catalog are checked in the list, so also are subject references used in the catalog. This shows the librarian which of the references have been

made.   If it is decided to discontinue a heading in the catalog,
this checked list will be a guide to removing the reference to
that heading.

The rule is: Mark with a check ($\checkmark$) at the left the
subject heading used and the references which have been
made to it; turn to each reference in its regular alphabetical
place and check it and the subject heading used.   The checks
on the page reproduced from Sears indicate that there are
entries in the catalog under WATER SUPPLY and that a reference has been made from WATERWORKS.

Adapting Subject Headings

As discussed above, it is sometimes necessary to introduce
headings for new subjects not included in the latest edition
of the list used by the library.   There may be other reasons
for modifying the official list, however.   For example, a library which serves children may find that the young user
often does not "think Sears"--a child who wants a book about
secret codes is not likely to look under CRYPTOGRAPHY;
one who wants a book on body building is not going to find
it under that heading in many libraries that use Sears, unless the idea of looking under PHYSICAL EDUCATION AND
TRAINING or EXERCISE occurs to the child.   The latest
edition of Sears has corrected subject headings for women
and blacks in response to criticism of racist and sexist headings in earlier editions.   The Library of Congress is also
continuing to revise obsolete and offensive subject headings,
but the task is much larger, and therefore is proceeding at
a slower pace.   The fact that librarians do not have to ac-
cede to insulting and outdated terminology has been amply
demonstrated by the impact that Sanford Berman's Prejudices
and Antipathies[5] and Joan Marshall's On Equal Terms[6]
have had on subject heading practice.   Much remains to be
done, however.   As Emmett Davis points out, the treatment
of people with disabilities in subject heading lists still leaves
much to be desired.[7]

Because the small library frequently depends on centralized or commercial cataloging, it faces a serious problem when it discovers that certain subject headings are a
disservice rather than an aid to library users.   If cards are
to be changed, additional staff time--and consequently, funds
--must be spent.   These costs must be weighed against the
negative impression created by offensive headings or lack of

access to materials caused by unfamiliar terms. A library may find that while it cannot afford to give personal assistance to every catalog user, it can manage to make at least those adjustments in subject headings which will best serve its particular clientele.

An excellent source of suggestions for alternate headings is Hennepin County Public Library's Cataloging Bulletin.[8] Using this on a regular basis to modify the library's official list occasionally, or at least to add extra see references, should not be prohibitively expensive and may prove to be a good investment in better access to materials and improved public relations. Card 71, below, is an example of a printed card modified for local use by changing the LC subject headings to Sears headings.

643.7 **Green, Floyd.**
   You can renovate your own home . a step-by-step guide to major interior improvements / Floyd Green and Susan E. Meyer ; with photos. by Susan E. Meyer. — 1st ed. — Garden City, N.Y. : Doubleday, 1978.

   302 p. : ill. ; 29 cm.

   Includes index.
   ISBN 0-385-12304-3 : $14.95

   Houses--Maintenance and repair
  1. ~~Dwellings--Remodeling~~ I. Meyer, Susan E., joint author. II. Title.
  TH4816.G73   643'.7   77-83939
                      MARC

  Library of Congress   77[7911]

Card 71. Printed LC card; Sears subject headings substituted for LC headings.

Subject Authority File

Instead of checking a printed list of subject headings, the special library for which no single printed list is adequate may have a subject authority file on cards. This type of file has one card for each subject heading used in the catalog, and on this card is a record of all references made

to that subject. When a subject heading is not taken from
an adopted printed list of headings, the source is given on
the card. There is also a card corresponding to each reference card in the catalog. Cards 72-75 are sample subject
authority cards.

The scope or explanatory note such as that given below some headings in Sears, e.g. under BUYING (see p. 133)
in the paragraph beginning "Use for works ...," may be entered on the subject authority card. The paragraph beginning
See also does not need to be given on the authority card, as
its use is in deciding whether to use this heading or one of
those suggested. When the question comes up again as to
whether to use a certain heading, the original source may be
consulted. Likewise, only the see and see also references
which are made for the catalog are listed on the authority
card. In other words, in choosing a heading, a printed list
is used for its scope notes, see also's, and its suggested
references to that subject. The authority file is used to show
which headings have been used and which references have
been made to them. If all suggested references were put
on the authority card it would be necessary to check those
which had been made.

```
Buying

             Refer from
     x  Purchasing
    xx  Consumer education




```

Card 72.   Subject authority card.

The reference cards in the subject authority file are
made exactly as those for the catalog, except that the subject

headings are not in full capitals. Subject headings in the
public card catalog need to be distinguished in some way
from other headings for the convenience of users. In most
catalogs, full capitals are used for this purpose. As the
subject authority file is only for the use of the librarian, the
terms are given with only the first letter of each heading or
subheading capitalized. Cards 74 and 75 are sample reference cards for the subject authority file.

```
Watergate affair, 1972-                    (LC, 8th ed.)

            Refer from
      xx Corruption (in politics)
      xx Political crimes and offenses
```

Card 73. Subject authority card showing source of heading.

```
                    Purchasing

                       see

                    Buying
```

Card 74. See reference card for subject authority file.

The major advantages of a subject authority file on cards are that it is always up to date, it gives space in the proper alphabetical place for new subjects and for headings chosen from other sources, and that it saves having to transfer information from one printed list to another when a new edition comes out. In view of the work entailed in the preparation of an authority file on cards, these advantages apply primarily to the special library whose area of concentration would require the addition of many specialized headings not included in printed lists of subject headings. For most other libraries, use of a printed list such as Sears or LC as an authority file is the method to be preferred.

```
                    Corruption (in politics)

                    see also

                    Political crimes and offenses
                    Watergate affair, 1972-
```

Card 75. See also reference card for subject authority file.

Even when a library relies on a centralized or commercial source for most of its cataloging, it is necessary to know when a heading is being used for the first time in that library's catalog, so that see and see also references can be considered. This does not require the time-consuming process of checking the headings on all cards received against the printed list or other authority file. Instead, it can be accomplished in connection with filing the cards in the catalog. Since both filer and reviser must check the catalog card which comes before, and the one which comes after each new card to be filed, a subject entry can be put aside for checking whenever it constitutes a heading which is not duplicated on the card before or after.

References

1. Sears List of Subject Headings. 11th ed., edited by Barbara M. Westby (New York: H. W. Wilson Co., 1977).

2. Library of Congress Subject Headings. 9th ed. (Washington, D. C.: Library of Congress, Subject Cataloging Division, 1980), 2v and supplements.

3. Subject Headings for Children's Literature. 2d ed. (Washington, D. C.: Library of Congress, Cataloging Distribution Service Division, 1975).

4. Working List of Subject Headings for Children's Literature. (Washington, D. C.: Library of Congress, Cataloging Distribution Service, 1982).

5. Sanford Berman, Prejudices and Antipathies; A Tract on the LC Heads Concerning People. (Metuchen, N. J.: Scarecrow Press, 1971).

6. Joan K. Marshall, On Equal Terms: A Thesaurus for Nonsexist Indexing and Cataloging. (New York: Neal-Schuman, 1977).

7. Emmett Davis, "Disability-related Subject Cataloging: Defective, Deformed, Degenerate, Delinquent," HCL Cataloging Bulletin 38: 27-31.

8. HCL Cataloging Bulletin. (Edina, MN: Hennepin County Library, Technical Services Division, bimonthly).

Chapter 8

In the words of John Cotton Dana, "to classify books is to place them in groups, each group including, as nearly as may be, all the books treating a given subject, for instance, geology; or all the books, on whatever subject, cast in a particular form, for instance poetry; or all the books having to do with a particular period in time, for instance, the Middle Ages.... Its purpose is ... to make ... books more available."[1]

If a miscellaneous collection of books is to be used with ease, it must be arranged in some way. Medieval libraries sometimes arranged books according to size, a not unreasonable practice given the extreme variations in dimensions of handwritten books and manuscripts. But while this may have been physically practical for shelving arrangements, it must have been exhausting for the scholar who needed to consult numerous volumes on the same topic but of varying sizes. Books could be sorted and put on the shelves in alphabetical order according to their authors. Of course, this would be fine for the reader who wished to see all the novels by Thomas Hardy, but pity the plight of the student of English history, whose materials would be scattered to the far corners of the alphabet. Although a collection arranged alphabetically would be many times more useful than one without any arrangement, the collection arrangement which is the most desirable is a classified one. Libraries are consulted more for material on a given subject than for any other purpose. Readers like to have the books on the same subject together, as they much prefer examining the books to searching a list or a catalog.

As well as bringing together different materials on the same subject, classification can also serve to show relationships between subjects. Geometry, algebra, and calculus are all related as members of the mathematics family,

147

which in turn is related to astronomy, physics, geology, and the other sciences. The obsession of early philosophers with trees of knowledge and other such constructs suggests the extent to which classification of knowledge is a prerequisite for broader understanding. The establishment of interdisciplinary studies programs at colleges and even some elementary schools in recent years signifies continued and increased recognition of the interrelatedness of branches of learning. Classification helps the library borrower to locate a book more readily, but it also helps the library present the written record of human endeavor in a logical interrelated pattern that has itself evolved with the growth of human knowledge.

Book classification systems invariably employ a number or other symbol to represent each subject. This has the advantage of permitting a considerable amount of information to be represented in a tiny space on a catalog card and on the spine of the book, providing a quick means of identifying that a particular book corresponds to a particular catalog entry, and presenting a sequential arrangement (numerical or alphabetical) which is universally understood.

Dewey Decimal Classification

In order to classify books by subject, some scheme or system of classification must be adopted. The system most widely used in the United States, especially in public and school libraries, is Melvil Dewey's Decimal Classification (DDC). It has also been adopted by many libraries in other countries. The American Library Association's The Booklist, Bowker's American Book Publishing Record (BPR), The H. W. Wilson Company's Standard Catalog series, and many other library publications which provide cataloging information use this classification system. Even though the Library of Congress (LC) uses its own classification scheme, the appropriate Dewey Decimal number is included on most LC printed catalog cards. The DDC is published in two forms, the unabridged[2] and the abridged[3]; both versions are revised and issued in new editions periodically. The abridged edition is intended for the use of small general libraries of all kinds, but particularly for public and school libraries. In this manual, the discussion of the DDC and the examples, unless so noted, refer to the eleventh abridged edition.

The system is called a decimal system because it divides all human knowledge into ten classes, with each class

subdivided into ten divisions, each subdivision into ten further ones, and so on beyond the decimal point, the numbers being considered as decimals, not consecutive numbers. One of the great advantages of this system is that it permits infinite expansion after the decimal point whenever a subject gains such complexity as to require further subdivision. Moreover, while any classification system would enable books on the same subject to be kept together, the sequential harmony of decimal numerals also permits relative proximity of books on related topics.

The ten main classes of the system are:

000	Generalities	500	Sciences
100	Philosophy and related disciplines	600	Technology (Applied sciences)
200	Religion	700	The arts
300	Social sciences	800	Literature (Belles-lettres)
400	Language	900	General geography and history

One hundred three-digit numbers are the notation used to designate each class, e.g., 500-599 for the sciences. The first division of each class is used for general works on that class, e.g., 500-509 for general works on the sciences; the subsequent divisions for the main divisions of the subject, e.g., 510-519 for mathematics, 520-529 for astronomy and allied sciences, 530-539 for physics, etc. In turn, each subdivision is divided into ten sections, e.g., 511 for works on mathematical generalities, 512 for works on algebra, 513 for works on arithmetic, 514 for works on topology, and so on. The system can be further subdivided by adding a decimal point after any set of three digits from 000 to 999. Adding as many digits as are required, e.g., 513.26 (in the unabridged edition) for works on fractions; 523, descriptive astronomy; 523.7, the sun; 523.78 (in the unabridged edition), eclipses. The abridged edition of the Dewey Decimal Classification shortens or reduces the numbers (and occasionally changes them), hence neither 513.26 nor 523.78 are in the eleventh abridged edition. Similar omissions will be found throughout the abridged edition.

A general library of 10,000 or 15,000 volumes would probably find the degree of subdivision provided by the abridged version adequate. In a typical library of such size, a book on eclipses could readily be found in a quick search through its collection of astronomy books. But a larger

library with dozens of books on astronomy would find the search for titles on eclipses a somewhat time-consuming and frustrating exercise. In general, a public or school library of 20,000 volumes or more--or one which expects to grow to that extent--will need the degree of categorical subdivision provided by the unabridged version of the DDC. The following example shows how much more detailed the unabridged edition can be:

Abridged DDC	.7	Sun
		Including charts, photographs; spectroscopy
		Class solar wind, zodiacal light in 523.5
	.702 2	Illustrations
		Class charts and photographs in 523.7
	.702 8	Techniques, procedures, apparatus, equipment, materials
		Class heliographs, coronagraphs, heliostats in 522; spectroscopy in 523.7

Unabridged DDC	.7	Sun
	.702 12	Formulas, specifications, statistics
		Class tables in 525.38
	.702 22	Pictures and designs
		Class charts and photographs in 523.79
	.702 8	Techniques, procedures, apparatus, equipment, materials
		Class heliographs, coronagraphs, heliostats in 522.5, spectroscopy in 523.77
	.71	Constants and dimensions
		Size, mass, gravitation, location, parallax
	.72	Optical, thermal, electromagnetic, radioactive phenomena
		Class zodiacal light in 523.59
	.73	Apparent motion and rotation
	.74	Photosphere, sunspots, faculae
	.75	Prominences, chromosphere, flares, corona
		Class solar wind in 523.58
	.76	Internal constitution
	.77	Spectroscopy
	.78	Eclipses
	.79	Charts and photographs

If a miscellaneous collection of books is to be classified according to the decimal system, the books will be grouped by their subject matter, with general books on all or many subjects (e.g., encyclopedias) in one group, books about philosophy in a second, books about religion in a third, and so on. Books in each general subject group will be sub-

divided into groups representing more specific aspects of that
subject. The divisions of the social sciences (300-399) illustrate the principle of subdivision by more specific subject:

300	The social sciences	350	Public administration
310	Statistics	360	Social problems & serv-
320	Political Science		ices
330	Economics	370	Education
340	Law	380	Commerce (Trade)
		390	Customs, etiquette, folk-
			lore

Additional subdivisions continue the progression from the
general to the specific. Economics, for example, is further
divided as follows:

330	Economics	335	Socialism & related sys-
331	Labor economics		tems
332	Financial economics	336	Public finance
333	Land economics	337	International economics
334	Cooperatives	338	Production
		339	Macroeconomics & re-
			lated topics

An illustration of one more level of breakdown is given for
Labor economics (331):

331.1 Labor force and market
331.2 Wages, hours, other conditions of employment
331.3 Workers of specific age groups
331.4 Women workers
331.5 Special categories of workers
331.6 Categories of workers by racial, ethnic, national
      origin
331.7 Labor by industry and occupation
331.8 Labor unions (Trade unions) and labor-management
      (collective) bargaining
331.9 [open]

Of course, no classification scheme is perfect. The
range of human knowledge and speculation cannot be reduced
to neat pigeon-holes without conflict or overlap. Most major
divisions of the 300's are recognizable as branches of the
social sciences, but they are hardly equal branches. One
could argue that Commerce (380) should really be a subdivision of Economics (330), or that Folklore (390) does not
really belong in the 300's at all. History is generally con-

sidered to be one of the social sciences, but in the DDC it is a separate class (900-999), far removed from its sister disciplines. The separate status of history is more than justified, of course, by the volume of published material. So, while logical foundations are important to the scholarly integrity of a classification scheme, its practicality as a tool of organization is not undermined by occasional lapses from structural perfection. In fact, even if there could be devised a system devoid of logical inconsistencies, books themselves would continue to cut across subject lines in defiance of the cataloger's wishful demands that they fall neatly into convenient categories.

From class to class in the DDC there are variations in the pattern of subdivision. In literature (800-899) one might logically expect to find division by poetry, prose, drama and other major branches. Instead, recognizing that library users will more often seek English poetry rather than all poetry, or French literature rather than one literary form in all national literatures, the DDC divides literature first by language and nationality:

800	Literature (Belles-lettres)
810	American literature in English
820	English & Anglo-Saxon literatures
830	Literatures of Germanic languages
840	Literatures of Romance languages
850	Italian, Romanian, Rhaeto-Romanic
860	Spanish & Portuguese literatures
870	Italic literatures Latin
880	Hellenic literatures Greek
890	Literatures of other languages

On the other hand, in the 700's (the arts), nationality is ignored and the subdivision is basically by form:

710	Civil & landscape art
720	Architecture
730	Plastic arts Sculpture
740	Drawing, decorative & minor arts
750	Painting and paintings
	... etc.

It is at the next level of subdivision that books in the 800's are grouped by literary form:

820	English & Anglo-Saxon literatures	821	English poetry
		822	English drama

823	English fiction	827	English satire & humor
824	English essays	828	English miscellaneous
825	English speeches		writings
826	English letters	829	Anglo-Saxon (Old English)

It would be surprising, indeed, if a group so individualistic as creative writers did not provide an occasional challenge to the neatness of the classification scheme designed by librarians to keep literary practitioners in their places. Take the Nobel Prize winner, Samuel Beckett. Although a native of Ireland and a disciple of James Joyce, he lives in Paris and writes in French. To complicate matters further, he translates his own French plays and novels into English. Clearly, this great international writer is the nemesis of perfectionist catalogers, but most libraries choose to honor the language of composition and place the works of Samuel Beckett in the literature of his choice, the 840's. T. S. Eliot, the American-born poet, never changed his language of composition, but he did choose citizenship as well as residence in England. While many American writers live abroad--in fact, the great American literary movement of the twenties was largely centered in France--and while many scholars insist that no governmental document can instantly transport a writer from one national literature to another, catalogers can be as human as writers, and Mr. Eliot is generally accorded his own national preference, the 820's.

It was certainly shortsighted on Mr. Dewey's part to have reserved so much of the 800's for the literature of Western Europe, leaving the literatures of East Indo-European and Celtic; Afro-Asiatic (Hamito-Semitic); Hamitic and Chad; Ural-Altaic, Paleo-Siberian, Dravidian; East and Southeast Asian; African; North and South American native, and all other literatures to be squeezed into the 890's. The Decimal Classification Committee may someday perform major surgery on the 800's, but the enormous cost to libraries that such a major re-classification would represent is a powerful deterrent. All libraries except those specializing in East Asian or other non-Western literatures are well advised to make do with the present imperfect scheme, rather than risk the considerable expense and confusion which are likely to result from haphazard tampering with the DDC.

In classifying works of literature, as we have seen, one must first determine the nationality of the author and then the branch of literature (poetry, for example) which the book at hand represents. However, there is one major exception

to this policy which is made by nearly all public and school libraries, and that is in the case of fiction. Theoretically, American fiction is 813, English fiction is 823, German fiction is 833, and so on. But, putting practicality above theory --which is what the service-oriented cataloger should do--it is clear that most library patrons are interested in the form (fiction) first, rather than nationality. To make the reader of novels go to one national literature for Hemingway, another for Graham Greene, and still another for Franz Kafka would not be good public service. So, most libraries file all fiction together in one section, arranging the books alphabetically by author without assigning a classification number.

Standard Subdivisions

Although classification is generally by subject, subarrangement is often desirable by the form of presentation of a subject, e.g., a dictionary of medicine, a periodical of history, a work on how to teach mathematics. These various forms or methods of treatment of a subject are shown in "Table 1. Standard Subdivisions." Earlier editions of the DDC called them "form divisions." These major subdivisions are:

-01	Philosophy and theory	-06	Organizations and manage-
-02	Miscellany		ment
-03	Dictionaries, encyclo-	-07	Study and teaching
	pedias, concordances	-08	open
-04	Special topics of gen-	-09	Historical and geographi-
	eral applicability		cal treatment
-05	Serial publications		

The dash (-) preceding each number in this table emphasizes the fact that these standard subdivisions are never used alone but may be used with almost any number from the classification schedules, e.g., 513, arithmetic; 513.07, study and teaching of arithmetic. Analyzing the number for mathematics 510: 5 indicates that it is in the general class of the pure sciences, 1 that it is in the division for mathematics, 0 that it is general mathematics not limited to arithmetic, algebra or any one of the other sections. In "synthesizing the notation," or "building the number," duplicate zeros are cancelled; thus 510 (mathematics) and -07 (study and teaching) become 510.7, not 510.07. Although standard subdivisions are always preceded by a zero, if a zero is already there to round out the number to three digits, it is unnecessary to add another zero, and thus 07 or 0.7 may mean study and teaching when added to the number for a subject.

Note that standard subdivision -07 is for books on how to study or how to teach, not for textbooks on the subject; e.g., 507 would be for a work on how to teach science, not for a textbook on science, which would go in 500. In the first instance, the content of the book is methods of teaching; in the second the content is science.

The following is an example of how the standard subdivisions are applied in the 900's:

900 General geography and history and their auxiliaries
901 Philosophy and theory of general history
902 Miscellany of general history
903 Dictionaries, encyclopedias, concordances of general history
904 Collected accounts of specific events
905 Serials on general history
906 Organizations of general history
907 Study and teaching of general history
908 [open]
909 General world history

Standard subdivisions are always preceded by a zero, but zero and a figure do not always mean a standard subdivision; e.g., under 759, .01-.07 signify periods of development, not limited geographically--e.g., 759.05 is used for painting and paintings of the period, 1800-1900. Standard subdivisions under the numbers for European history have two zeros; e.g., 941.003 would be the number for an encyclopedia of the history of Scotland; 944.005, for a serial publication on French history. This is necessary since .01-.09 are used for period divisions of history; e.g., 941.103 is the number for the Early period of independence, 1314-1424, of the history of Scotland; 944.05 for the First Empire, 1804-1815, in the history of France. Standard subdivisions should be used with great care, first making sure that the numbers have not been used for some other purpose.

Another method of differentiating between books on the same subject is possible when a book's treatment of a topic is confined to a particular geographical location. The notations to be used are given in "Table 2. Areas," and, as in the case of the standard subdivisions, are never to be used alone, and are therefore preceded by a dash, e.g., -7, North America. However, unless the schedule specifically allows these notations to be added directly, the standard subdivision -09 must be interposed between the number in the

schedule and the area notation. A library having many books on a subject, several of which are on a given continent, country, or locality may expand the number for that subject by using the area notation. For instance: the number for agriculture is 630, with no instruction to add area notations directly. Thus one begins by adding -09. Then, turning to the Area Table, one finds -6 Africa, and adding these one has 630. 096 for agriculture in Africa; or for Tanzania, 630. 09678. The latter number is rather long for a small library and would only be used if the library had quite a large collection of books on agriculture, many of which were on African agriculture in specific locales, and it was desirable to bring them together.

In addition to the standard subdivision and area tables, the eleventh abridged edition includes two auxiliary tables: "Table 3. Subdivisions of Individual Literatures" and "Table 4. Subdivisions of Individual Languages." As in the first two tables, the notations are preceded by dashes and are not intended to be used alone. A major difference is that the notations of Tables 3 and 4 are to be used only when permission to do so is specifically given in the 800 and 400 schedules.

In addition to the four tables, the DDC provides another way to expand some numbers via the direction "add to." For example, under 560. 9, Historical and geographical treatment of Paleontology, we find: "Add to base number 560. 9 the numbers following 547. 9 in 574. 909-574. 999, e. g. , marine paleontology 560. 92." In earlier editions of the DDC, the corresponding instruction was "divide like" (a specific span of numbers). The principle involved has not changed, but the new and more detailed instructions are less confusing and easier to use.

Just to suggest the lengths to which the DDC system can be carried for the purpose of specifying the exact subject of a book, consider the following highly unabridged example which--due to changes in the schedule--is no longer valid today:

> A staff member of the Northwestern University Library Cataloging Department has identified what is believed to be the longest Dewey number ever under serious consideration for assignment: a 23-digit monster for <u>Arab Attitudes Toward Israel</u> by Yehosafat Harkabi, 301. -15433012917492705694.

The meaning of the number can be broken down as follows: 301--Sociology; 1543--Opinions, attitudes, beliefs on specific topics (Add 001-999); 301--Sociology; 29--Historical and geographical treatment (Add "areas"); 174--Regions where specific racial, ethnic, national groups predominate (Add from Table 5); 927--Arabs and Maltese; 0--General relations between two countries (Add "areas"); 5694--Palestine, Israel. In other words: Historical and geographical treatment of opinions on countries where Arabs predominate, and their relations with Israel. [4]

Reduction of Numbers

In a classification system using Arabic numerals for the symbols of the classes and the decimal principle for subdivision of those classes, numbers grow in length as the classification is expanded to make a place for divisions of a subject. The library which does not need these subdivisions simply uses the broad number, omitting any figures at the end which it does not need. For example, the number for the period of United States history when Franklin Delano Roosevelt was president is 973.917, but the small library with a limited number of books on U.S. history may use only 973.9, Twentieth century, 1901- , or 973.91, Early twentieth century, 1901-1953.

Whenever a cataloger considers shortening a classification number, two important factors must be kept in mind. The first question is how many titles on the subject the library is likely to own within some reasonably projected time span. Currently the library may have only three books about American history during FDR's administration, but a few years from now it might have ten different titles and would find it a nuisance to have those ten scattered throughout several shelves of books dealing with half a century's worth of American history. The second question has to do with the cataloger's ability to shorten a number in a manner consistent with the internal logic of the classification scheme adopted by the library and compatible with general policy decisions governing the degree of breakdown needed in the various classes. For example, the cataloger may have a book, Great Cases in Psychotherapy, for which the DDC number suggested by the Library of Congress is 616.89'14'0926. The apostrophes indicate logical places at which the number may be cut.

If the library is a small one, and uses the eleventh abridged DDC, the cataloger will find that the schedule does not include the number 616. 89'14'0926, case histories in psychotherapy, nor 616. 89'14, psychotherapy. The schedule gives only 616. 89, psychiatric disorders, which specifically includes psychotherapy and would be the correct number to use.

Another example: the full number for a book entitled Morristown, the War Years, 1775-1783 is 973. 3'09749'74. For a library using the abridged DDC, area notations from Table 2 may be used to the point of indicating a specific state. Therefore, the cataloger may choose to use 973. 3 (Revolutionary War, no area subdivision), 973. 30974 (-09 for the standard subdivision plus -74 for the northeastern U.S.), or 973. 309749 (New Jersey). The unabridged DDC permits the number to be extended to specify Morris County.

The degree to which the library extends numbers should be based on a specific policy that reflects the nature of that library's collection. It is quite likely that a library in Morris County would want to extend the DDC number for the book mentioned above to its fullest length, even if it uses the abridged edition, so as to collocate materials of local interest, of which it probably owns a considerable number. On the other hand, a library in California would be content with 973. 30974. Ordinarily, breaks shown by the apostrophes should be preferred, but above all, the breaks should be logical and conform to the internal structure of the DDC (973. 3097, Revolutionary War, historical treatment, North America, would make no sense).

Whatever policy decision a library makes about the degree to which it wants to extend certain numbers, it should be recorded in the schedules. Thus a library in Morris County might annotate its edition of DDC (as on opposite page):

When reducing a number provided by a cataloging aid or a centralized service, it is extremely important that the cataloger always check the shortened number with the annotated schedule in order to maintain consistency in the library's practice and to ascertain the suitability of the derived number.

In addition to the above precautions, keep in mind that a number should never be shorter than three digits and should not end in a zero beyond the decimal point. Make the number as specific as possible, i. e. , use 510, 520, 511, etc. , rather than putting everything in 500, and make sure that the short-

973   **United States**

For specific states, see 974-979

.01-.09   Standard subdivisions and persons

As enumerated under 930-990

▶   **973.1-973.9 Historical periods**

Class comprehensive works in 973

.1   **Period of prehistory, discovery, exploration to 1607**

Class period of prehistory, discovery, exploration of North America to ca. 1599 [*all formerly* 973.1] in 970.01

.2   **Colonial period, 1607-1775**

Class here King William's War, Queen Anne's War, King George's War, French and Indian War; if preferred, class in 971.01

Class local history in 974-975

.3   **Revolution and confederation, 1775-1789**

Social, political, economic, diplomatic, military history; causes, results

Including celebrations, commemorations, memorials, prisons, health services, secret service and spies, propaganda

for Morris County, use 973.30974974

for New Jersey, use 973.309749

---

ened number makes sense.   Record all decisions for reduction in the schedules.

The Relative Index

One of the important features of the Dewey Decimal classification system is its relative index.   D. J. Haykin [5] defined a relative index as one "which will show under each entry the different senses in which the term is used and the diverse aspects of the subject with their appropriate places in the classification system."

In order to select a class number for The Saturday Night Special, a book urging control of small cheap handguns, the classifier might begin by looking in the index under "handguns." Finding that there is no such heading in the index, the classifier would think of other possible headings to search and would discover the following entries:

Crime   364
   correction   364. 6

```
        prevention
            criminology                      364. 4
            pub. admin.  see Welfare
                services

    Firearms
        art metalwork                        739. 7
        other aspects see Guns

    Guns
        control                              363. 3
            law                              344
        pub. admin.  see Public
            safety
        hunting & shooting sports            799. 202  8
        s. a.  Small arms

    Pistols  see  Small arms

    Public
        safety
            law                              344
            pub. admin.
                central govts.               351. 75
                local govts.                 352. 93

    Revolvers  see  Small arms

    Small
        arms
            art metalwork                    739. 7
            hunting & shooting sports        799
            manufacturing                    683. 4
            mil. eng.                        623. 4
```

The number for gun control, 363. 3, seems to be the most
specific, but it should not be assigned without going back to
the schedules and examining the context. In reading back up
the schedule from 363. 3 (Other aspects of public safety), one
finds the centered entry, 362-363 Special social problems and
services. A centered entry represents "a concept for which
there is no specific number in the hierarchy of notation, and
which, therefore, covers a span of numbers. "[6] A note under the 362-363 heading explains the scope:

> Social causes and effects; extent, distribution, se-
> verity, incidence; control through standards, mon-

> itoring, surveillance, reporting ... prevention,
> safety measures ...

The note under 363.3 tells the cataloger that control of ex-
plosives and firearms is covered by that number, along with
disasters, censorship and control of information.

If the cataloger feels that the thrust of Saturday Night
Special is crime prevention, the number 364.4 would be
checked for its context and notes. Criminology is the subject represented by 364, and 364.4 Prevention of crime and
delinquency has the following note:

> Prevention police work, counseling, guidance, en-
> vironmental design; welfare services, e.g., recre-
> ational services; identification of potential offenders

When the two public safety numbers are checked, 351.75 and
352.93, it is found that while both specifically include firearms control, the context is that of agency administration.

This example should show that a tentative choice of
class number may be confirmed or altered by an examination
of its relationship to surrounding numbers in the schedule,
or instructions or annotations in the schedules may lead to
a further search. It cannot be emphasized too strongly:
never classify from the index. Instead, begin with the schedules, skimming the summaries first, if necessary, and checking the index only to ascertain whether you have covered all
aspects of the subject.

Classification Aids

At this point in the discussion, the reader has no doubt come
to the conclusion that classification must be one of the most
time-consuming and therefore costly of library chores. For-
tunately, this need no longer be the case, for an increasing
variety of cooperative cataloging services and reference aids
are available. Small libraries can have their books processed
by a larger library or by a regional processing center, can
buy their books pre-processed from a jobber, or can order
catalog cards from the Library of Congress or other sources,
as discussed in chapter 11.

Even when cataloging is done by the library, there
are a number of tools available which can ease and speed

the cataloger's work. The cataloging job can be initiated at
the time that a title is ordered. For example, if a library
uses The Booklist as a major selection aid, the typist who
prepares the order slips can add the classification number
and subject headings suggested by The Booklist to the duplicate slip which is retained by the library as a record of the
order, so that cataloging can be speeded when the item arrives. When material is selected for purchase from another
reviewing source, it may be checked against American Book
Publishing Record (BPR) or the Weekly Record for suggested
class numbers and other data at the time of ordering or when
the material is received. When the library uses a retrospective selection aid such as H. W. Wilson's Standard Catalogs,
Bro-Dart's The Elementary School Library Collection, or one
of the other classified sources listed in Appendix C, the cataloging data can be noted at the time the order is placed, as
suggested in connection with The Booklist, above; or the
checked copy of the selection aid can be used by the cataloger
when the material comes in.

An increasingly helpful aid is the Cataloging in Publication (CIP) program, which began in 1971. Over 2,500 publishers submit material in galley form or provide publication
data (approximately 27,000 titles in 1981)[7] to the Library of
Congress, whose catalogers determine the classification numbers and catalog entries for the book. Thus when the book
is published, this data appears on the verso of the title page
and can be used for the preparation of catalog cards when the
book arrives in the library.

Whether a library buys catalog cards or uses the various aids mentioned above, the classification number should
be checked with the library's official, annotated copy of the
DDC to insure consistency. This is especially necessary if
a library uses the abridged edition, for many aids give unabridged DDC numbers. Moreover, different aids may show
complete agreement or considerable variation as to the number for a given title. To return to the example of The Saturday Night Special, the number assigned to it by Book Review Digest is 623.4, while LC and The Booklist chose 363.33,
and Wilson's Public Library Catalog has it under 363.3.
Since 623.4 represents Ordnance, under Military and Nautical
engineering, the Book Review Digest cataloger apparently interpreted the author's intent differently. The local cataloger
must examine the book and judge which number is better,
keeping in mind local needs and policies.

The various aids will be found very useful as a check

on one's classification and may suggest more desirable classification numbers when the specific topic is not included in the index to the tables. If one is continually in agreement with the aids, presumably one knows how to classify. In case of doubt always consult the aids. But having consulted the aids, be sure to consider the particular library's collection and see that the number suggested is in accordance with its practice and is the best place for the given book in that library.

An aid may change its policy, as The Booklist has done in regard to the use of 810 and 820. At one time all literary works of American or English authors were put together, and 821 (English poetry) was used for both American and English poetry. The seventh edition of the Public Library Catalog has Irving Adler's 1974 revised edition of Thinking Machines under 519. 4, while the 1959-1963 Catalog had the earlier edition in 510. 78. The change reflects the revision of the DDC, and should therefore not come as a surprise to the cataloger. If a library is to adopt such a change in policy, all of the books and records involved should have the classification numbers changed, while bibliographies such as the Standard Catalogs may ignore their earlier practice and simply be consistent in present and future issues. It is a saving in time for the library to make the change when the aid first makes it. Otherwise the library using it in its cataloging must assign different class numbers to all books issued after a change is made by the aid, and if the library purchases printed cards it must then revise them.

General Rules for Classifying

Once the cataloger is thoroughly familiar with the classification system, has examined the auxiliary tables and read the introductory matter, is aware of the various aids available, and understands the library's policies, the work can begin. The first step in determining the class number for a title is to find out what classification information is already at hand. If a card set has been obtained from a cooperative or commercial source, the number suggested should be checked against the library's annotated copy of the schedules, for it may need to be shortened or modified in some other way. If cards are not available, check the back of the title page for CIP data, and if that fails, check BPR or a similar aid, and proceed as above.

If no classification information is available, the book which is to be classified should be carefully examined to see what it is about, what the author's purpose was in writing it, what class of readers will find it most useful. To do this, read the title page, preface, all or part of the introduction, look over the table of contents (as this spreads out before the examiner the skeleton of the book), and scan parts of the book itself. Having determined to what main class the book belongs, e.g., history, turn to the table for that class--in this case, 900. An examination of the table shows that 900 is divided according to place and time. Such questions arise as: what country or section of a country is the book about? Does it cover the entire history of that country or section, or only a specific period? Of course, if it covers the entire world from creation to the present time, it goes in the general number, 909. But if the book is limited to United States history, it will go in 973. The figure 9 indicates that it is history, 7 that it is limited geographically to North America, and 3 that it is further confined to the United States. The 900 class, which includes history, geography, and biography, is a good one with which to begin the study of classification. It is readily determined whether or not a book treats of history, geography, or biography; and if it is history, the country and period of time covered are usually clearly indicated.

If the book is one of literature, the first deciding factor is the nationality of the author; the second, the literary form. Thus Masefield's poems are put with other books of English literature and in the section for poetry, 821. A book on the theories of electricity and electronics would go in the main class science, the division for physics, and the section for electricity and electronics, 537.

The figures are the symbol of the class; e.g., 620 stands for engineering and allied operations, and all general books on that subject would be so marked. If a book is on a specific kind of engineering, the third figure changes to show that fact; e.g., 621 represents applied physics, which includes mechanical, electrical, and other types of engineering. Having discovered what a book is about and its place in the classification scheme, one puts the number representing that subject in the system (the notation) in the book and on its cover, so that all books may be kept together on the shelves in the order of their classes.

Many books are on two or more subjects, or two or

more aspects of the same subject.   To give an illustration,
a book on farming may treat of both the economics and the
technology of farming; a work on wine, its commercial and
domestic manufacture and public health measures regarding
it.   There is no single number for farming or for wine, as
the DDC system is designed to categorize material according
to fields of knowledge or disciplines rather than by specific
topics.   Thus the book on farming should be thought of as
being either an economics or a technology book and classified accordingly.

In some cases where two numbers might serve equally
well, the schedules themselves provide help by means of tables
of precedence.   For example, under criminology, the following instructions are given:

364	*Social problems and services; association*	364

364   Criminology

Crime and its alleviation; extent, incidence, distribution of crime

Class here comprehensive works on criminology and criminal law

Unless other instructions are given, observe the following table of
precedence, e.g., punishment of specific types of offenders 364.6
(*not* 364.3)

Penology	364.6
Treatment of discharged offenders	364.8
Offenders	364.3
Prevention of crime and delinquency	364.4
Causes of crime and delinquency	364.2
Criminal offenses	364.1

For criminal law, see 345

.09   Historical and geographical treatment of criminology
as a discipline

Class historical and geographical treatment of crime and its
alleviation in 364

In addition, when two or more standard subdivisions could
be used to extend a number, the preferred choice is specified by a precedence list at the beginning of the standard
subdivision table.

Having determined the subject and the aspect of it
covered, and the discipline within which it falls, the next
step is to locate the classification number for it in the
schedules.   As indicated in the Second Summary (the 100
divisions), 630 in Technology (applied sciences) is the division for the technology of farming; 330 the division for economics.   The Third Summary shows that 338 is the number
for production.   Turning to 338 in the schedules, one finds

338.1, Agriculture (including food supply); turning to 630, one finds 631.3 Agricultural tools, machinery and equipment. But which of these numbers should one use if the book discusses both the price of crops and the various types of harvesters? The choice depends upon the relative emphasis given by the author to the two aspects of his subject, as explained in the following guidelines.

The rules below are adapted from W. C. B. Sayers [8] and Lake Placid Club Education Foundation's Guide. [9] The classifier should also read carefully the "Editors' Introduction" to the eleventh Abridged DDC, which is very helpful.

1. Subject versus form: Class a book first according to its subject, and then by the form in which the subject is presented, except in generalia and in literature, where form is the distinguishing element. For example, Grove's Dictionary of Music and Musicians would be given the number 780.3; 78 shows that it is about music, 0 that it is not limited to one or more particular aspects of music, and 3 that it is in the form of a dictionary. Masefield's poems would be given the number 821; 8 showing that it is literature, 2 that it is by an English writer, and 1 that it is poetry. The literary form here determines its symbol, not the subject matter.

2. Subject emphasis: In determining the subject, consider the main emphasis or purpose of a book. For example, in the introduction to John K. Cooley's Baal, Christ, and Mohammed: Religion and Revolution in North Africa, the author states that he has "tried to set out some main themes in the relationship between religious faith, alien imperialism, and the native Berber revolutionary spirit." An examination of the table of contents and further reading in the introduction show that the book treats of the religion of North Africa, missions in North Africa, and analyzes the reasons for the Islamic dominance in North Africa. Hence Cooley's book would be classified in 209.61, the history of religion in North Africa; or in the very small library, simply in 209.

3. More than one subject: If a work deals with two subjects; class with the one emphasized most; e.g., class the effect of one subject on another with the subject affected. If the emphasis is equal, class with the one treated first. If the emphasis is about equal and both subjects are treated concurrently, class with the subject coming first in the schedules. If a work deals with three or more subjects, these

same principles apply, except that if the emphasis is about equal but the subjects are subdivisions of one broader subject, class with the broader subject. For example, the preface to M. S. Stedman's Religion and Politics in America states that "the purpose of this book is to advance an understanding of the relationships between religion and politics on both the empirical and the theoretical level...." Stedman would be classified in 261.7, Christianity and political affairs. Skilling and Richardson's Sun, Moon and Stars deals with the sun, moon, planets, stars, astronomers and observatories, with about equal space and emphasis on each. All sections are subdivisions of the broad subject, descriptive astronomy, and therefore this book would be classified in 523.

4. Contrasting opinions or systems: If a work treats of two different opinions or systems, with about equal treatment of each, but advocates one, class with the one advocated; but if more attention is paid to one, class with it, regardless of advocacy. For example, a book discussing capitalism and communism would be classed in 335.4, Marxian systems, if the bulk of it dealt with communism, even though the author clearly preferred capitalism. But a book which dealt equally with the two and also advocated capitalism would go in 330.12, Free-enterprise economic systems.

5. More than one aspect: A work may deal both with the theory or basic principles of a process and with its application to a specific subject. If the theory is preliminary to the application, and the author's purpose is to describe the application, class with the application, but if the "application" is only an example (with much less space given to it) and the author's purpose is to describe the theory, class with the theory. How to Fix Your Own TV, Radio, and Record Player contains general information about TV, radio and record players, so that when repairing them the worker can understand and recognize the parts and their relation to one another. It also includes material on how to diagnose the trouble and how to locate, remove, replace, or repair the faulty part. This book would be classified in 621.38, Electronic and communication engineering, rather than in 537.5, Electronics. Similarly, a book about the theory of electrodynamics would go in 537.6, but its application as in a book about electric trains, would go in 621.33.

6. Subject not provided: Do not make up a number for a new subject which does not appear in the DDC. A new edition may use that number for something else. Follow the

usual procedure for classifying and stop when you locate the most specific number that will contain the subject of the book, even if it is only a three-digit number.   Later, if the number for that subject is worked out by the DDC editors, you can add to the number already assigned to the book.   For example, a number for backgammon, 795.1, is specified for the first time in the eleventh edition, but there were many books published on this subject before the new DDC appeared. A classifier using the tenth abridged edition who wanted to bring together books on backgammon might have been tempted to establish a new number.   In the tenth edition, the number for checkers and similar games was 794.2, and 794.3 through 794.5 were unassigned.   If the cataloger had picked 794.3 as the class for backgammon, it would have been a mistake. The eleventh edition uses that number for darts, and assigns backgammon its own number, 795.1, under Games of chance. Even if the cataloger had agreed with the DDC editors that backgammon is a game of chance first and a board game second, the books should have been placed in the broad number for games of chance, 795, rather than assigned a new number.   It is easier to add to a number when a new schedule is published, than to change the entire number.

7.   General versus specific: Class in the most specific number that will accommodate a book.   If a subject is limited by place, form or other aspect and there is a number in the schedules for that more precise aspect, prefer the specific to the more general number.   Thus James Truslow Adams' Provincial Society, 1690-1763 would be classified 973.2, the number for colonial history of the United States, not 973, the general number for United States history; Maeterlinck's The Life of the Bee, 595.7, Insects, not 592, Invertebrates.   The closeness of the classification, however, also depends upon the amount of material the library has on the subject or is likely to have in the future.   Hence Maeterlinck's book in small libraries using the abridged DDC could go in 595.7, whereas larger libraries using the unabridged edition would put the book in 595.799.   Formerly, all books on Southeast Asia in the average public or school library were put in 959, but with the recent importance of that region to Americans, closer classification became necessary in order to bring together books on Vietnam, Cambodia, etc.

8.   Evaluations: The classifier is not a critic nor a judge, but sometimes must make an evaluative decision as to which of two or more numbers will be best.   For example, I Never Danced at the White House, a collection of columns by

Art Buchwald, might go in 817, as he ranks as a humorist of some merit. As a general rule, however, a journalist's columns would be classified in the 070's.

Always record in the schedules all decisions on optional numbers, reductions, and other variations. Place a book where you think it will be most useful, but avoid changes in recommended DDC practice.

When ready to classify a collection of books, first sort them by general groups, then examine those in each group carefully to see precisely what they are about. This is much easier than taking books as they come and switching one's thoughts from science to religion, to drama, to electronics, and so forth. A knowledge of the rules for classifying will be found very helpful, but one learns to classify by classifying. Keep in mind the purpose of classifying, namely, "to make books more available" to the readers for whose benefit classification is used. Be as consistent as possible; if in doubt about a class for a certain book, see what other books owned by the library are in that class, or consult bibliographic aids which include classification numbers.

Changes and Choices

The eleventh abridged DDC is a true abridgement of the full nineteenth edition, in contrast to the previous abridged edition. The tenth was an adaptation, which all too often used numbers that departed somewhat from those used in the unabridged edition for the same subjects. This meant that libraries dependent on LC cataloging could no longer routinely shorten the DDC numbers suggested by LC.

The eleventh abridged DDC reflects the numerous changes in the complete new DDC, but does not incorporate numbers which differ from those in the nineteenth. The two latest editions are entirely congruent, except in the amount of detail and the length and specificity of class numbers. The most notable changes in the new sets of schedules occur in the 300s, where Sociology, formerly 301, has been expanded to include 302-307 and where 324 has been completely revised, incorporating the old 329. For a helpful discussion of how to cope with the changes, see the HCL Cataloging Bulletin # 35 (July-August 1978). [10]

In "DDC 19: An Indictment," [11] Sanford Berman

complains that changes of such magnitude are too expensive
to implement and are confusing to users. Speaking from the
vantage point of a small library, Anne Reynolds' reply to
Berman [12] argues that the 302 to 307 adoption is not as impossible as it may seem at first, especially since the range
of numbers was vacant for many years. The smaller a library's collection and the more often it is weeded, the easier it is to adapt to changes in the schedules.

As new editions come out, they should be purchased
and adopted by even the smallest library, not only for the
purpose of keeping up to date as new subjects appear and
are incorporated, but also so that advantage may be taken
of time-saving cataloging aids and centralized services, which
usually reflect the latest editions of DDC.

If the library has a very small amount of material on
a subject the number for which has been changed in the tables, it would be well to change it immediately; if a great
deal of material, the amount of work involved may make it
impossible. In the case of such an extensive change as that
represented by the entirely new schedules for law and mathematics introduced in the 10th edition, it was not always wise
to attempt to change the classification numbers of books already cataloged. The new schedules should have been adopted,
however, and while the library will have arithmetic books
under both 511 and 513 for some years, the discrepancy will
eventually disappear as the old books in 511 are worn out and
discarded.

For new subjects, however, it is often worth changing
the number, as there is likely to be less material on hand.
If a new subject has been classified broadly at its first appearance, later--when the nature of it is more apparent and
when the library has more on it--the subject may be divided
to better advantage. This is easily done by adding numbers
after the decimal point. The number of new subjects unpro-
vided for in the classification system increases as the scheme
grows older. This is why it is so necessary for a library
to get the new editions as they appear.

As a result of changes in the numbers from one edition of the DDC to another, sometimes there are different
numbers given for the same subject in different aids and on
printed cards. When the Library of Congress adopts a new
edition of the DDC, it does not (and cannot) revise the numbers previously assigned to books in subject categories for

which the DDC has provided new numbers. Therefore, a library which orders LC cards for two books on the same subject which were published several years apart could very well discover that the class number for one is not the same as the number assigned to the other. For example, if a library ordered two books on ethnicity, Nathan Glazer's Beyond the Melting Pot, and a recent title from Greenwood Press, America's Ethnic Politics, and also ordered cards for them from the Library of Congress, it would find that LC suggests 301.451 for Glazer but 305.8'00973 for America's Ethnic Politics. The Glazer book was cataloged by LC in 1970, before the phoenix schedule for 301-307 was published. The new book has been assigned a class that conforms with the nineteenth edition of DDC. It is up to the cataloger to catch the difference when the cards arrive, and to change the number for the Glazer book to reflect the new schedule.

Not only is the classifier faced with changing class numbers from edition to edition, but also with varying options in choices of numbers. For example, the tenth edition allowed the option of classifying geography and travel along with the history of a specific place, so that a cataloger could have put all books on French history, geography, and travel in 944 rather than dividing them between 914.4 and 944. The eleventh edition has rescinded this option, along with others that were available previously.

Considerable discretion is still allowed, however, and the cataloger must face these changes and choices in order to keep the library's materials consistently classified. Whenever a decision is made, it should be noted in the appropriate places in the schedules. For example, if one chooses to class sacred vocal music in 784 rather than 783, both numbers should be annotated to that effect. The decision should take into account the habits of the library's users and the economic implications of departing from preferred Dewey numbers.

A major change introduced in the eleventh edition concerns the treatment of North American native races. A new number, 970.004, has been introduced for comprehensive works, but the option of using the old number (970.1) is allowed. Similarly, vacated numbers 970.3, 970.4, and 970.5 may continue to be used for specific tribes, places, and government relations, but DDC now prefers classing specific tribes in 970.004, tribes in specific places in 971-979 with the subdivision of 004, and government relations in 323.1.

In effect, the editors have decided to treat native races in a
manner more consistent with the overall approach of the
scheme, i.e., classification by discipline, rather than by
subject.

Among other options provided for in the schedules
are: laws of a specific subject may be classed under the
subject, using 026 from Table 1; bibliographies may be
classed with the subject, using 016 from Table 1; 298 and
289.2 can be used for locally important religions or sects
not separately provided for.

Probably the greatest number of options offered by
the DDC is in the 920's for biographies. Many small libraries choose to treat biographies and autobiographies of indi-
viduals somewhat in the manner of fiction, marking them B
or 92 and arranging them alphabetically by the name of the
biographee rather than the author. Collective biographies
can all be put in 920, or can be divided according to pro-
fession, e.g., 925 for scientists. Another possibility is to
classify biographies of people closely identified with a specific field in the number for that subject, so that the reader
who looks on the shelf for baseball would find biographies of
players along with other books on the sport. A disadvantage
of this method, if one wishes to identify the biographical nature of a work, is that it requires the addition of the standard subdivision -092, which can result in a rather long number, such as 796.357092 for a biography of a baseball player.
However, when a book deals more with the work a person
has done in a particular field than with that individual's life
as a whole, it should be classed with the subject rather than
relegated to the 920's. Thus a book about how Einstein developed the theory of relativity should go in 530.1092, but a
book which told his life story might go in the general biography section. Again, the policies adopted by a library for
biographies should reflect user preferences, should be spelled
out in the cataloger's copy of the classification schedules,
and should also be communicated to the public services staff.

Shelf Arrangement of Books Within a Class

The larger the number of books within any one class the
more need there is for some symbol which can be used in
arranging the books within that class. Another factor to consider besides the size of the collection is the actual need for
keeping the books in exact order on the shelves. Many li-

braries use no symbol whatever on the spines of the books of fiction, though fiction may comprise a rather large number of books even in the small library. A book with no symbol on its spine is understood to be fiction and is to be arranged alphabetically by author on the shelf.

Other libraries use a symbol for fiction, F or Fic, and many of these add the author's surname to the spine if it is not there originally or wears off. For instance $\frac{F}{Milne}$ on the spine of Milne's Winnie the Pooh makes it easy to shelve and locate this book. The catalog cards would have the symbol F or Fic on them. Some libraries use SC (Short Story Collection) to designate books of short stories and shelve them immediately following the books of fiction. In public libraries juvenile fiction may be designated by a J or some other symbol. Similarly, a different symbol may be used to indicate a picture book for young children, because the shapes and sizes of these books make it desirable to keep them on specially built shelves. Reference books are usually marked with an R above the classification number in order to indicate that they are not shelved with other books of that number, but are kept in a section of the library devoted to reference works.

In the case of nonfiction, library practice varies. In order to provide sub-arrangement by author, some libraries use "book numbers" as well as classification numbers. Book numbers do have the advantage of making it possible to keep the books within a class--i.e., those having the same content and therefore the same classification number--in exact order with a minimum of difficulty. When added to the class number (usually directly below it as a second line of the call number), the book number can also provide for each volume a distinctive symbol (or call number) which can be used for circulation control, record and inventory purposes, as well as for shelf location. However, the amount of work involved in determining and applying the number, plus the confusion which it sometimes causes patrons, reduces the advantages for small libraries. Public and school libraries of 75,000 volumes or fewer can usually manage to do without book numbers, and even many larger libraries use them only for certain sections of their collections.

A book number basically is a combination of letters and figures taken from an alphabetic order table, such as the Cutter-Sanborn table. [13] In fact, this system became so widely used in the early part of the century that the term

"cutter number" is often used to describe a great variety of book number symbols. The basic elements of the revised Cutter book number system consist of an initial letter followed by numerals to represent a name. This provides an alphabetic arrangement by means of an author symbol which is usually much shorter than the author's name. The figures are also treated as decimals, so as to make possible the insertion of a new name between any two combinations already used. For example, consulting the Cutter-Sanborn Table, one would assign book numbers as follows:

Miles	M645
Millikan	M654
Mills	M657

If just two numerals are used, the above book numbers would be M64 for Miles and M65 for Millikan, but M657 for Mills in order to distinguish between it and the Millikan book if the titles being cataloged have the same classification number. However, if the book by Millikan is classified in 530 and the one by Mills in 591.5, M65 may be used for both, since the classification numbers differ.

Books of individual biography in the collection should be arranged by the name of the subject of the biography (the biographee, not the biographer), so that all of the biographies of one person will come together on the shelf. Therefore, many book numbers may begin with the same initial letter or letters. To illustrate: Agassiz, A262; Allen, A425; Arlis, A724; or, shortening them to two figures: A26, A42, A72. Thus they may be distinguished with three symbols. By adding the initial letter of the biographer's name, one may readily differentiate several biographies of the same person and arrange them in alphabetical order by author: e.g., Goss's biography of Johann Sebastian Bach would have the book number B11G and Wheeler and Deucher's B11W; Dan Beard's autobiography, B36, and Clemens and Sibley's biography of Beard, B36C. Note that the autobiography has no letter added after the number B36 and would therefore stand before the biographies on the shelf.

Many libraries have found the first letter or the first three letters of the author's surname a satisfactory substitute for Cutter numbers and use author letters for both fiction and nonfiction. Thus Stevenson's <u>Treasure Island</u> might be marked $\frac{F}{S}$ or $\frac{F}{STE}$ on the spine, the same symbol being used on the catalog cards to show the location of the book.

In the class of individual biography there are likely to be some cases of persons with the same surname or surnames beginning with the same letter or letters. To illustrate, Franklin D. Roosevelt's biographies might be marked ROO; if the library also has biographies of Eleanor Roosevelt and Theodore Roosevelt, one way to differentiate among them is to add a comma and the initial of the first name. But it is highly questionable whether such minute differentiation is necessary in most small libraries. Another illustration may be drawn from the Adamses: Henry Adams' Letters (1892-1918); Mrs. Henry Adams' Letters, 1865-1883; and J. C. Miller's Sam Adams, Pioneer in Propaganda. They could all be assigned the class symbol B for biography or 92 with A, A1, and A2 as book numbers. If the Cutter-Sanborn tables are used, the books present no problem if three figures are used; the books would be marked A213, A215 and A217 respectively, below the class number. There are not likely to be many such cases in the small general library. Cutter-Sanborn numbers may be used for individual biography even though just the initial letter is used in other classes.

If book numbers are not used, individual biographies should have the biographee's name underscored on the spine of the book for convenience in shelving. It should be added where it does not appear; for example, Eaton's Leader by Destiny should have "Washington" written on the spine and be shelved under Washington's name, rather than Eaton's. Also, in the case of literary and art criticism, it is the subject of the book instead of the author whose name should determine shelf arrangement.

The name by which the book is to be shelved should also be added if necessary and underscored on the spine in the case of books with editors, translators, joint authors, pseudonyms, or whenever there may be doubt as to the choice of name. If fiction is published anonymously but the author is known and the book is entered in the catalog under the name, it should be added to the spine.

References

1. J. C. Dana, A Library Primer (Boston: Library Bureau, 1920), p. 98.
2. Melvil Dewey, Dewey Decimal Classification and Relative Index. 19th ed. (Albany, N.Y.: Forest Press Division, Lake Placid Education Foundation, 1979), 3 v.

3. Melvil Dewey, Abridged Dewey Decimal Classification and Relative Index. 11th ed. (Albany, N.Y.: Forest Press Division, Lake Placid Education Foundation, 1979).

4. American Libraries, 6:588, November 1975.

5. D.J. Haykin, Subject Headings: A Practical Guide (Boston: Gregg Press, 1972), p. 2.

6. Melvil Dewey, Abridged Dewey Decimal Classification and Relative Index. 11th ed., p. 37.

7. Kathryn Mendenhall, Final Report of a survey of the Cataloging in Publication Program to the Library of Congress Cataloging in Publication Division (Washington, D.C.: Library of Congress, 1982), p. A-2 and p. H-1.

8. W.C.B. Sayers, An Introduction to Library Classification. 9th rev. ed. (London: Grafton, 1954), pp. 179-180.

9. Lake Placid Education Foundation, Guide to Use of Dewey Decimal Classification: Based on the Practice of the Decimal Classification Office at the Library of Congress (Lake Placid Club, N.Y.: Forest Press, 1962).

10. John P. Comaromi, "DDC 10: The Reclass Project," HCL Cataloging Bulletin, 35:12-15, July-August, 1978.

11. Sanford Berman, "DDC 19: An Indictment," Library Journal, 105:585-589, March 1, 1980.

12. Anne L. Reynolds, "Implementing 'DDC 19,'" Library Journal, 105:1444, July 1980.

13. Distributed by Libraries Unlimited, PO Box 263, Littleton, CO 80160

Chapter 9

AUDIOVISUAL AND OTHER "NONBOOK" MATERIALS

In "Part I, Description," AACR2 treats separately seven
categories of materials which share a common characteristic,
if only in a negative sense: cartographic materials, sound
recordings, motion pictures and videorecordings, graphic materials, machine-readable data files, three-dimensional artifacts and realia, and microforms. What sets these categories
apart from those treated in the chapters for books, pamphlets,
and printed sheets; manuscripts; music; and serials, is that
catalogers perceive them as characterized by something other
than words (or musical notes) on paper.

"Nonbook," "nonprint," "audiovisual," are terms which
have been used to label materials which have found their way
into library collections, but have not been accommodated easily by cataloging rules developed historically for books and
other "ink-print" materials. None of the terms proposed as
a catch-all for the great variety of materials acquired by libraries that do not fall into the ink-print category has met
with general approval. "Nonbook" is really a "nonword,"
"nonprint" is too ambiguous, and "audio-visual" is too specific. In The Concise AACR2, Michael Gorman solves the
semantic problem by simply calling his condensation of
AACR2's Part 1 "The description of library materials."

Why then do the authors of Akers' Simple Library Cataloging persist in the separation between formats? Partly
because the last two editions treated AV materials separately,
and because the book's readers are likely to find the division
useful in sorting out similarities and differences in the rules
for print and other materials. However, the main reason for
the retention of this chapter is that sound recordings, art reproductions, filmstrips, etc., still pose special problems--
despite the rationalization of the rules in AACR2.

The most serious difficulty is the paucity of commer-

mercial cataloging for items other than books, requiring the
library to do much more original cataloging. In addition, the
physical formats of various media frequently call for organization and storage differing from those for books. For these
reasons--and for the purpose of raising issues related to the
handling of various materials in libraries--this chapter has
been retained. The intent is not to reject the integrated approach of AACR2; rather, it is to assist librarians toward
adoption of a common code for all materials.

The librarian's approach to the organization and cataloging of audiovisual and other nonbook formats will depend
on the community served. The following questions should be
asked:

- Who will use the material (staff, students, general
public, researchers, etc.)?

- What is the function of the material in terms of the
goals of the institution (reference, program support,
enrichment, teaching aid, etc.)?

- What special storage, maintenance, and security
problems does a particular medium pose?

A library in a school or community college committed
to the multimedia approach to teaching and learning might
choose to handle all materials uniformly, shelving them together and interfiling catalog cards so as to bring attention
to all print and nonprint items on a given topic. A public
library, however, might include entries for all types of materials in its central catalog but house audiovisual material
separately in order to minimize storage space or maximize
security. It would follow that the school library with the
integrated collection would have to classify all types of media
in the same way as books, but that the public library with
separate collections could use two or more different systems.
In choosing forms of entry, however, each library would have
to use headings and styles of entry for its nonbook materials
that are compatible with those for books in order to bring all
items on the same subject or by the same person together in
the catalog. On the other hand, a special library of material
in a single format, such as a picture collection, or a library
devoted to a single field but requiring a mixed media collection, such as a music library, might need to develop special
classification and indexing schemes in order to provide a sufficiently detailed breakdown of the collection's contents.

Even in these cases, it is desirable to adopt the AACR2 rules for description, headings, uniform titles, and access points. The more specialized a library is, the more likely it is to have unique holdings of interest to researchers. Consequently, participation in bibliographic networks is important, and that participation demands conformance with AACR2. For example, the holdings of the small but important Institute of Jazz Studies at Rutgers University are slowly becoming accessible to scholars as recordings are cataloged and entered into the OCLC database.

Most small libraries, of course, do not have unique collections and are not likely to have the resources to participate in large networks. However, local cooperation is becoming increasingly feasible and desirable, especially as the costs and problems of automation decrease, while the prices of materials increase. Just as at the national level, local resource sharing is facilitated by the use of standards. AACR2, in providing rules for cataloging all kinds of materials in a consistent format, makes it possible for small libraries to join the network movement at a grass roots level.

When a library adopts AACR2 for cataloging all its materials, it should also adopt a subject heading list which serves for all formats. If Sears is used for books, it should also be used for sound and videorecordings, art reproductions, and so on. Media format subdivisions of subject headings should be avoided. The ideal is to interfile entries for all kinds of materials in one central catalog, so that the patron looking for presidential inaugural speeches will discover that not only can these be read in print but also can be heard on a recording. But how does this patron know that one entry refers to a book and the other to a recording? AACR2 provides the option of using a "general medium designation" after the title proper, enclosed in brackets. Thus the entry might read "Inaugural speeches [sound recording]" in the title and statement of responsibility area, with the physical description area clarifying the fact that the item is actually on two cassettes. If the library user is not interested in a recording, he or she need read no further. Color coding of catalog cards or the use of symbols in place of fully spelled out media designations are not recommended, because they emphasize form over content and confuse the catalog user.

Although the ideal of emphasizing content over form has come closer to realization with the publication of AACR2, a few anomalies remain. The rules demand that the cataloger

describe the item in hand: a slide of a map is to be treated
as a slide. Any reproduction or facsimile is to be described
as such, and the details on the original are supplied in a
note. The problem of multimedia kits has not been solved
entirely by AACR2. The rule states that an item containing
parts in two or more media where no part predominates
should be handled as a kit (1. C4), while if one part does
appear to be predominant, that part is the one that is cataloged, with the rest handled as accompanying material. Either way, there will be instances where the patron's access
to content will be restricted.

While small libraries will generally want to use the
first level of description for books, they should give serious
consideration to providing more detail for audiovisual materials. The second level of description suggested by AACR2
calls for more information on series and edition than is generally required for AV materials, but the first level does
not allow for sufficient data in the physical description area.
The description of a nonbook item should tell enough about
the format and content to enable the potential user to decide
whether or not it is suitable. The physical description area
must include sufficient detail to indicate what type of machine
is required for playback, projection, etc. Contents notes
must be comprehensive enough to minimize the need for au-
diting or viewing the item in order to determine whether or
not it will indeed meet the needs of the patron. Facilities
for this may not be readily available, the user may not have
the time to do it, or the item may not lend itself to exces-
sive handling. Consequently, the physical description and note
areas for audiovisual material should be as specific as possible, while the rest of the description can follow the first
level format.

Where handling of the material is not a problem,
description can be abbreviated to first level, or even elim-
inated. For example, single maps, charts, pictures, transparencies, and similar flat items can be housed in a vertical
file under the appropriate heading. Small browsing collections of art reproductions, toys, or games might be most
effectively presented to users by means of a notebook of
photographs of the items. Whereas a school media center
may need to have detailed subject access to all its materials
in order to facilitate instruction, a public library may decide
that some categories of material need not be treated in the
standard way. Anything that is perceived by the library and
the user as an "extra" rather than a basic resource, a found

rather than sought item, can receive modified inventory and cataloging treatment. The question of who is going to look for what and why should determine the amount of time and effort a library spends on cataloging.

Description

The following general rules are a review of AACR2 rules, with the focus on application to audiovisual and other non-traditional materials. Amplification, exceptions, and examples will be given in the sections on the various media. The elements, arrangement, and style of the catalog record for non-book materials are essentially the same as for books and it is assumed that the reader of this chapter is familiar with the preceding chapters.

The first step in preparing a catalog record for any item is to decide what the item is. Is it a monograph or a serial, a microform, a filmstrip or a multimedia kit, model, etc. ? The nature of the item will determine the specific rules to be applied. Once it is decided what type the item is, the sources of information which one can use to create the record can be ascertained from the rules. In addition, the "general material designation" (GMD) will have been established, and a decision as to whether or not to use it made. Every library should have a policy governing the application of GMDs, and the level of description for the various kinds of materials it acquires.

Sources of information. For description of audiovisual materials, the general rule for chief source is to use the item itself in the case of graphic, cartographic, motion picture, video, and three-dimensional materials. For sound recordings, the two labels affixed to a disc or cassette constitute the chief source. The specific sources for various parts of the description will be listed under the headings for the types of materials covered in this chapter. When information from a source other than that prescribed has to be used, it should be enclosed in brackets and the source given in a note.

Main entry. In line with the effort to achieve consistency, AACR2 has a single chapter of rules for "choice of access points" for all kinds of materials, which includes rules for choice of main entry. The definition of authorship has been stretched somewhat to include performers as authors of sound recordings, films, and videorecordings under certain

circumstances. For the full definition of personal authorship, see p. 49, and for a discussion of choice of main entry, see chapter 3. In most cases, audiovisual materials are characterized by the kind of diffuse and extensive collaboration which makes author main entry inappropriate.

Title and statement of responsibility. The title is transcribed as it appears in the chief source of information, although punctuation and capitalization may be adjusted if necessary. If the chief source of information does not yield a satisfactory title, as is sometimes the case with audiovisual materials, the cataloger may use secondary sources, as prescribed below. Some materials, such as realia, may need to have titles created by the cataloger. In such cases, the supplied title must be bracketed and a note made (see card 136).

After the title proper, the cataloger has the option of inserting a "general material designation" in order to alert the user to the type of format:

> Julius Caesar [sound recording]
> Julius Caesar [motion picture]

```
    Lee, Harper.
       To kill a mockingbird. -- Philadelphia :
    Lippincott, 1960.
       296 p. ; 21 cm.




    I. Title
```

Card 76. Entry for book (GMD omitted).

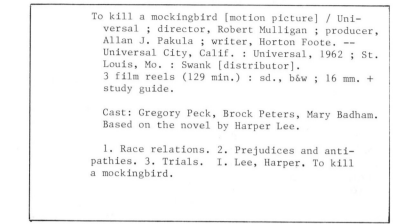

To kill a mockingbird [motion picture] / Universal ; director, Robert Mulligan ; producer, Allan J. Pakula ; writer, Horton Foote. -- Universal City, Calif. : Universal, 1962 ; St. Louis, Mo. : Swank [distributor]. 3 film reels (129 min.) : sd., b&w ; 16 mm. + study guide.

Cast: Gregory Peck, Brock Peters, Mary Badham. Based on the novel by Harper Lee.

1. Race relations. 2. Prejudices and antipathies. 3. Trials. I. Lee, Harper. To kill a mockingbird.

Card 77.   Entry for motion picture based on book.

To kill a mockingbird [filmstrip] / Films Incorporated. -- Cambridge, MA : Films Inc., 1980. 2 filmstrips (362 fr.) : b&w ; 35 mm. + 2 cassettes (42 min. : 1 7/8 ips, mono.) + 1 teacher's guide + 1 paperback. -- (Movie-Strip)

Edited from the 1962 motion picture based on the book: To kill a mockingbird / Harper Lee. Sound accompaniment compatible for manual and automatic operation.

1. Race relations--Fiction. 2. Prejudices and antipathies--Fiction. 3. Trials--Fiction. I. Lee, Harper. To kill a mockingbird.

Card 78.   Entry for filmstrip based on motion picture.

AACR2 specifies these GMDs for North American use:

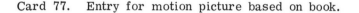

art original
chart
diorama
filmstrip

flash card
game
globe
kit

machine-readable data file	picture
manuscript	realia
map	slide
microform	sound recording
microscope slide	technical drawing
model	text
motion picture	transparency
music	videorecording

British catalogers are to use an abbreviated list which sub-
sumes globes and maps under "cartographic material"; art
originals, charts, filmstrips, flash cards, pictures, slides,
technical drawings, and transparencies under the term "graphic";
and dioramas, games, microscope slides, models, and realia
under the term "object." There is a great deal to be said
for the more concise and generic British approach, and the
chapter headings in Part I of AACR2 reflect the British groupings. The wisdom of the British version of GMD is especially
apparent in the "object" category, where the rules leave the
choice of specific material designation in the physical description area up to the cataloger, acknowledging the impossibility
of designating the entire range of terms that may be required,
and leading to some confusion in the choice of GMD.

On the whole, however, the North American list of
GMDs will serve quite well in giving the library user an in-
stant signal about the nature of the item being described.
Compare, for example, cards 76, 77, and 78. Most libraries will not bother with the GMD [text] for the book version,
but will want to draw attention to the other formats in as
conspicuous a manner as possible. The typical catalog user
probably does not look beyond the author and title information, and would fail to read the physical description areas
which would differentiate between the three formats.

Most libraries still have collections that are composed
largely of books, periodicals, and other "text" materials.
Consequently, they will omit "text" as a GMD, on the assump-
tion that patrons will consider anything that is not flagged to
be print. Manuscripts are unlikely to be found in small libraries, and printed music, in most cases, does not need to
be differentiated from other monographs. All other North
American GMDs, however, are quite likely to be of use in
small multimedia collections, such as those found in schools.

While the point has been made earlier in this chapter,
it should be noted here that the choice of GMD is determined
by the physical nature of the object in hand, rather than by

its contents. Thus art reproductions in microform should be given the GMD [microform] rather than [picture] and a chart on a transparency should be designated [transparency] rather than [chart].

After the GMD, give parallel and other title information if access to the item will be improved. For small libraries following AACR2 rules, subtitles will seldom be necessary, but the English translation of a title in another language may sometimes be advisable.

When an item has no collective title, the GMD follows the last title or title/statement of responsibility (see card 83).

For audiovisual materials, the statement of responsibility tends to be more extensive than for books, as many people and organizations are frequently involved in creating a sound recording, film, or filmstrip. The AACR2 concept of responsibility is broader than it was in previous rules. Chapter 12 of AACR1 (revised) essentially limited statements of responsibility to those considered to be of primary significance in the identification of the work. The new rules define statement of responsibility as "a statement transcribed from the item being described, relating to persons responsible for the intellectual or artistic content of the item, to corporate bodies from which the content emanates, or to the persons or corporate bodies responsible for the performance or the content of the item." (AACR2, p. 571)

For example, in the chapter on motion pictures and videorecordings, the rule says to record statements "relating to those persons or bodies credited ... with participation in the production of a film ... who are considered to be of major importance to the film and the interests of the cataloging agency." (7. 1F1) The effect of the phrase "relating to" is to give the cataloger greater leeway in using whatever attribution of responsibility appears in the chief source of information, and thus to exercise less judgment in determining "authorship." In addition, the idea that a performer can be assigned the major responsibility for a work is formally acknowledged in the new definition.

Judgment must still be used to differentiate between persons and bodies with primary responsibility and those whose contribution is less important. While The Concise AACR2 says "always record the statement of responsibility

which appears first in the chief source of information, unless
the name of the author, publisher, etc., has already appeared
in the title," (p.18) how much to include in the responsibility
statement, what to omit, and what to put in a note will vary
according to the needs of different libraries and their users.

Edition. The rules for the edition area pose no special problems and are applied to audiovisual materials in the
same way as for monographs. Following the edition area,
there is a special area which allows certain information to
be presented for two types of materials, serials and cartographic materials. This will be discussed below as it applies to the latter.

Publication, distribution, etc. The place of publication is now required for audiovisual as well as print materials. When more than one place is shown in the chief source
of information or accompanying material, record 1) the first
named place, 2) the most prominently displayed place, if different from the first, 3) the first named place in the country
of the library, if different from the above. The rules for
recording the publisher or distributor follow the same pattern
as those for place. When both publisher and distributor are
given, but the functions are not clear, they can be stated in
brackets (see card 77). The date shown should be the one
of the particular edition being cataloged. If there is no edition statement, use the year of first publication found on the
item. If not on the item itself, the date on accompanying
material may be used. If a copyright date is used, it should
be preceded by a "c" (see card 79).

Physical description. Formerly called the "collation,"
the physical description area is that part of the cataloging
record which often seems to be the most intimidating to the
novice audiovisual cataloger. Without question, a failure to
familiarize oneself with the essential physical characteristics
of the various media and with the standard equipment required
for playing or viewing different media will cause problems.
The cataloger must give enough information in this area to
permit the potential user to determine whether an item is
usable with equipment at hand, and will fit the show or play
time available. In addition, standard details about number of
pieces, color, size, etc., are important for identification,
inventory, storage and other purposes. The "extent of item"
data also gives the potential user a clue to the depth or
scope of the contents.

The type and range of information presented in this area of the record will vary with the various media, and will be discussed in greater detail in succeeding sections of this chapter. The following is simply a list of the most common descriptors required:

1. Number of pieces and type of medium (specific material designation). It is optional to omit the specific material designation [SMD] if it is the same as the GMD, and to omit the first word or prefix if it is the same as in the GMD. For example, if the GMD is [sound recording], it is permissible to use "1 disc" or "2 cassettes," etc., in the extent of item area. Where components of a unit are in different formats, each is enumerated and described, as in card 78.

2. Length, such as the running time of a film, number of frames of a filmstrip, playing time of a sound recording, etc., enclosed in parentheses. Time is given in minutes, rounded off to the next highest minute, except when the total time is under five minutes, in which case minutes and seconds are given.

3. Sound or silent in the case of films and videorecordings.

4. Color (or black-and-white) is indicated for motion pictures, videorecordings, and graphic materials, and three-dimensional objects. Sepia, tinted, or the actual color may be used when appropriate. (8.5C)

5. Material of which an object is made, when appropriate, as in the case of some objects and art originals.

6. Size. For two-dimensional items, give height x width, and for three-dimensional, height x width x depth; for tape and film, give width; for globes, give the diameter; etc. Metric measurements are used in most cases, but the measurement system most commonly associated with an item is preferable, e.g. millimeters for film width, inches for audio tape width. Dimensions for standard 2 x 2 inch slides are not spelled out, but are assumed as given.

7. Playback speed and recording mode for sound recordings.

8. Accompanying material, such as a teacher's guide. If important information about the nature of accompanying

material cannot be stated briefly in the physical description area, it may be given in a note.

Series. This presents no special problems for audio-visual materials. Discretion should be used, however, in deciding whether or not to list a series, and only those which will be of real assistance to the user need to be indicated.

Notes. This area can be as simple or as elaborate as it needs to be. The amount of information, as always, should be governed by the needs of the user. Secondarily, the nature of the format may require greater detail in the note area than is necessary for a book. Thirdly, the purpose the item serves in a given collection may warrant extra information in the cataloging record. Because some media are expensive and relatively fragile, additional time spent in providing contents notes and summaries may be justified.

Information which cannot be fitted into the standard parts of the record, but which is needed to clarify the description or indicate how the item is to be used should be given in a note. The following is a list of commonly used notes:

1. Nature, scope, or artistic form of the item; language; relationship to other works; titles other than the title proper.

2. Credits and other statements of responsibility: persons or organizations who participated in the creation or performance of a work, to the extent that they are felt to be significant to the user.

3. Edition, publication, and distribution details which are important, but which do not fit into the main description.

4. Physical details and accompanying material not included in the physical description area, due to their unusual or cumbersome nature.

5. Educational level or special audience for which the item is intended.

6. Availability of the same item in a different format (e.g. if a library has the same recording on both disc and tape).

7. Summary, in those cases where the title or contents note will not adequately describe an item. This should be brief and objective.

8. Contents, where parts of the unit cataloged have distinctive titles; often, a listing of contents will obviate a summary.

9. Holdings: if the library is missing part of the item, specify what is lacking.

10. "With" notes: when there is no collective title for an item made up of several works and separate entries are made for each, make a note about the other work (see cards 92 and 93).

In the sections on specific types of media which follow below, not all areas of description are covered in every instance. It is assumed that the reader will refer to the general rules in this and previous chapters.

Cartographic Materials

AACR2 defines these as:

> ... all materials that represent, in whole or in part, the earth or any celestial body. These include two- and three-dimensional maps and plans (including maps of imaginary places); aeronautical, navigational, and celestial charts; atlases; globes; block diagrams; sections; aerial photographs with a cartographic purpose; birds-eye views (map views); etc. (3.0A)

These materials are to be assigned either the GMD [map] or [globe], and described by one of the following terms (specific material designation) in the physical description area:

aerial chart	celestial chart
aerial remote sensing image	celestial globe
	chart
anamorphic map	globe (other than celestial)
atlas	
bird's-eye view or map view	hydrographic chart
	imaginative map
block diagram	map

map profile
map section
orthophoto
photo mosaic (con-
    trolled)
photo mosaic (uncon-
    trolled)
photomap

plan
relief model
remote-sensing image
terrestrial remote-
    sensing image
topographic drawing
topographic print

Explore it [map] : Philadelphia style : official
map of Philadelphia / Scarfo Productions. --
Rev. 11/80. -- Scales vary. -- Philadelphia :
Philadelphia Convention and Visitors Bureau,
1980, c1978.
2 maps on 1 sheet : col. ; 23 x 45 cm. and
28 x 21 cm. on sheet 47 x 30 cm.

Inset: Atlantic City, N.J.
Includes key to hotels and points of interest
in Philadelphia.

1. Philadelphia (Pa.)--Maps. 2. Atlantic City
(N.J.)--Maps. I. Scarfo Productions.

Card 79. Entry for maps with varying scales.

The whole earth globe [globe]. -- Scale
1:41,817,600. 1 in. to 660 miles. -- Northbrook, Ill. : Hubbard Scientific, [196-].
1 globe : col., plastic, mounted on metal
cradle base ; 31 cm. in diam. + 1 lesson plan.

1. Earth. 2. Globes.

Card 80. Entry for globe.

```
The new international atlas / Rand McNally. --
   1980 ed. -- Scale 1:75,000,000-1:300,000.
   -- Chicago : Rand McNally, 1980.
   1 atlas (xiv, 320, 232 p.) : 205 col. maps ;
38 cm.




   1. Atlas.   2. Geography.   I. Rand McNally.
```

Card 81.   Entry for atlas; GMD omitted.

If none of the above terms is suitable, an appropriate term
may be coined (see card 82).   Small libraries will have few
of these categories, and will not have substantial numbers of
items within the ones they do have.   A library that has three
globes, a relief model, and a couple of wall maps will have
these so prominently displayed as to eliminate the need for
cataloging.   Individual maps frequently can be incorporated
within the vertical file under a place name or other subject
heading, and thus do not need to be cataloged, either.

If a library has a significant number of large maps
that cannot be folded and are of long-term value to the collection, flat storage in a cabinet specifically designed for this
purpose is advisable.   The maps can be arranged alphabetically by area, making it unnecessary to assign a call number
or to catalog them, beyond what might be desirable for inventory purposes.   Maps may be arranged by: 1) continent, 2)
country, 3) state, province, etc., 4) county, 5) city or town.
For instance:

> North America.   United States.   North Carolina.
> Wake.   Raleigh.

However, integrated media centers may wish to have
catalog entries for cartographic materials, and therefore a
brief review of the rules is given below.   Special libraries

with large collections of maps will want to consult other manuals, as well as AACR2. A good starting point is Maxwell's Handbook for AACR2,[1] which has an excellent capsule history and summary of the problems of map cataloging.

Prescribed sources of information. The chief source is the item itself. When it is in parts, the entire set, including the title sheet, is treated as the chief source. Secondarily, the container, or the cradle or stand for a globe, may be used. If the necessary information is not in any of these sources, accompanying printed material may be used. Title and statement of responsibility should be taken from the chief source of information. Edition; mathematical data; publication, distribution, etc.; and series are derived from the chief source plus accompanying material. The physical description and notes may be derived from any source.

Main entry. As Maxwell points out, AACR2 does nothing to change the time-honored Cutter rule that "the cartographer is the author of maps."[2] The only help provided by AACR2 in decreasing the absurdity of cartographic entry rules is a result of the changes in corporate authorship, which means that there will be more title main entries and fewer Rand McNally Co. entries. However, if the cataloger is careful to provide the appropriate subject headings, the user will still find the material, and thus it is easier to follow the usual rules than to substitute a special set of rules, at least for collections where cartographic materials are not the predominant format.

Title and statement of responsibility. These are recorded as usual, with one important exception: If the title gives no information about what geographic location is covered by the map or globe, add this in brackets, as in the AACR2 example:

Vegetation [GMD] : [in Botswana]

If there is no title, the cataloger may supply one in brackets, being sure to include the name of the area.

Sets of maps may be treated individually or as a unit, depending on which approach is likely to be more useful in a given library. For a set lacking a collective title, separate cataloging records may be made for the parts, and linked by notes, or one description can be made, listing the parts in order. The third alternative applies only to a large number

New Jersey [map]. -- Scale 1:175,000.   1 in.
  to ca. 2 3/4 miles. -- Morrisville, PA :
  Relief-Technik, [ca. 1980]
  1 relief wall map : col., synthetic rubber ;
  169 x 133 cm.

Card 82.   Entry for wall map.

of physically separate parts, for which a collective title may
be supplied by the cataloger.

     Mathematical data.   Following the edition area, and
parallelling the "numeric and/or alphabetic, chronological,
or other designation area" for serials, description of cartographic materials calls for a "mathematical data area." The
data pertain to scale, projection, and coordinates and equinox.
A statement of scale should always be given, with a few exceptions noted below.   The scale is to be expressed as a
ratio (1:   ), and preceded by the word scale.   It is to be
included even when already stated in the title.   For example:

       Bartholomew one inch map of the Lake District
    [map]. --Rev. --Scale 1:63, 360. --

Weihs suggests the following method for converting graphic
scales to fractions:

     If scale is given in terms of miles to an inch,
     multiply the number of miles per inch (1 in. =
     43 mi.) by the number of inches in a mile
     (63, 360 in.) For example, 43 x 63, 360 = 2,
     724, 480 is listed as Scale 1:2, 724, 480. [3]

Other ways to determine scale are to use a bar graph or a
grid, or to compare with a map of known scale, and to show

the result as approximated, e.g. , "Scale ca. 1:63,360. "
When there is no way to approximate, use the phrase "Scale
indeterminable. " Use brackets when the scale has been derived from a source other than the chief source of information. It is optional to add a comparative measurement, as
in card 80.

For celestial charts, maps of imaginary places, views,
and maps with nonlinear scales, give the scale only if it appears on the item. When you know that a cartographic item
was not drawn to scale, use the phrase "Not drawn to scale. "

For three-dimensional cartographic material such as
relief models, it is optional to add the vertical scale after the
horizontal.

The statement of projection is to be given when it is
found on the item, container, or accompanying material, but
small, non-specialized libraries can omit this. The statement
of coordinates and equinox is optional in any case.

Physical description. This area encompasses a description of the number and nature of the items, color, material (if other than paper), type of mounting (when applicable),
dimensions, and accompanying material.

If there is more than one map (or chart, etc.) on a
sheet, or if the item is in parts that are meant to be fitted
together, express this as follows:

> 2 maps on 1 sheet
> 1 plan in 4 sections

When you are describing separately one part of a multipart item with no collective title, show this by a phrase such
as:

> on 1 side of 1 map
> on sheet 3 of 3 plans

If an item is in color, even if only in part, state so.
The material and mounting can be indicated when the cataloger
feels that the information is important.

Dimensions are given in height x width for flat items,
height x width x depth for relief models (optional), and diameter for globes. Generally, the measurements are expressed
in centimeters.

Atlases are a special case. They are described both as cartographic material and as a book. The mathematical data area is included, and the physical description area shows volumes and pagination. In addition, the number of maps in an atlas is given, and the book's dimensions. Most libraries will choose to omit the GMD for atlases, if they do so for books, as an atlas is generally thought of and handled like a book (see card 81).

Sound Recordings

A sound recording is a medium on which "sound vibrations have been registered by mechanical or electronic means so that the sound can be reproduced." (AACR2 glossary, p. 570) The most frequently used SMDs are sound disc, sound cassette, sound reel, and sound cartridge.

Prescribed sources of information. Use the labels affixed to a disc as the chief source of information. In the case of cassettes, cartridges, and reels, use both labels and the reel, cassette, or cartridge. If necessary, use accompanying textual material, the container, and other sources, in that order.

The title and statement of responsibility must come from the chief source. Edition, publication, and series may be taken from the chief source, accompanying textual material, or the container. Notes and physical description may be taken from any source.

When a sound recording has a collective title that appears in textual material or on the container, but not on the labels, the collective title may be used without brackets, but a note should be made indicating the source.

Main entry. 1) A recording or set of recordings (musical or spoken) containing a single work, several works or excerpts by one composer or author is entered under the name of that person (e.g. cards 83, 84, 98). 2) A recording containing works by different composers or authors, but performed by one person or group, may be entered under the name of the performer. Whether or not to enter under performer depends upon the purpose of the recording. Michael Gorman recommends that one should enter under performer when

the wording, layout, typography, etc., of the chief

```
Bach, Johann Sebastian.
  [Suites, orchestra, BWV 1067, B minor]
  Suite no. 2 in B minor, BWV. 1067 ; Brandenburg
concerto no. 5 in D, BWV. 1050 [sound recording]
/ J. S. Bach. -- Hollywood, Calif. : Seraphim,
c1980.
    1 disc (ca. 44 min.) : 33 1/3 rpm., mono. ;
12 in. -- (Great recordings of the century)
    Seraphim : 60357.
    Marcel Moyse, flute ; Adolf Busch, violin (2nd
work) ; Rudolf Serkin, piano (2nd work) ; Adolf
Busch Chamber Orchestra ; Adolf Busch, conductor.
    1. Suites (Orchestra).  2. Concerti grossi.
I. Moyse, Marcel.  II. Busch, Adolf.  III. Ser-
kin, Rudolf.  IV. Bach, Johann Sebastian.  Bran-
denburgische Konzerte. Nr. 5  V. Brandenburg
concerto no. 5 in D, BWV. 1050
```

Card 83. Two works by one composer.

```
Rossini, Gioacchino.
  [Guillaume Tell. Italian]
  Guglielmo Tell [sound recording] = William Tell
/ Rossini ; [text by] Jouy, Bis. -- New York :
London Records : Distributed by Polygram, c1980.
    4 sound discs (ca. 234 min.) : 33 1/3 rpm.,
stereo. ; 12 in. + 1 libretto.
    London: OSA 1446 (OS 26647-OS 26650)
    Opera in four acts, sung in Italian.
    Mirella Freni ; Luciano Pavarotti ; Sherrill
Milnes ; Nicolai Ghiaurov ; Ambrosian Opera
Chorus ; National Philharmonic Orchestra,
Riccardo Chailly, conductor.

    1. Operas.  I. Freni, Mirella.  II. Pavarotti,
Luciano.  III. Ghiaurov, Nicolai.  IV. Title.
V. Title: William Tell.
```

Card 84. Entry for sound recordings of an opera performed
          in language other than the original.

source of information or the container clearly
present the activity of the performer(s) as the
major purpose of the recording, rather than the
presentation of particular verbal or musical content.
[4]

```
Temple, Shirley.
    On the good ship lollipop [sound recording] /
  Shirley Temple. -- New York : Movietone Records,
  c1965.
    1 disc (26 min.) : 33 1/3 rpm ; 12 in.

    Movietone Records: MTM 1001
    Songs from motion pictures, sung by Shirley
  Temple.




    1. Music, Popular (Songs, etc.).  2. Children's
  Songs.  I. Title.
```

Card 85.   Entry under performer.

Thus it is appropriate to enter under Shirley Temple in the
example shown in card 85; under Shearing in card 86; and
under Horowitz in card 87.   It would not be appropriate to
enter the recording described in card 91 under the Wiener
Philharmoniker or Karl Böhm, as the principal purpose of
the recording is to present the music of Schubert and Schumann, and only secondarily the artistry of the orchestra and
conductor.   If there are two or three principal performers,
enter under the first named (see card 88).   3) A recording
containing works by different people performed by more than
three principal performers is entered under the collective title
(see cards 89 and 90).   If there is no collective title, use
the main entry for the first work on side 1 (see cards 91
and 96).   4) Optionally, a recording with no collective title,
but containing several works, may be given a separate catalog
entry for each work (see cards 91-93).

   Title and statement of responsibility.   In the title
proper for musical works, include medium of performance,
key, date of composition and/or number whenever the title
would be an indistinctive, type-of-composition term.   If the
title is distinctive, give the medium of performance, etc., as
other title information:

   Symphony no. 3, A major, op. 56 [GMD]

   Easter fresco [GMD] : for soprano, flute, horn,
     harp, and piano

```
Shearing, George
  George Shearing, Brian Torff in concert at the
Pavilion [sound recording] / George Shearing,
Brian Torff. -- Concord, Calif. : Concord Jazz,
c1980.
  1 disc (ca. 43 min.) : 33 1/3 rpm ; 12 in.

  Concord Jazz: CJ 132
  Title on container: On a clear day.
  Contents:  Love for sale / Cole Porter (9 min.,
30 sec.) -- On a clear day / Burton Lane (6 min.,
11 sec.) -- Brazil '79 / Brian Torff (5 min., 35
sec.) -- Don't explain / Arthur Herzog, Jr. (6
min., 6 sec.) -- Happy days are here again /
Milton Ager (2 min., 51 sec.) -- Have you met
Miss Jones / Richard Rodgers (3 min., 47 sec.)
                        (Continued on next card)
```

```
Shearing, George [sound recording]. (Card 2)

            Contents--Continued.

-- Blue island blues / Brian Torff (3 min., 3
sec.) -- Lullabye of Birdland / George Shearing
(5 min., 29 sec.)




  1. Jazz music.  2. Music, Popular (Songs, etc.).
I. Torff, Brian.  II. Title.  III. Title: On a
clear day.
```

Card 86.   Entry under performer; cover title as added entry;
durations in contents.

If a musical work has titles that vary in phrasing and
language, it is best to use a uniform title. The rule for
choice of language is to use the composer's original title in
the language in which it was formulated, unless a later title
in the same language is better known:

    Mozart, Wolfgang Amadeus
      [Die Zauberflöte]
      The magic flute

Horowitz, Vladimir.
  The Horowitz concerts 1979/80 [sound recording].
-- New York : RCA Red Seal, c1980.
  1 sound disc (ca. 45 min.) : 33 1/3 rpm,
stereo. ; 12 in.

    RCA Red Seal: ARL1-3775
    Piano: Vladimir Horowitz.
    Contents: Fantasiestücke : op. 111 ; Nacht-
stücke : op. 23 / Schumann (17 min.) -- Scherzo
a capriccio / Mendelssohn (6 min.) -- Sonata
no. 2 in B flat minor, op. 36 / Rachmaninoff
(22 min.).
                            (Continued on next card)

Horowitz, Vladimir. [sound recording]. (Card 2)

    1. Piano music. 2. Sonatas (Piano).
I. Schumann, Robert. Fantasiestücke, piano,
op. 111. II. Schumann, Robert. Nachtstücke.
III. Mendelssohn-Bartholdy, Felix. Scherzo a
capriccio. IV. Rachmaninoff, Sergei. Sonatas,
piano, no. 2, op. 36, B flat minor.

Card 87. Entry under performer.

The rules for establishing uniform titles given in AACR2
aim to bring together and organize a composer's work by
musical form, except where a composition is generally referred to by a distinctive title, as in the Mozart example
above. The rules also deal with standardized terms applying
to the instrumental and vocal medium of performance, and
with other identifying elements such as keys and opus numbers. These rules do not lend themselves to succinct explanation, but it is important for even the smallest library that

Sims, Zoot.
 Just friends [sound recording] / John Haley
Sims and Harry Sweets Edison. -- Beverly Hills,
CA : Pablo, c1980.
 1 sound disc (ca. 41 min.) : 33 1/3 rpm ; 12 in.
 Pablo: 2310-841.
 John Haley Sims, tenor saxophone ; Henry Sweets
Edison, trumpet ; Roger Kellaway, piano ; John
Heard, bass ; Jimmie Smith, drums.
 Recorded Dec 18 and 20, 1978, at Group IV
Studios, Hollywood, Calif.
 Contents: Nature boy / Eden Ahbez (5 min., 38
sec.) -- How deep is the ocean / Irving Berlin
(6 min., 52 sec.) -- My heart belongs to daddy /

                    (Continued on next card)

Sims, Zoot. [sound recording]. (Card 2)

                    Contents--Continued

Cole Porter (5 min., 2 sec.) -- I understand /
Kim Gannon, Mabel Wayne (3 min., 12 sec.) -- Just
friends / John Klenner, Samuel Lewis (5 min.,
11 sec.) -- Blue skies / Irving Berlin (6 min.,
18 sec.) -- Until tonight / Mauve (4 min., 47
sec.) -- A little tutu / Harry Sweets Edison
(3 min., 42 sec)

 1. Jazz quintets. I. Edison, Harry, 1915-
II. Title.

Card 88.   Entry under first principal performer.

has a collection of classical recordings to have a clearly
thought out and consistent approach to what it has.

    If the library buys its recordings from a jobber who
can supply catalog card sets with every item, the library
simply accepts the decisions made by the jobber's cataloger
and adapts its in-house cataloging of recordings acquired
through other sources to the jobber's practice. Similarly,
if the library buys cards, or if it participates in a regional

processing system, it must accommodate its policies accordingly. When a recording has to be cataloged at the local level, the cards produced in-house should be compatible with those obtained from the outside source, and therefore the same authority file for uniform titles should be followed at the local level.

```
        The Christmas revels [sound recording]. -- Cam-
           bridge, Mass. (Box 502, Cambridge 02139) :
           Revels Records, c1978.
           1 sound disc : 33 1/3 rpm ; 12 in. + texts
        ([4] p. ; 22 cm.)

           Revels Records : RC 1078.
           Subtitles on container: In celebration of the
        winter solstice; traditional and ritual carols,
        dances, and processionals.
           Various ensembles under the auspices of Revels,
        Inc. ; John Langstaff, director.
           Recorded 1978, Sanders Theater, Harvard Univ.
           Program notes by Susan Cooper on container.

           1. Christmas music. I. Langstaff, John M.
        II. Revels, Inc.
```

Card 89.   Entry under collective title.

When a library chooses to do its own cataloging but does not subscribe to LC's card service or music catalog, [5] it needs some other aid in establishing an authority file for names and uniform titles.   The Schwann Record and Tape Guide [6] can be used for this purpose, for while its choices do not always coincide with LC's, Schwann's entries are familiar to most recording borrowers, and the Guide is readily available, cheap, and easy to use.   For example, if you have a recording labeled "Beethoven's Emperor Concerto," you will find it in Schwann not under "Emperor" but under Concerti for piano and orchestra, No. 5 in E flat, Op. 73.   This information should be used to form the uniform title, arranged in the following order:

-form:	concerto
-medium of performance:	piano, orchestra
-number:	no. 5
-opus:	op. 73
-key:	E flat major

Concert favorites [sound recording]. -- Los
  Angeles, Calif. : Mace, c1978-
  2 sound discs (ca. 94 min.) : 33 1/3 rpm,
stereo. ; 12 in.
  Mace: MAC 9116, MAC 9125.
  Original works and arrangements.
  Various orchestras and conductors.
  Program notes on containers.
  Contents: v. 1. Bolero / Maurice Ravel (15 min.,
53 sec.). Pavane for a dead princess / Maurice
Ravel (5 min., 40 sec.). Capriccio espagnol /
Nicolai Rimsky-Korsakov (8 min., 34 sec.). Flight
of the bumblebee / Nicolai Rimsky-Korsakov (1 min.,
33 sec.). Song of India / Nicolai Rimsky Korsakov

(Continued on next card)

Card 00.   Entry under collective title.

If the labels, textual material, or jacket of the recording
had omitted any mention of the concerto's number, key, or
opus number (a highly unlikely event), the information can
be obtained from a source such as Berkowitz's Popular Titles
and Subtitles of Musical Compositions.[7] The catalog entry
would look like this:

> Beethoven, Ludwig van
>   [Concertos, piano, orchestra, no. 5, op. 73,
> E-flat major]
>   Emperor concerto

Note that the uniform title is bracketed and given on the line
between the main entry and the title as it appears on the recording label.   For composers whose works are regularly
cited by standard index number, (such as Koechel numbers in
the case of Mozart, Deutsch in the case of Schubert, BWV
for Bach, etc.), include the number in the uniform title, preceding the key (see card 91).

There is one major problem in using Schwann as a
guide to uniform titles, and that is choice of language.
Schwann contradicts AACR2 in preferring popular usage in
the U.S. to the composer's language.

Uniform titles are required for musical compositions
whenever a composition is identified by form, genre, or

generic term, e.g., canon, cantata, chaconne, chorale, chorale-prelude, concerto, divertimento, duet, fantasia, fugue, mass, motet, oratorio, overture, passacaglia, quartet, quintet, rondo, scherzo, sonata, song, suite, symphony, trio, variation. As a rule, the plural form is used in the uniform title, unless the composer wrote only one work of the type.

```
Schubert, Franz, 1797-1828.
  [Symphonies, D. 485, B-flat major]
  Symphonie Nr. 5 B-Dur, D. 485 / Franz Schubert.
Symphonie Ur. 4 d-Moll, op. 120 / Robert Schu-
mann [sound recording]. -- West Germany :
Deutsche Grammophon, c1980.
  1 sound disc (ca. 60 min.) : 33 1/3 rpm,
stereo. ; 12 in.
  Deutsche Grammophon : 2531 279.
  Wiener Philharmoniker ; Karl Böhm, conductor.
  Durations: ca. 29 min. ; ca. 32 min.
  Program notes in German by Hans Kohlhase with
English and German translations on container.
  1. Symphonies. I. Böhm, Karl, 1894-    II.
Schumann, Robert, 1810-1856. Symphonies, no. 4,
op. 120, D minor. 1980. III. Wiener Philharmoniker
```

Card 91.   Entry under composer of first work.

In some cases, the form does not have to be followed by the medium of performance. For example, it is understood that a mass is performed by voices, a symphony by an orchestra, etc. The medium can be omitted also for works which are a set for different media, or which are not designated for any specific media by the composer, or which are more easily identified by a thematic index number, e.g.:

Mozart, Wolfgang Amadeus
[Divertimenti, K. 251 ...]

Do not give more than three media of performance, and give them in the following order: voices, keyboard instrument, other instruments. For the following conventional combinations, use the uniform titles given in brackets:

string trio (violin, viola, violincello) [Trios, strings ...]

    string quartet (2 violins, viola, violincello) [Quartets, strings ...]
woodwind quartet (flute, oboe, clarinet, bassoon) [Quartets, woodwinds ...]
wind quintet (flute, oboe, clarinet, horn, bassoon) [Quintets, wind ...]
piano trio (piano, violin, violincello) [Trios, piano, strings ...]
piano quartet (piano, violin, viola, violincello) [Quartets, piano, strings ...]
piano quintet (piano, 2 violins, viola, violincello) [Quintets, piano, strings ...]

Other chamber music combinations must be given in full, even when there are more than three media.

```
Schubert, Franz.
  [Symphonies, no. 5, D.485, B-flat major]
  Symphonie Nr. 5 B-Dur, D. 485 [sound recording].
-- West Germany : Deutsche Grammophon, c1980.
  on side 1 of 1 disc (ca. 29 min.) : 33 1/3
rpm, stereo. ; 12 in.

  Deutsche Grammophon : 2531 279.
  Wiener Philharmoniker ; Karl Böhm, conductor.

  With: Symphony no. 4, op. 120, D minor /
Robert Schumann.


  1. Symphonies.  I. Böhm, Karl.
```

Card 92.   Entry for one work on disc containing two works.

If a work is an arrangement or translation, note that in the uniform title:

    Berlioz, Hector
      [Le corsaire; arr.]
      The corsaire : overture for concert
    band / transcribed by Gunther Schuller

    Bizet, Georges
      [Carmen.   German]

```
Schumann, Robert.
   [Symphonies, no. 4, op. 120, D minor]
   Symphonie Ur. 4 d-Moll, op. 120 [sound record-
ing]. -- West Germany : Deutsche Grammophon,
c1980.
   on side 2 of 1 disc (ca. 32 min.) : 33 1/3
rpm, stereo. ; 12 in.

   Deutsche Grammophon: 2531 279.
   Wiener Philharmoniker ; Karl Böhm, conductor.

   With: Symphony no. 5, D. 485, B-flat major /
Franz Schubert.


   1. Symphonies.  I. Böhm, Karl.
```

Card 93.   Entry for second work on disc described in cards
            91 and 92.

For a collection of a composer's complete works, the
uniform title is [Works].   Use [Selections] for extracts or
for three or more compositions in different forms.   Use the
medium if all the selections are for a general or specific
medium of performance or type of composition:

broad medium:	[Chamber music]
	[Choral music]
	[Instrumental music]
	[Keyboard music]
	[Vocal music]
specific medium:	[Brass music]
	[Orchestra music]
	[Piano music]
	[Piano music, 4 hands]
	[Piano music, 2 pianos]
	[String quartet music]
	[Violin, piano music]
works of one type:	[Concertos]
	[Operas]
	[Polonaises, piano]
	[Quartets, strings]
	[Sonatas]
	[Sonatas, violin, piano]
	[Songs]

206 / Simple Library Cataloging

Add "selections" if the uniform title is for an incomplete collection, or give the consecutive numbering:

[Organ music. Selections]

[Sonatas, piano, no. 21-23]

For a discussion of uniform titles for non-musical works, see Chapter 4. The GMD may be given as the last item in the uniform title, as well as after the title proper, but most libraries will want to follow the Library of Congress which gives it only after the title proper:

> Mendelssohn-Bartholdy, Felix
> [Ein Sommernachtstraum]
> Ein Sommernachtstraum [sound recording] :
> Musik zu Shakespeares Schauspiel = A midsummer
> night's dream

Note that other title information is transcribed after the title proper to which it pertains.

When a sound recording has a collective title, use this as the title proper, and give the titles of the individual works in a contents note (1.1B10), as in card 90.

The statement of responsibility should give the composer, or in the case of spoken sound recordings, the writer shown on the label. Collectors of field material, lyricists, and others who bear responsibility beyond performance or interpretation are also given if they appear prominently on the label (see cards 84 and 97).

When a sound recording contains several works, the treatment depends on whether one work predominates, whether there is a collective title, whether there is a principal performer who is the major reason for the recording, and to what degree the individual works are to be traced.

If there is no collective title, but there is a predominant work, treat the title of the predominant work as the title proper, and give the other works in a note (see card 94).

In the Chabrier example, the other works are not traced. Another example with a predominant work and no collective title is shown in card 95. Here the decision has

been made to give all the works in the title/statement of
responsibility area.   One could, however, list the other
works in a contents note.   Either way, the individual works
can be traced.

```
Chabrier, Emmanuel.
  [Selections]
  Espana [sound recording]. -- Chicago : Wing,
[1968?]
  1 disc (44 min.) : 33 1/3 rpm, stereo. ;
12 in.

  Mercury: Wing WC 18068
  Detroit Symphonie ; Paul Paray, conductor.
  Also contains Suite pastorale, Danse village-
oise, Sous bois, Scherzovalse, Fete pollonaise,
Overture to "Gwendoline," Danse slave.

  I. Detroit Symphony.  II. Paray, Paul.
III. Title.
```

Card 94.   Entry for recording of several works by one composer, where one work predominates (others not
traced).

```
Albinoni, Tomaso.
  Adagio in G minor / Albinoni (arr. Giazotto).
Serenade no. 13 in G, K.525 ("Eine kleine Nacht-
musik") / Mozart. Canon / Pachelbel.  Concerto
grosso in G minor, op. 6, no. 8 ("Christmas Con-
certo") / Corelli [sound recording]. -- Holly-
wood, Calif. : Seraphim, [197-?].
  1 sound disc : 33 1/3 rpm, stereo. ; 12 in.
  Seraphim: S-60271.
  Toulouse Chamber Orchestra ; Louis Auriacombe,
conductor.
  Durations: 8 min., 18 min., 5 min., 16 min.
  I. Mozart, Wolfgang Amadeus. Kleine Nachtmusik.
II. Pachelbel, Johann. Canon in D.  III. Corelli,
Arcangelo. Concerto grosso, no. 8, op. 6, G minor.
```

Card 95.   Entry under predominant work.

Verdi, Giuseppi.
    [Quartet, strings, E minor]
    Streichquartett e-Moll / Giuseppi Verdi.
Streichquartett D-Dur, op. 11 / Peter Tchaikow-
sky [sound recording]. -- [Hamburg] : Deutsche
Grammophon, c1980.
    1 sound disc (ca. 50 min. : 33 1/3 rpm,
stereo. ; 12 in.

    Deutsche Grammophon: 2531 283.
    Amadeus Quartet.

    1. String quartets. I. Tchaikowsky, Peter
Ilich. Quartets, strings, no. 1, op. 11, D major.
II. Amadeus Quartet.

Card 96.   Entry under composer of first work.

7M
STRAWBE
K 63   STRAWBERRY Shortcake in Big Apple City.

    Original soundtrack recording; writer and lyrics, Romeo Muller;
music written and performed by Flo & Eddie. Disc 12 in. 33 rpm.
stereo Kid Stuff KSS-163. Cassette KST-940.
    Contents: What a Day; Big Apple City; New Friends; Bake Off;
Strawberry Land; and others.

    1. Children's Stories 2. Motion Picture Soundtracks I. Muller,
Romeo

Copyright 1982   00-1603
Professional Media Service Corp.

Card 97.   Commercial card (not in AACR2 format).   State-
           ment of responsibility includes composers and
           writer.

    When no part of the recording can be said to be pre-
dominant, list the titles and corresponding statements of responsibility in the order in which they appear, as in cards

83 and 96. Note that a space-semicolon-space is used to separate titles of works by the same person (see card 83), but that a period-space-space is used to separate statements when the authors or composers are different.

Shands, Harley C.
  The doctor talks to you about understanding phobias [sound recording] : a discussion / by Harley C. Shands. -- Bayside, N.Y. : Soundwords, c1979.
    1 cassette (30 min.) : 1 7/8 ips, mono.

  Interview.
  Intended audience: Ages 16 through adult.

  1. Fear. 2. Neuroses. I. Title. II. Title: Understanding phobias.

Card 98. Cassette entered under personal author.

When there is no collective title, the cataloger may make separate entries for each work, linking them by a "with" note. Cards 92 and 93 represent a typical example, where the Schubert piece takes up one side of the disc and the Schumann the other side. Both are given equal prominence, and the decision to make a unit entry or separate entries is not a crucial one. A unit entry will require fewer cards, but separate entries may be slightly easier for the catalog user, or may allow more detail to be presented for each work.

Publication, distribution, etc. Where a sound recording label shows both a company and a "brand" or subdivision, use only the latter. For example, if the label reads "Decca Record Company/Ace of Diamonds," record this as London : Ace of Diamonds. If it is not clear whether a name applies to a subdivision or a series, treat it as a series. If the publisher and distributor are not the same, add a statement of function, as in card 84.

Sound recordings may show several dates, or no date

at all. Copyright, recording, release and other dates may appear, but it is not always clear which is which. Fleischer and Goodman point out the following:

> Since 1972 the familiar symbol for copyright © does not apply to sound recordings. The correct symbol is ℗. The Rules prefer a publishing date, but allow a copyright to be used in case it is the only available date (1.4F6). This is entered as a lower case (small) c followed by the date, whether the item cataloged is printed or recorded. When two copyright dates are found on a sound recording, one a © and the other a ℗, the latter refers to the recording itself. The other date may deal with the lyrics of a song, accompanying text, or some other written data that may or may not be treated in the catalog record.[8]

When the only available date is the recording date, it may be given in brackets as the probable publication date.

Key to Rebecca [sound recording] / by Ken
   Follett ; read by Anthony Quayle. -- Downs-
   view, Ont. ; Lewiston, N.Y. : Listen for
   Pleasure Limited, 1982.
   2 sound cassettes (150 min.) : 1 7/8 ips., mono.

TC-LFP 7015
   Text of original novel abridged by Edward
Phillips.
   Dolby system recording.

   I. Quayle, Anthony. II. Follett, Ken. The key
to Rebecca.

Card 99. Entry for recorded abridgement of novel.

Physical description. This should describe the format sufficiently to enable the user to know what kind of equipment is needed for playback. The following information is given in the order listed: number of cartridges, cassettes, discs, or

reels; playing time, in parentheses (if readily available); playing speed; recording mode (e. g. , stereo.); diameter of discs and tape reels. Dimensions of cassettes and cartridges are given only if they are not standard. Accompanying material is listed as usual.

Notes. Because the label number is so important to the identification of a sound recording, it is given at or near the beginning of the notes, rather than at the end. Next in importance in most cases are the performers and their medium of performance. Durations may be given for parts of the item being described. Audience level and summaries may be useful in some cases. The contents note may combine titles of individual works, statements of responsibility, performers, and duration (see cards 86 and 90). The "with" note is generally the last item in the note area.

Motion Pictures and Videorecordings

While the techniques used to create these two formats are entirely different, film and video share characteristics which require similar descriptive cataloging. The primary similarity is that both contain images in motion. In addition, a theatrical film or documentary originally shot in 35 mm. frequently is also available as a 16 mm. film for the educational market, and as a videocartridge or videodisc for the home viewer who owns a video player.

A motion picture is a series of still pictures on film which, when projected, gives the illusion of motion. An optical or magnetic sound track may appear as a strip down one side of the film. Various sizes of film can be used (8, 16, 35, 55, 70 mm.), and the film can be mounted on reels, in cassettes or cartridges. A loop film has the start and end spliced together and is designed to run continuously without rewinding; it is usually mounted in a cartridge. The width of the film and the type of mounting determine the kind of machine needed for projection.

A videorecording contains electronic signals on magnetic tape, on disc, or other material, designed to be played back on television equipment. Videotape varies in width and may be on reels or in cassettes or cartridges. As new formats continue to be developed, it is essential that the catalog description specify the kind of playback machine required.

The following GMDs and SMDs are prescribed by AACR2:

GMD	SMD
motion picture	film cartridge
	film cassette
	film loop
	film reel

videorecording	videocartridge
	videocassette
	videodisc
	videoreel

The fragile and costly nature of film requires a minimum of handling and therefore a maximum of description in the cataloging, especially in terms of contents. The practice of using separate printed book catalogs for public library film and/or video collections is almost universal, and will be discussed below. However, the availability of a separate book catalog for films and/or video should not rule out the provision of subject entries in the general catalog in order to alert the library's patrons to all holdings on a given topic. Media centers should interfile full card sets in their general catalogs, whether or not they also choose to print a separate list of films and/or videorecordings.

Media centers should use the same classification system as that chosen for other materials, and should consider the possibility of intershelving with other media. Most public libraries keep 16 mm. films in locked storage, arranged alphabetically by title or by a code based on reel size and accession number. They tend to treat 8 mm. film and videodiscs more casually, allowing the original illustrated container to take the place of a catalog, since the films and discs are considered to be a browsing collection intended primarily for entertainment.

Prescribed sources of information. The chief source is the item itself, specifically the title frames at the beginning and end. When the container, such as a cartridge, is an integral part of the item, it can also be considered as the chief source. If the information is not available from the chief source, use accompanying textual material, the container (if not integral), and other sources, in that order. The

chief source is prescribed for the title and statement of responsibility area. For the edition, publication, and series
areas, the chief source plus accompanying material may be
used. Any source may be used for the rest.

```
Bozzetto, Bruno.
   Happy birthday [motion picture] / Bruno
Bozzetto. -- New York : Janus Films [distributor],
1980.
   1 film reel (10 min.) : sd., col. ; 16 mm.

   Title from data sheet.
   Summary: A man goes to surprise a birthday
celebrant, only to find the house mysteriously
empty. The event turns into a tale of horror.


   I. Title.
```

Card 100.   "Author" main entry for film (Bozzetto responsi-
             ble for story and animation).

```
The Merchant of Venice [videorecording] / BBC
   and Time-Life Television ; executive producer,
   Jonathan Miller. -- New York : Time-Life
   Video, 1980.
   3 videocassettes (Sony U-matic) (157 min.) :
sd., col. ; 3/4 in. -- (The Shakespeare plays)

   Cast: Warren Mitchell, Gemma Jones, John
Franklyn-Robbins.



   I. Miller, Jonathan.   II. Shakespeare, William.
Merchant of Venice.   III. Series.
```

Card 101.   Entry for videorecording (held by library in one
             format only).

Main entry. Because the making of a film or video program is a collaborative effort, it is seldom possible to attribute "authorship" to an individual. Occasionally, particularly in the case of animated films, there is one person who is clearly the creator. When the concept, art work, photography, editing, and sound track can all be attributed to an individual, the entry should be under the name of that person (see card 100).

```
    She drinks a little [motion picture] / Martin
      Tahse Productions ; producer, Martin Tahse ;
      director, Arthur Allan Seidelman ; screenplay,
      Paul W. Cooper. -- New York, NY : Learning
      Corp. of America, 1981.
      1 film reel (30 min.) : sd., col. ; 16 mm. +
    1 teacher's guide. -- (Learning to be human)
      Title from data sheet.
      Cast: Amanda Wyss, Bonnie Bartlett, Elliot
    Jaffe, Michael Leclair.
      Based on:  The first step / Anne Snyder.
      Summary:  A teen-ager is burdened and trauma-
    tized by an alcoholic mother.  Exposure to organ-
    izations such as Alateen helps her to cope.
      1. Alcoholics--Fiction.  2. Mothers and daugh-
    ters--Fiction.  I. Snyder, Anne.  First step.
```

Card 102.   Entry for film based on book.

Title and statement of responsibility. Generally, the producer and director are given in the statement of responsibility (see cards 77, 101, 102). The animator and the writer may also be important enough to be included. If the nature of the responsibility is not clear, insert the proper phrase in brackets. Other credits can be given in a note. The interests of the collection's users should influence the cataloger's decision as to what names should be in the catalog record.

Publication, distribution, etc. Producer and distributor or releasing agency are given. If the distribution date is not the same as the production date, the earlier date may be given in a note (see card 103). When the distribution date is not known, but the original production date is, the former may be omitted, as in card 77.

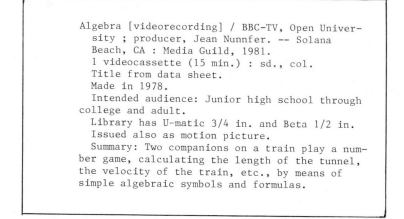

Algebra [videorecording] / BBC-TV, Open Univer-
sity ; producer, Jean Nunnfer. -- Solana
Beach, CA : Media Guild, 1981.
1 videocassette (15 min.) : sd., col.
Title from data sheet.
Made in 1978.
Intended audience: Junior high school through
college and adult.
Library has U-matic 3/4 in. and Beta 1/2 in.
Issued also as motion picture.
Summary: Two companions on a train play a num-
ber game, calculating the length of the tunnel,
the velocity of the train, etc., by means of
simple algebraic symbols and formulas.

Card 103.   Card for videorecording owned in several formats.

Physical description.   The number of units of a film
or videorecording is followed by the appropriate SMD.   In
the case of videorecordings, add the trade name or other
technical specification in parentheses, if this affects use (see
card 101).   Duration is given in parentheses, followed by

Rewiring a lamp [motion picture]. -- New York :
Universal Education and Visual Arts, [ca. 1970]
1 film cartridge (Kodak) (3 min.) ; si., col. ;
super 8 mm. -- (Basic home electrical and
wiring)

Film guide on container.

1. Electric wiring.   I. Series

Card 104.   Entry for film loop in cartridge.

sound, color, and speed characteristics. Sepia is treated as black and white. For material which is partly color and partly black and white, use a phrase such as "col. with b&w sequences." The revolutions per minute are indicated for videodiscs, and sometimes projection speed in frames per second (fps) may be needed for silent film. The width of videotape and the diameter of videodiscs are given in inches, but film gauge is given in millimeters. For 8 mm. film, precede the gauge by single, standard, super, or Maurer (see card 104).

```
The Puzzle of the Tacoma Narrows Bridge collapse
  [videorecording] / Robert Fuller ; Dean Zoll-
  man ; Thomas Campbell. -- New York : Wiley
  Educational Software, c1982 ; John Wiley & Sons
  [distributor]
    1 videodisc (Pioneer laser) (ca. 27 min.) :
  sd., col., 1800 rpm ; 12 in.
    Documentary film footage of 1940 bridge
  collapse.
    In 19 chs. with 71 picture stops.
    Summary: Presents the collapse as an example
  of an oscillation problem for study by physics
  and engineering students.
    ISBN 0-471-87320-9
    1. Tacoma Narrows Bridge (1940). 2. Bridges.
  I. Fuller, Robert. II. Zollman, Dean. III.
  Campbell, Thomas.
```

Card 105. Entry for videodisc.

Notes. Names of persons not included in the statement of responsibility but likely to be of interest to the user may be given under a heading such as cast or credits. Other titles under which an item has been released, relationship to other versions, and significant physical details not already specified can be included in the note area. When a library owns a title in several formats, these are given in a note (see card 103). A brief, objective summary should be given, including enough information to permit the prospective user to judge suitability.

Book catalogs. Where film and/or video collections have developed independently, are housed apart from the library's overall collection, or are the only holdings (as in a regional AV center), the book catalog has proven to be the

most efficient means of access for the borrower who comes seeking film or video specifically (see pages following).

The same information which would be given on a catalog card is included in a book catalog format, with the exception of medium designation and film width or video format (where all are the same), which are given only once, on the cover or in the introduction. Descriptions are more likely to be annotations than summary notes, since they can be longer and less formal, and because the catalog also serves as a promotional tool. Tracings take the form of an index to the catalog, which may include names of filmmakers, performers, etc., in the same alphabetical sequence as subjects or in a separate "name" index. If the films and/or videorecordings are housed in a library and serve only that library's borrowers, the same subject heading list used for other materials in the collection should be used, and--ideally--subject and selected added entries should be filed in the central catalog. Where a film/video collection is a separate, independent entity, or where it serves several institutions, a list such as Public Library Subject Headings for 16mm Motion Pictures [9] may be used as a guide for developing a subject heading authority file.

Graphic Materials

This is a large and not entirely coherent category of materials, characterized mainly by pictorial content in a two-dimensional format. The glossary in AACR2 defines a graphic as:

> A two-dimensional representation whether opaque (e.g., art originals and reproductions, flash cards, photographs, technical drawings) or intended to be viewed, or projected without motion, by means of an optical device (e.g., filmstrips, stereographs, slides). (p. 566)

Microforms, maps, broadsheets, and microscope slides, although appearing to fit into the above definition, are not considered to be graphics. Transparencies and charts may not contain any pictorial matter. Some graphics are to be viewed as they are, others need to be projected by means of a machine providing a light source and magnification. Thus neither type of content nor method of viewing provide a single unique element unifying this category, in contrast to such categories as cartographic materials or sound recordings.

GUIDE TO ABBREVIATIONS

The following explains the symbols and abbreviations used in the title section.

Film Description ——————┐

Film Title

AN OLD BOX.

An old man rescues a box from a garbage pile and turns it into a music box. However, his modest amusement cannot compete with a noisy street fair. Cold and alone, he climbs into the box, where suddenly, in a psychedelic swirl, Christmas scenes materialize. In the end, the old man becomes a star which takes its place in the firmament. Such a bare description does not really do justice to the charm and delicacy of the graphic style, which make the film a moving parable for any season. A film by Paul Driessen. 1976.

FILM STUDY - ANIMATION; CHRISTMAS.

2840   ya   color 11 min.

p - primary
c - children
y - young adults
a - adults

Film Number

Subject Headings

Audience Level

Release Date

Color or Black and white

Running Time

26

THE DOONESBURY SPECIAL.
The comic strip "Doonesbury" is the basis for this animated film by John and Faith Hubley. Casual, ironic vignettes touching on feminism, anti-war activism, communes, and college sports recreate the lost world of the activist sixties. Funny and nostalgic, and very naturalistic, in the style of the Hubleys.
HUBLEY, JOHN & FAITH; FILM STUDY · ANIMATION; HUMOR & SATIRE; SOCIAL COMMENT.
4713   ya   color 26 min.

DOROTHY AND THE ABC'S.
An animated film for children about a bold and curious little girl and her clever and resourceful pet parrot. 1980.
CHILDRENS FILMS · ANIMATED.
0112   pc   color 9 min.

DOUBLE DRIBBLE.
Basketball never had it so bad as the tense moments before Merithew, a pint-sized Goofy, enters the game and saves the day. 1946.
DISNEY, WALT · ANIMATED; CHILDRENS FILMS · ANIMATED.
2029   cya   color 8 min.

DOUBLETALK.
A humorous situation in which a young man calls on a girl for their first date. We hear not only the spoken words, but the unspoken thoughts of all.1976.
HUMOR & SATIRE; ADOLESCENCE.
4534   ya   color 9 min.

DOUGHNUTS.
The adventures of Homer Price and his uncle's doughnut-making machine which refuses to stop making doughnuts. From the book by Robert McCloskey. 1963.
CHILDRENS FILMS · LIVE ACTION.
1217   s   color 26 min.

THE DOVE.
A right-on-the nose parody of the films of Ingmar Bergman, especially Wild Strawberries and The Seventh Seal. An old professor stops at his family's abandoned summer house. Sitting in the outhouse, he recalls his youth, his incestuous love for his sister, and her badminton game with death. Throughout, the pidgin Swedish spoken by the characters is dutifully translated in the subtitles, even when the cow says "Moo." 1968.
HUMOR & SATIRE; FILM STUDY · DRAMATIC.
2585   ya   b/w 15 min.

DR. JEKYLL AND MR. HYDE (1932).
When MGM purchased the rights to this story (for their 1941 film starring Spencer Tracy), the earlier version disappeared and was not seen anywhere for many years. Not only is it a highly entertaining horror film, but a remarkable technical achievement as well. Director Rouben Mamoulian's experiments with subjective camera and synthetic sound make the first transformation scene, in particular, quite frightening. Fredric March (who won the Academy Award for his performance), Miriam Hopkins, and Rose Hobart star. 1932.
FEATURE FILMS · HORROR; FILM STUDY · HISTORY; LITERATURE · FILM ADAPTATIONS.
2588   ya   b/w 90 min.

DR. JEKYLL AND MR. HYDE. (ABRIDGED).
Adaptation of Robert Louis Stevenson's story about the hapless doctor who succeeds in separating the good and evil natures of man. Considered by many to be the first great American horror film. With John Barrymore. Silent. 1920.
HORROR FILMS; LITERATURE · FILM ADAPTATIONS; FILM STUDY · HISTORY; HALLOWEEN FILMS; BARRYMORE, JOHN.
1220   ya   b/w 25 min.

DR. LEAKY AND DAWN OF MAN.
Certain that Africa is the cradle of civilization, the late archeologist Louis Leaky and his wife Mary spent over forty years in painstaking excavation at East Africa's Olduvai Gorge. Their persistence and conviction were rewarded in 1959 when they unearthed the remains of man's earliest known ancestor. 1967.
ANTHROPOLOGY; AFRICA; ARCHEOLOGY; EVOLUTION.
1221   ya   color 26 min.

DR. MARTIN LUTHER KING, JR.: AN AMAZING GRACE.
Introduced by Gil Noble, this film uses historic footage to chronicle the career of his extraordinary black leader. Probably the most moving of the films about Dr. King.
BIOGRAPHY (KING, MARTIN LUTHER); BLACK HISTORY & CULTURE; DISCRIMINATION & PREJUDICE; RACE RELATIONS.
0104   ya   color 62 min.

DR. SEUSS ON THE LOOSE.
Presents three short stories by the famous children's author, "Sneeches," "The Zax," and "Green Eggs and Ham." 1974.
DR. SEUSS; CHILDRENS FILMS · ANIMATED.
1222   pc   color 25 min.

DRACULA.
This first screen version of the classic horror tale was made in 1922. An acknowledged masterpiece, directed by F. W. Murnau, the film evokes a magnificent spirit of malevolence and impending doom, while the grim scenes of the vampire stalking his victims in the deepening shadows of night have never been equalled for sheer visual terror. From the History of the Motion Picture Series. 1962.
FILM STUDY · HISTORY; HORROR FILMS; HALLOWEEN FILMS; MURNAU, F. W.
2587   ya   b/w 26 min.

DRACULA HIGHLIGHTS.
This film spotlights the high points from "Dracula." Bela Lugosi's first appearance as the famous malefactor. 1931.
HORROR FILMS; HALLOWEEN FILMS.
8118   cya   b/w 17 min.

THE DRAGON OVER THE HILL.
Unusual animation using metal sculptures is the medium for telling a lighthearted story about two blacksmiths and their encounter with a firebreathing dragon. The film is excellent too, for encouraging young children to make up stories of their own. 1977.
CHILDRENS FILMS · ANIMATED; FILM STUDY · ANIMATION.
0106   pc   color 8 min.

DRAGON STEW.
Animated tale of a king who loves food, a royal cook who never cooks, and a small, fat dragon who is designated to be the main ingredient of a secret recipe. From the book by Tom McGowen. 1972.
CHILDRENS FILMS · ANIMATED.
1223   pc   color 14 min.

DRAGON'S TEARS.
Animated version of a Japanese story about a ferocious dragon and the magic that takes place when a little boy invites him to his birthday party. From the story by Hirosuke Hamada. Narrated by Robert Morse. 1962.
CHILDRENS FILMS · ANIMATED.
1224   pc   color 6 min.

DREAM OF THE WILD HORSES.
Slow motion photography, soft-focus background and an original musical score combine to produce a mood-evoking piece of art on the movement of horses running wild and free. Made in Southern France. 1960.
FILM STUDY · SPECIAL EFFECTS; HORSES.
1226   ya   color 9 min.

Sample page of title section.

Sample page of index.

The following GMDs and specific material designations (SMDs) are to be used:

GMD	SMD
art original	art original
chart	chart
	flip chart
	wall chart
filmstrip	filmslip
	filmstrip/filmstrip
	cartridge
flash card	flash card
picture	art print
	art reproduction
	photograph
	picture
	postcard
	poster
	study print
slide	slide
	stereograph/sterograph
	reel
technical drawing	technical drawing
transparency	transparency

AACR2 allows the option of substituting from another category or adding more precise terms to the above SMDs. For example, flannel board pieces might be used as an SMD, with [picture] or [chart] as the GMD.

Many of the materials which fall into the graphics category can be handled quite simply by keeping them in the vertical file, or picture file, if a separate file is kept. Even small sets of slides mounted in protective plastic envelopes and individual transparencies, protected by tissue, can go into the vertical file. Charts, study prints, art reproductions --if they are small enough or can be folded--can be handled in the same way. If the same subject heading list as for other materials in the collection is used, a set of guide cards can be filed in the central catalog to refer users to the vertical file or picture file. It is helpful to incorporate see and see also references directly into the file itself. For a separate picture collection, an alternative is to use Dane's The Picture Collection [10] as an authority list.

Large unframed and unmounted pictures and charts can

present special problems for storage and retrieval. When creasing is undesirable for vertical file storage, flat storage in horizontal map cases is probably the best solution.

Boxed sets of study prints, flash cards, transparencies, slides, etc., which most likely will be used as a unit, should be cataloged. Framed works of art require separate storage and are usually valuable enough to warrant cataloging. A public library which provides a circulating art collection will find that in addition to cards in the catalog, borrowers who wish to place reserves will appreciate a separate list of holdings, especially if it is illustrated with photographs of the works.

Prescribed sources of information. The item itself, including permanently affixed labels, is the chief source. If the container is an integral part of the item (the frame of a painting, for example), it is also considered a chief source. When the item consists of several parts separately labeled, but only the container has a collective title, the container is the chief source. If the information needed does not appear on the chief source, it can be taken from the container, accompanying textual material, and other sources, in that order. The prescribed sources for the various areas of description are:

AREA	SOURCE OF INFORMATION
Title and statement of responsibility	Chief source
Edition	Chief source, container, accompanying material
Publication, distribution, etc.	Chief source, container, accompanying material
Physical description	Any source
Series	Chief source, container, accompanying material
Note	Any source
Standard number, terms of availability	Any source

Main entry. Original works of art--paintings, drawings, photographs, etc.--are entered under the name of the

artist. Reproductions are also entered under the artist responsible for the original, unless the reproduction is actually
an adaptation of a work. For example, an engraving made
by an artist from a painting by another artist would be entered under the engraver, who has, in effect, created a new
work. However, a slide or other mechanical reproduction
would be entered under the name of the person who created
the original work, just as the facsimile of a book would be
entered under the author of the original book.

Filmstrips, study prints, and similar materials are
almost always the result of collaborative effort between script
writers, photographers, graphic artists, researchers, and so
on. Consequently, they are most often entered under title.

   Title and statement of responsibility. Record the title
from the chief source, as described above. In some cases
there will be no title information from any source. The cataloger must then supply a brief, but descriptive title in brackets:

> [Photograph of Ronald Reagan]
> [Driver education transparencies]

Record the statement of responsibility if there is a person
or corporate body prominently shown on the chief source of
information.

   Publication, distribution, etc. Art originals, unpub-
lished photographs, and similar works will not have a "publisher." However, the date of creation should be given.
For commercially produced graphic materials, the usual rules
apply.

   Physical description. The specific elements needed
to describe the various graphic materials will be discussed
below. As always, this area must answer the questions:
how much of what, what size, what color, what accompanying
material is there.

   Notes. For graphic materials, the note area is used
to clarify the artistic form when the physical description area
does not do this adequately; to give additional important title
information; to list credits; to cite donors and previous owners of original art; to clarify the history of an item and to
describe the original work, if the item being cataloged is a
reproduction; and to give physical details which are important

but not readily fitted into the proper area. Intended audience, summary, or contents, can be given when desirable.

```
            Gaydos, Tim.
              [Dormer] [art original]. -- 1974.
              1 art original : oil on canvas ; 71 x 46 cm.

              Title supplied by cataloger.
              Detail of house on Block Island.
              Presented to library's Local Artists' Collec-
            tion by J. Q. Citizen, December 1981.
              Size when framed:  75 x 50 cm.
```

Card 106.   Entry for original painting.

Art original.   Most small libraries are not so fortunate as to own original works of art, but those that do will want to have as complete a record for each work as possible. This is important not only because of the present or potential value of a work (monetary or historical), but because it is unique, and no other description of it may exist. Drawings, paintings, and architectural renderings are cataloged according to the general rules for graphics, but a few special situations should be noted.

Artists do not always give a title to their work, and thus all other information assumes greater importance in its identification. If the work is representational, the cataloger can supply a title which briefly describes the subject of the picture (see card 106). If it is abstract, the cataloger could enter it as untitled. In both cases, the supplied title should be in brackets.

The physical description area should indicate the materials used by the artist: the medium (acrylic, pastel, oil, etc.) and the base (canvas, paper, wood, etc.). Give the height x width of the work in centimeters, excluding the mounting and frame.

```
    Fractional parts [chart] : circles. -- Paoli,
    Penn. : Instructo, [196-]
      1 flannel board set (various pieces) : flannel ;
    col.

    Contains circles divided into parts for learn-
    ing fractions such as halves, thirds, quarters,
    fifths, sixths, eighths.



    1. Mathematics.
```

Card 107. Entry for flannel board set.

The note area should provide the following information:

- The nature or form of the work, if that is not obvious from the description.
- The source of the title, if it is not from the chief
  source.
- Name/s of person/s associated with the work, as
  in the case of an unsigned painting tentatively attributed to a particular artist.
- Donor or source; previous owners, if any, and the
  relevant dates.
- Framed size; other physical details of importance
  that are not in the physical description area.

Chart. A chart is an opaque sheet, either flat or
relief, which presents information via graphs, pictures, tables,
diagrams, or outlines. Flannel or magnetic board sets can
sometimes also be categorized as charts, when the contents for
for a particular display are stored as an entity (see card
107). The boards themselves are considered equipment, and
are not cataloged. Do not confuse charts which are carto-
graphic--aeronautical charts, for example--with those in the
graphic category. Another specific material designation besides chart, flip chart, wall, chart, flannel board set, and
magnetic board set, is relief chart.

A chart's physical dimensions--height x width--should

be given in centimeters. When a chart is printed on both sides, this is indicated as "double sides." For flip charts, the number of sheets is given.

Vision [chart]. -- New York : Better Vision
    Institute, c1956.
    1 flip chart : double sides, col. ; 102 x
152 cm.

    Summary: Contains information about sight,
visual disorders, lenses, etc.; includes examples of optical illusions.

    1. Eye. 2. Optical illustions. 3. Optics.

Card 108.   Entry for flip chart.

An Introduction to word processing [filmstrip] /
    Prentice-Hall Media, Inc. ; [produced by] Cal
    Industries Inc. ; writer, Gil Klevins. --
    Tarrytown, NY : Prentice-Hall Media, 1981.
    3 filmstrips (ca. 53 fr. each) : col. ; 35 mm.
+ 3 sound cassettes (ca. 41 min. : 1 7/8 ips,
mono.) + 3 reproducible masters + 1 instructor's
guide. -- (Word processing)
    Title from data sheet.
    Credits: Consultant, Eileen Tunison.
    Sound accompaniment compatible for manual and
automatic operation.
    Intended audience: Senior high school, junior
college, and vocational education students.
    1. Business education. I. Series: Word pro-
cessing (Prentice-Hall Media).

Card 109.   Filmstrip set; physical description includes ap-
            proximate number of frames and minutes.

Filmstrip.   A filmstrip is a strip of film with still

pictures and/or captions meant to be projected in sequence, frame by frame. The film is usually 35 mm. and--if cut apart and mounted--could be turned into slides. Interdependent scripts or sound recordings accompanying the filmstrip are considered to be part of the cataloging unit. If accompanying materials are designed to be used independently of the filmstrip, treat the unit as a kit (see p. 262). Many filmstrips are issued as sets which are clearly meant to be used as such (see card 109). However, when each part of a set is able to stand on its own, without reference to the other parts, you may choose to enter each filmstrip separately, unless the sound accompaniment for several filmstrips is on a single disc or cassette (see cards 110 and 111).

```
        Drug information [filmstrip] / Guidance Associ-
     ates. -- Mt. Kisco, N.Y. : Guidance Associ-
     ates, 1980.
        4 filmstrips (366 fr.) : col. ; 35 mm. + 4
     sound cassettes (52 min. : 1 7/8 ips, mono.) +
     4 teacher's guides.
        Title from data sheet.
        Rev. ed. of the filmstrips issued separately
     under title: Drug information series, 1970.
        Sound accompaniment compatible for manual and
     automatic operation.
        Intended audience: Junior high school students
     through college.
        Contents: Sedatives -- Narcotics -- Stimulants
     -- Psychedelics.
        1. Drug abuse.   I. Drug information series.
```

Card 110.   Filmstrip set cataloged as a unit.

For certain kinds of projectors, filmstrips may be mounted in cartridges. In that case, the SMD "filmstrip cartridge" is used. The only other format in this category is the filmslip, which is a very short filmstrip mounted in a rigid frame.

The filmstrip itself is the chief source of information, and its title, credit and end frames should be examined by the cataloger. However, if the container provides a collective title for a multipart item that you want to treat as a unit, use the title on the container.

```
    Narcotics [filmstrip] / Guidance Associates. --
      Mt. Kisco, N.Y. : Guidance Associates, 1980.
      1 filmstrip (ca. 90 fr.) : col. ; 35 mm. +
    1 sound cassette (ca. 13 min. : 1 7/8 ips,
    mono.) + 1 teacher's guide. -- (Drug informa-
    tion)

      Rev. ed. of filmstrip issued in 1970.
      Sound accompaniment compatible for manual and
    automatic operation.



      1. Drug abuse.  I. Series.
```

Card 111.   Separate entry for one filmstrip in a series.

Filmstrips are usually entered under title, as responsibility tends to be diffuse.   There is a sizable body of filmstrips made from children's picture books, where the illustrations are reproduced exactly as they appear in the book, and
the full text is recorded.   The question of main entry for
these filmstrips is affected by AACR2 rule 21.9, which states
that if the medium of expression has changed, an item ought
to be entered under the heading appropriate to the new work.
When a book is presented in the filmstrip/sound mode, the
principal creative responsibility is still that of the book's
writer and illustrator, but additional people are involved in
the production: photographer, reader, and producer, for
example.   One could, therefore, argue for main entry under
author, but the collaborative nature of filmstrip production
makes a stronger case for entering under title, with a name/
title added entry for the original book (see cards 112 and
113).

The degree of detail provided in the physical description area depends on the local situation.   In an integrated
media center where students and teachers are apt to go directly to the shelves to select materials, and where equipment is limited to a few standard models, a minimal description such as that shown in card 113 may suffice.

In card 113, it is assumed that the filmstrip is the

standard 35 mm. gauge and that the cassette is also standard.
The number of filmstrips, the color, and the accompanying
material should always be given.

```
The Happy owls / by Celestino Piatti.   The three
   robbers / by Tomi Ungerer. -- Weston, Conn. :
   Weston Woods, [196-]
   1 filmstrip (44 fr.) : col. ; 35 mm. + booklet.

   Filmstrip adaptation and photography by Vir-
   ginia Shippey; producer, Morton Schindel.


   I. Piatti, Celestino. The happy owls. II. Un-
   gerer, Tomi. The three robbers.  III. Title:
   The three robbers.
```

Card 112.   Entry for two items on one filmstrip.

```
Henry Huggins by Beverly Cleary [filmstrip] /
   Random House/Miller-Brody Productions. --
   Westminster, MD : Random House School Division,
   1980.
   1 filmstrip : col. + 1 sound cassette + 1
guide.



   1. Dogs--Fiction.  I. Cleary, Beverly. Henry
Huggins.
```

Card 113.   Minimal description of filmstrip.

While The Concise AACR2 does not call for the number

of frames for filmstrips, this is easy to determine and very
helpful to the user who wants an idea of the scope and depth
of the content. Some filmstrips have numbered frames, and
accompanying manuals frequently give frame totals. Where
neither of these sources of information exist, Olson suggests
the following:

> A piece of white tape can be fastened to the edge
> of a work table, marked off in frame lengths, and
> covered with clear plastic or clear tape. A film-
> strip can then be stretched out against this (like
> measuring yard goods) and the frame count read
> directly. [11]

```
    The Story of Illinois [filmstrip] / International
        Film Bureau Inc. -- Chicago, IL : The Bureau,
        1971.
        6 filmstrips (373 fr.) : col. ; 35 mm. + 3
    sound cassettes (87 min. : 1 7/8 ips, mono.)
        Title from data sheet.
        Sound accompaniment compatible for manual and
    automatic operation.
        Intended audience: Intermediate grades through
    senior high school.
        Contents: pt. 1. The beginnings of Illinois
    (64 fr., 14 min.) -- pt. 2. Illinois under the
    French flag (60 fr., 11 min.) -- pt. 3. Illinois
    becomes a state (66 fr., 14 min.) -- pt. 4. The
    Illinois of Lincoln (82 fr., 18 min.)
        1. Illinois--History. I. International Film
    Bureau.
```

Card 114. Contents note incorporates length.

When a library has a variety of filmstrip sets--some
in cartridges, some with 7-inch discs, others with cassettes,
still others with 12-inch discs with automatic advance signals
--it is useful to have enough information in the catalog record
to indicate what equipment is needed. Also, many borrowers
will want to know how much time is required to use a given
item, and therefore duration of sound accompaniment for filmstrips should be provided whenever it is readily available.
Citing the number of frames and minutes of sound accompaniment for a set can be simplified by giving the range where it
is not too varied (e.g., 52-56 fr., ca. 50 fr. each, 12-14
min.), or by including the information in the contents note.

If a filmstrip is captioned, that can be indicated in a note.
(See cards 114-116.)

Tales of a fourth grade nothing [filmstrip] /
    Pied Piper Productions. -- Verdugo City, CA :
    Pied Piper, 1980.
    1 filmstrip (86 fr.) : col. ; 35 mm. + 2 cas-
settes (24 min. : 1 7/8 ips) + 1 teacher's guide
+ 1 author biography sheet. -- (First choice
authors and books ; unit 15)
    Title from data sheet.
    Based on: Tales of a fourth grade nothing / by
Judy Blume.
    Filmstrip recording (13 min.), interview re-
cording (11 min.).

    1. Brothers and sisters--Fiction. 2. Family
life--Fiction. 3. Humorous stories. I. Blume,
Judy. II. Blume, Judy. Tales of a fourth grade
nothing.

Card 115. Note clarifies contents of cassettes.

Valentine songs that tickle your funny bone
    [filmstrip] / Michael Brent Publications ;
    Ruth Roberts, Bill Katz. -- Port Chester,
    NY : Michael Brent Publications, 1980.
    4 filmstrips (55 fr. each) : col. ; 35 mm. +
2 sound cassettes (32 min. : 1 7/8 ips) + 1
script + 1 teacher's guide + 1 songbook. --
(Songs that tickle your funny bone)
    Title from data sheet.
    With captions.
    Sound accompaniment for automatic operation
only.
    Intended audience: Primary and intermediate
grades and junior high school students.
    1. Valentine's Day--Songs and music. 2. Holi-
days. 3. Songs. I. Series.

Card 116. Entry for captioned filmstrip set.

    Flash card. A flash card is printed with numbers,
letters, words, or graphics, and is intended for brief display

(manual or mechanical) for drill purposes. The cards come in sets and may be coordinated with sound, in which case they may require a special audiocard player. A flash card set will usually have a title main entry, unless responsibility is very clearly attributed to one person. The physical description should give the number of cards, color, size in centimeters, and accompanying material (see card 117).

Classification and opposites [flash card] :
    pictures for pegboard. -- Oak Lawn, Ill. :
    Ideal School Supply, c1964.
    231 cards : b&w & col. ; 10 x 9 cm. + 2 guide
cards.

    Words and pictures printed on cards for use on
pegboard or as flash cards.

    1. Reading.   2 Vocabulary.

Card 117.   Entry for flash card set.

Szutter, Martin F. W. J.
    Amerikan granduer [art original] / M. Szutter.
  -- [197-]
    1 art print : screenprint, col. ; 63 x 50 cm.

    11th of 50 prints, signed by artist in pencil.
Size when framed: 85 x 72 cm.

    1. Title.

Card 118.   Entry for signed screenprint; GMD [art original] used instead of [picture].

```
        Antonello da Messina.
          Madonna and child [picture]. -- Washington,
        D.C. : National Gallery of Art, [19-]
          1 art reproduction : photolith, col. ;
        36 x 28 cm.




          1. Art, Renaissance.   2. Mary, Virgin.
        I. Title.
```

Card 119.   Entry for art reproduction.

```
        Eyewitness to space [picture] / NASA. -- Wash-
          ington, D.C. : U. S. Government Printing
          Office, 1969.
          12 art reproductions : col. ; 51 x 46 cm. --
        (NASA picture set no. 3)

          Reproductions of paintings inspired by the
        activities connected with the moon launch.




          1. Apollo project.   2. Moon--Exploration.
        I. Series.
```

Card 120.   Card for set of art reproductions.

        Picture.   A picture is defined by the AACR2 glossary
as:

        A two-dimensional visual representation visible to
        the naked eye and generally on an opaque backing.

> Used when a more specific term (e.g. art original,
> photograph, study print) is not appropriate. (p. 569)

Thus, the GMD [picture] is used to encompass any sort of
graphic that is not an art original, chart, filmstrip, flash
card, slide, technical drawing, or transparency. The most
common SMDs are: art print, art reproduction, photograph,
postcard, poster, and study print. The term "picture" is
also used as SMD when none of the others is appropriate, or
when cataloging a mix of reproductions of drawings, photographs, etc.

```
Wildsmith, Brian.
  [Brian Wildsmith posters] [picture]. -- New
York : Franklin Watts, c1970.
  4 posters : col. ; 92 x 61 cm.

  Title supplied by cataloger.
  Each poster is an enlargement of an illustra-
tion from a Wildsmith picture book.
  Contents: The snow queen -- Aladdin --
Hansel and Gretel -- Sleeping Beauty.


  1. Children's literature.  2. Picture books
for children.
```

Card 121.   Set of posters treated as a unit.

There is some confusion about art prints and art originals. A print is produced directly from a plate made by
the artist, usually in a limited quantity, numbered, and signed
by the artist. Lithographs, serigraphs or silkscreens, wood-
cuts, and etchings are some of the types of prints. The
plate, block, or screen prepared by the artist is indubitably
an art original, but whether the images (prints) drawn from
that should be given the GMD [art original] or [picture] is a
matter of interpretation. Maxwell uses [picture], [12] while
Fleischer prefers [art original].[13] Art reproductions are
mechanically produced copies of art works, usually by a
photographic process, and therefore the GMD [picture] is
clearly appropriate. In deciding whether to treat an item
as an original work of art, or as a reproduction, look for

the following: an artist's signature and a number; signs of commercial production or distribution; and information about technique. For example, in discussing serigraphy, the Murrays state that an artist using the silk-screen method can achieve "variations ... in the prints which can remove serigraphy from the more mechanical process of printing such as those employed in lithography."[14] Consequently, it seems correct to treat the print described in card 118 as an art original.

Photo-story discovery set no. 1 [picture]. -- Rochester, N.Y. : Eastman Kodak, 1969, c1967. 29 photos. : b&w ; 9 x 9 cm. + teacher's guide.

Summary: Several sequences of pictures tell stories about common experiences in children's lives; intended to stimulate visual literacy and oral expression.

1. Pictures. 2. Stories without words.

Card 122. Card for set of photographs.

When a picture is commercially distributed, it may or may not be an "original." In case of doubt, use the GMD [picture] and the SMD art print or art reproduction.

Posters are sometimes difficult to define as posters, as they may have the characteristics of art reproductions or other kinds of graphic material. It is helpful to keep in mind the function of posters, which is to send a message, to announce or to advertise something. Thus while a poster announcing a gallery exhibit may also be an art reproduction showing one of the artist's works, it is primarily a poster. A blowup of a photograph of a rock star is a promotional item, and should be described as a poster rather than a photograph.

Photographs of the usual sort present no special

problems. Should a library discover examples of early photography in its collection, it should seek expert advice on care
and preservation. Photographs and postcards are usually incorporated into a vertical file, unless they are acquired as
sets which will be more useful if cataloged as units (see
card 122).

```
        Black abc's [picture] / author, June Sark Hein-
          rich ; consultant, Bernadette H. Triplett.
          -- Chicago : Society for Visual Education,
          c1970.
          26 study prints : col. ; 46 x 33 cm.

        Captioned photographs designed to help teach
        letters of the alphabet and the speech sounds
        they represent, and to develop appreciation and
        respect for "being black."  Teaching suggestions
        on back of each print.


          1. Reading.  2. Alphabet.  3. Blacks--Pictorial
        works.  I. Heinrich, June Sark.
```

Card 123.   Entry for study print set; main entry under title,
             as responsibility extends to photographer and
             others.

```
        The Story of milk [picture] / by Judy. --
          Minneapolis, Minn. : The Judy Co., c1968.
          1 story board (12 inserts) : composition
        board, col. ; 33 x 35 cm. -- (See-Quees 12, no.
        7)

          Summary: Inserts showing various activities re-
        lated to milk production may be manipulated to
        aid sequential narration.


          1. Milk.  2. Stories without words.
```

Card 124.   Entry for a special-purpose visual aid.

Study prints combine pictorial and textual matter for instructional purposes and usually identify themselves as such. Again, sets significant to the collection may be cataloged as units, while single items can go in the vertical file.

Burnout on the job [slide] / IBIS Media ; producer and writer, Carol Ann Mangano. -- Pleasantville, NY : IBIS Media, 1982.
307 slides : col. + 4 sound cassettes (77 min. : 1 7/8 ips) + 1 program guide.
Title from data sheet.
Sound accompaniment compatible for manual and automatic operation.
Intended audience: Senior high school through college and adult.
Contents: pt. 1. Understanding the symptoms -- pt. 2. Burnout cycle -- pt. 3. Learning to refuel -- pt. 4. Prevention and the work environment.

1. Stress. I. Mangano, Carol Ann.

Card 125. Entry for slides with sound accompaniment.

Crowther, Richard L.
Holistic energy architecture [slide] / Richard L. Crowther. -- Glendale, CA : KaiDib Films International, 1980.
130 slides : col. + 1 instructor's guide.
Title from data sheet.
Intended audience: College and professional audiences.
Summary: Details the conception, design, and construction of the author's latest residence and laboratory in Denver, Colo. Explains the concept of holistic energy as the interplay between thermal, magnetic, ionic, radiative, gravitational, and metabolic energies.
1. Architecture, Domestic. 2. Energy conservation. I. Title.

Card 126. Entry for slide set.

The physical description of pictures includes the number

of items; the process or method of production for prints and art reproductions; transparency or negative, when applicable to photographs; color; size, excluding mount or frame, given as height x width in centimeters. The note area should give information about the mounting, if this is of significance.

```
        Transportation fires [transparency]. -- Bowie,
            Md. : Robert J. Brady Co., 1970.
            43 transparencies (80 overlays) : col. ;
            31 x 26 cm. + instructor's guide. -- (Fire
        fighting practices ; unit 12)

            Title from data sheet.
            Contents: Automobile fires -- Gasoline tank
        truck fires -- Aircrash fire fighting and
        rescue.



            1. Fire fighting.  I. Series.
```

Card 127.   Entry for transparency set.

Slide.   The AACR2 glossary defines a slide as "transparent material on which there is a two-dimensional image, usually held in a mount, and designed for use in a projector or viewer." Most commonly, a slide is a single frame of 35 mm. film in a 2" x 2" mount. However, any transparent material can be used to create a slide. Lantern slides, for example, which were popular in the nineteenth and early twentieth centuries, are made of glass. Other special kinds of slides are stereographs, paired slides designed to be used with special viewers that create a three-dimensional effect, and sound slides, which allow brief commentary to be recorded on the slide mount, and also require special equipment.

Slides present few problems as long as they are stored, cataloged and circulated in boxed sets, arranged in trays or magazines ready for projection, or in plastic sleeves. When they are handled as a unit, each requires only one set of catalog cards and can be readily shelved with other media. However, this approach will not serve the user who wishes to

retrieve individual slides dispersed among several sets. Since cataloging every slide is expensive, most small libraries will either have to circulate sets only, or forego full cataloging but use a visual display system which allows users to scan the holdings within broad subject areas without actually handling the slides or needing a catalog entry for every single one. The slide sets would be classified using the same system as that chosen for other materials, with the individual slides in the set identified by their number within the set. Thus, if one wanted a slide of the Step Pyramid, one would look at the section of the display which houses ancient architecture and scan the slides until the appropriate one was found. When the slide is circulated, it is identified as part of the set, e.g. 722A3.

Slide sets that have accompanying sound are cataloged much in the same way as filmstrips with sound recordings (see card 125).

The physical description area does not need to include slide size if it is the standard 2" x 2" or 5 x 5 centimeters. For modern stereographs, the number of reels and frames are given.

In the note area, the type of slide tray in which sets are mounted might be named, as a convenience to the user. If a projector of a special or unusual kind is needed, this should be stated in a note. When the contents of a set of slides is not clear from the title, and there are too many slides to list individually, give a brief description of the nature of the set in a note.

Technical drawing. It is the rare small library that will need to catalog this kind of material. However, technical drawings might be important in vocational schools, and would certainly be of major concern in libraries of engineering and architectural firms. The best guidance in cataloging technical drawings is found in Weihs' Nonbook Materials.[15]

Transparency. A transparency is an image on transparent material, usually a sheet of clear acetate, designed to be projected by an overhead projector, or viewed over a light box. It may be mounted in a cardboard frame, with overlays hinged to one side of the frame. Single transparencies or small sets may be incorporated into the vertical file, while larger boxed sets may be cataloged and stored as a unit.

In the physical description, give the number of overlays,

if there are any. When you give size, exclude the frame or mount.

Three-Dimensional Objects

Under this heading, AACR2 groups such things as models and dioramas, sculpture and crafts, specimens and realia. It really is a catch-all category, covering all the miscellanea not appropriate in any of the other groupings. Not even the characteristic of three-dimensionality is exhibited by all materials included. For example, jigsaw puzzles, some types of games, and certain paper crafts are two, rather than three-dimensional.

The following GMDs are allowed by AACR2, and the SMDs are those most likely to be useful in small libraries:

GMD	SMD
diorama	diorama
game	game
	jigsaw puzzle
microscope slide	microscope slide
model	mock-up
	model
realia	exhibit
	puppet
	toy

AACR2 prescribes only diorama, exhibit, game, microscope slide, mock-up, and model as SMDs, but adds: "If none of these terms is appropriate, give the specific name of the item or the names of the parts of the item as concisely as possible." (10.5B1)

As in the case of other materials, the library that owns only a few objects of a particular type will probably have the items on prominent display and will not need to catalog them. However, unique items and those of great value should be formally described, and those apt to be missed by a user searching the catalog under a specific topic should be given an entry.

Prescribed sources of information. Except for the physical description and note areas, information must be taken from the chief source. The chief source, however, is

broadly defined as "the object itself together with any accompanying textual material and container issued by the 'publisher' or manufacturer of the item." (10.0B1) In case of
discrepancy, the object itself is preferable. Permanently
attached labels are considered to be part of the object.

```
        Sinaiko, Arlie.
          The generation [art original] / Arlie Sinaiko.
        -- [196-]
          1 sculpture : bronze ; 91 x 49 x 7 cm.

          Donated by artist through Bodley Gallery in
        New York, 1968.
          Two abstract forms, one 91 cm. high, the other
        48 cm. high, on attached base, 5 x 60 x 28 cm.



          I. Title.
```

Card 128.   Entry for original sculpture.

```
        Farm life [diorama] / created by the third
          grade, Lincoln School. -- [1982]
          1 diorama (30 pieces) : cardboard, col. ; in
        box, 35 x 48 x 6 cm.

          Figures of animals, people, and farm implements;
        farmyard and stable background.



          1. Farms.
```

Card 129.   Entry for locally produced diorama.

Main entry. Just as the painter is the main entry
for an original oil, so a sculptor is the main entry for a
sculpture. Similarly, the creator of the original sculpture
would be the main entry for the reproduction. Original,
signed works of potters, weavers, silversmiths, etc., should
also be entered under the name of the creator. Some games,
such as simulations, may have a clearly established "author"
responsible for the intellectual content, and should be entered
under that person's name.

```
Brett, Peter A.
   Tuf [game] : the superlative mathematics game /
Peter A. Brett. -- Rowayton, Conn. : Peter A.
Brett, c1967.
   1 game (7 dice, 3 timers, rule book) ; in box,
22 x 21 x 4 cm.

   Intended audience: Grade 7 to adult.
   Summary: Series of games from simple to complex
develop ability to reason.



1. Mathematics. 2 Reasoning. I. Title.
```

Card 130. Entry for game.

Title and statement of responsibility. Realia will
often require a title to be supplied by the cataloger. The
supplied title should be as accurate and succinct as possible,
and must be enclosed in brackets. A statement of responsibility is not necessary, unless the information appears clearly
in the chief source.

The choice of GMD may be problematic in some cases.
For example, a handmade ceramic may be an object intended
for everyday use, or it may be a work of art of greater
aesthetic than utilitarian value. In the first instance, the
GMD would probably be realia; in the second, art original
would appear to be more appropriate, although AACR2 does
not list it as a GMD for objects. If the item is signed, if
the cataloger has evidence that the creator is a professional

artist, and if the item has been acquired for its aesthetic value, the cataloger may want to assign [art original] as the GMD. In doubtful cases, [realia] is the better choice.

```
Another world [game] / M. C. Escher. -- New
   York : Galling Gallery, c1977.
   1 jigsaw puzzle (500 pieces) : cardboard, col.
; in box 36 x 36 x 4 cm. -- (M. C. Escher jig-
saw puzzle collection)

Published in arrangement with G. W. Breughel
Publishers, Holland.
Completed puzzle size: 51 x 41 cm.




1. Escher, M. C.   I. Series.
```

Card 131.   Entry for jigsaw puzzle.

```
Milkmaid [realia]. -- India : [19-]
   1 doll : cloth and papier-mâché, col. ;
25 cm. high.









1. India--Social life and customs.   2. Dolls.
```

Card 132.   Entry for costume doll.

The appropriate GMD for toys and puppets may also

be a matter of debate. For example, in Nancy Olson's Cataloging of Audiovisual Materials, a bean bag and a hand puppet are assigned the GMD [game].[16] On the other hand,
Fleischer and Goodman in their Cataloging Audiovisual Materials use [realia] for a set of hand puppets.[17] Given the
way that AACR2 defines game, as a set of materials designed
for play according to prescribed rules (p. 566), puppets and
toys do not usually fit in that category. Moreover, the
AACR2 definition of realia as "actual objects (artifacts, specimens) as opposed to replicas" is broad enough to accommodate most puppets and toys.

```
        The Seeing eye [model]. -- Oak Lawn, Ill. :
        Educational Products, [ca. 1970]
        1 mock-up (13 pieces) : plastic, unpainted ;
        11 cm. high, in box, 25 x 19 x 6 cm. + instruc-
        tion sheet. -- (How we live)

        Twice actual size, with bony orbit of skull.
        Eyeball comes apart for study of detailed in-
        terior sections and moves in socket.



        1. Eye.  I. Series.
```

Card 133.   Card for mock-up.

        Publication, distribution, etc.   Many kinds of three-
dimensional materials that find their way into library collections are not obtained from a publisher or distributor.   Naturally occurring objects such as insects, plants, rocks,
fossils, etc., contributed to the library by a collector are
not "produced" or "distributed," and therefore do not require
the usual place, date, etc., of publication.   However, commercially distributed materials of this kind are treated in the
usual way.

        For artifacts such as costumes, furniture, implements,
etc., the cataloger should give the place and date of manufacture, if that can be determined or approximated in the publication area.

Physical description. As usual, the number of pieces and their nature, type of material, color, size, and accompanying material are given. The hardest decisions may be the selection of the best term to use for the specific material designation and the amount of detail to include in the description. Some definitions of typical SMDs will be given below. In regard to the amount of detail to provide, it may be simpler to give all that is readily evident than to spend time deciding what is essential and what is optional.

Vonnoh, Bessie Potter, 1872-1955.
   The dancing girl [model] / by Bessie Potter
Vonnoh. -- New York : Alva Museum Replicas,
[ca. 1980]
   1 statue : Alvastone ; 37 x 29 cm.

   Actual size reproduction of bronze original
made between 1900 and 1916; in the Art Institute
of Chicago.

   I. Title.

Card 134.   Entry for reproduction of a sculpture.

Art original. As suggested by the discussion above, the question of whether an item is art or realia entails judgment based on the cataloger's knowledge of who created the object and for what purpose. Critical opinion about what is art can pose problems. If a sculptor, potter, or other creator of three-dimensional objects professes to be a professional artist, then the cataloger should treat the object as an art original.

Diorama. The AACR2 glossary defines diorama as a "three-dimensional representation of a scene created by placing objects, figures, etc., in front of a two-dimensional painted background." (p. 565) When easily ascertainable, give the number of pieces in the diorama and the material of which it is made.

Echinoderm morphology collection [realia]. --
Northbrook, Ill. : Hubbard Scientific Co.,
[196-?]
7 specimens : dried ; in box, 40 x 30 cm. +
environment chart.

Contents: Common starfish -- Aztec starfish --
Purple sea urchin -- Giant urchin -- Sand
dollar --Brittle star -- Urchin mouthparts
(Aristotle's lantern).

1. Marine animals.

Card 135.   Entry for commercially distributed set of realia.

[Crabs] [realia].
4 crabs : dried ; in box, 24 x 18 x 4 cm.

Title supplied by cataloger.
Crabs collected on Long Beach Island, N.J.
Contents: Horseshoe crab -- Sand crab --
Fiddler crab -- Ghost crab.

1. Marine animals.

Card 136.   Entry for noncommercial realia.

Game.   The definition, "a set of materials designed
for play according to prescribed rules," may be stretched
somewhat to include items such as jigsaw puzzles or playing
cards.   While these do not necessarily have written instructions, the fact that they are intended for play in specified
ways is obvious.   The physical description will often be

insufficient to indicate the purpose of a particular game, and therefore a note explaining its use may be necessary.

```
    Balance scale [realia] / Ohaus Scale Corp. --
      Oak Lawn, Ill. : Ideal School Supply, [196?]
      1 scale, 2 pans, 8 weights (1 gram to 50
    grams) ; in box, 15 x 36 x 16 cm. + instruction
    sheet.




      1. Weights and measures.  2. Measuring instru-
    ments.
```

Card 137. Card for realia.

```
    The Cat in the hat [realia] / by Dr. Seuss. --
      New York : Eden Toys, c1980.
      1 toy : polyester fiber, col. ; 58 cm. high.




    I. Seuss, Dr.
```

Card 138. Entry for a stuffed toy representing a picture-book character.

Microscope slide. Usually, the material sandwiched

between two pieces of glass is a section of living matter which must be viewed under a microscope. Since these slides are most often used in the biology lab, libraries may not always catalog them. AACR2 rules can be easily applied, but Weihs suggests that the note area should include "type of stain and the particular aspect of the slide the stain highlights," and the "method of preparation, e.g., sectioning, orientation, material in which the specimen is imbedded, spread, smear," etc. [18]

Drosophila salivary gland chromosomes [microscope slide]. -- Burlington, N.C. : Carolina Biological Supply, [197?]
1 slide : stained ; 3 x 8 cm.

Smear.
Aceto-orcein stain shows giant polytene chromosomes with clearly visible banding.

1. Drosophila. 2. Chromosomes.

Card 139. Entry for microscope slide. [19]

Model. Defined as a "three-dimensional representation of a real thing, either of the exact size of the original or to scale," (AACR2, 568) a model may also be a representation of a concept, such as a set design or a theoretical chemical compound, or a replica of an art object. A model with moving parts meant to be manipulated, usually for training purposes, is a mock-up. For art reproductions, follow the same pattern as for graphics. It is usually helpful to give the scale in a note.

Realia. This is a large category which includes all real objects--manufactured, handmade, or occurring in nature. Anything three-dimensional that is not a replica, a model, a microscope slide, a game, or an original work of art will be given the GMD [realia]. Examples used in AACR2

range from paperweights to quilts. It might be helpful to define one common SMD that is not in the AACR2 glossary: exhibit. Maxwell uses the definition "a collection of objects and materials arranged in a setting to convey a unified idea."

Hand puppet family [realia]. -- Princeton, N.J.
: Creative Playthings, c1969.
5 hand puppets : rubber, col. ; each 20 cm.
long, in box, 28 x 23 x 14 cm.

Puppets represent mother, father, 2 children, and baby.

1. Puppets and puppet plays. 2. Family.

Card 140. Set of puppets treated as realia.

[North American Indian artifacts] [exhibit] /
assembled by Jane Smith.
1 exhibit (various pieces) : col. ; in box,
30 x 110 x 60 cm.

Donated by collector in 1979.
Includes arrowheads, beads, feather head-
dress, rattle, beaded bag; displayed against picture in bottom of display case showing scenes
of daily life. Top of case made of plexiglass.

1. Indians of North America.

Card 141. Entry for exhibit.

A collection is called an exhibit when no part predominates

over any other part, and the components are of the same
type. For exhibits composed of different kinds of materials,
Maxwell would use the GMD [kit]. [20] One could also make
a distinction between exhibits and kits on the basis of intended
use. An exhibit is generally meant to be viewed as a unit,
whereas a kit is usually designed to be used in parts in conjunction with various learning activities (compare cards 141
and 152). When cataloging objects not packaged for commercial distribution, place, name and date of "publication" are
omitted. For naturally occurring objects, no date is given.
However, the place, name, and date of manufacture is given
for artifacts, when that information can be determined.

Microforms

A microform is a miniature reproduction of graphic material
(print, pictorial, cartographic, etc.) which requires magnify-
ing equipment appropriate to each format to render it legible
to the eye. The medium may be transparent or opaque.
Among the transparent formats are microfilm, microfiche,
and aperture cards. Microfilm is a strip of 35 mm. or
16 mm. film mounted on a reel or in a cartridge. Microfiche is a sheet of film, usually 3" x 5" or 4" x 6", containing reproductions reduced in ratios up to 90 times. Ultra-
microfiche is a film sheet containing reductions 90 times or
greater. Aperture cards are computer cards (9 x 19 cm)
which contain keypunched data and one or more openings that
frame sections of microfilm. Opaque microforms include
microcards and microprints, which are cards or sheets containing printed reproductions of photographically reduced material.

AACR2 treats microforms in a manner similar to
facsimiles. The description is of the microform, and information about the characteristics of the original book, periodical, etc., is relegated to a note. The Library of Congress,
however, has adopted a policy requiring that the bibliographic
description of a reproduction in microform emphasize the original, and that publication data pertaining to the microform
be given in a note. LC justifies this decision on the basis
that different libraries may hold the same work in varying
microform or xerographic formats, and that identification of
the work itself--rather than a particular manifestation of it
--should be given precedence. This is a logical argument
from the point of view of the user, who seeks a specific title,
and does not care whether it is in macro- or microform

reproduction, as long as he or she can get access to it. The brief summary of rules presented here reflects AACR2, but cards 142 and 143 illustrate the different interpretations.

```
Shirley, James.
   The gentleman of Venice [microform] : a tragi-
comedie presented at the private house in Salis-
bury Court by her Majesties servants / written
by James Shirley. -- New York : Readex Micro-
print, 1953.
   1 microopaque ; 23 x 15 cm. -- (Three cen-
turies of drama.  English, 1642-1700)

   Reproduction of original: London : H. Moseley,
1655. 78 p. ; 18 cm.


   1. English drama.  I. Title.  II. Series.
```

Card 142. Entry for microform, using AACR2 rules (adapted from Hinton example [21]).

```
Shirley, James.
   The gentleman of Venice [microform] : a
tragi-comedie presented at the private house in
Salisbury Court by Her Majesties servants /
written by James Shirley. -- London : H. Moseley,
1655.
   78 p. ; 18 cm.

   Microopaque. New York : Readex Microprint,
1953. 1 card ; 23 x 15 cm. (Three centuries of
drama. English, 1642-1700)


   1. English drama.  I. Title.  II. Series.
```

Card 143. Entry for microform described in Card 142, LC rule interpretation.

Most small libraries will own little in the way of microforms, with the exception of newspapers and periodicals. If the library uses a simple holdings list for these, issues available in microform should be noted as part of the record. Small special libraries may need to acquire a variety of microform material to which access has to be provided through the catalog.

Prescribed sources of information. The title frame/s of a microform, or the title card in a set of cards, is the chief source of information. If the eye-readable heading at the top of a fiche or opaque or that on the container is more detailed than the title frame, use the source with the fullest information. If information is not available from the chief source, take it from the rest of the item, the container, accompanying eye-readable material, or any other source, in that order of preference. The chief source must be used for the title and statement of responsibility. For the physical description and note areas, any source may be used.

Main entry. The choice of main entry is generally not affected by the microformat and is almost always the same as for the original.

Title and statement of responsibility. This area is treated according to the general rules, except for the options regarding choice of chief source of information. As in the case of other formats, items lacking a collective title may be treated as a unit or separately, with linking notes.

Special data for cartographic materials and serials. If the work is a reproduction of a serial or map, the data about the original item should be given in this area.

Publication, distribution, etc. According to the AACR2 rules, the information given here must pertain to the microform, not the original. According to LC policy, just the opposite should be done.

Physical description. Give the number of units of microfilm, microfiche, microopaque, or aperture cards. Add cartridge, cassette, or reel, as appropriate. If the number of frames of a microfiche can be readily determined, give these in parentheses:

1 microfiche (120 fr.)

```
American libraries [microform] / American
   Library Association. -- Vol. 1, no. 1 (Jan.
   1970)-
   Ann Arbor, Mich. : University Microfilms,
   1971-
        microfilm reels : ill. ; 4 in., 16 mm. --
(Current periodical series)

   Issued every month except bimonthly July-
August.
   Continues: ALA bulletin.
   Includes index.
   Publication no.: 5731-S.
   ISSN 0002-9769.

   1. Library science - Periodicals. I. American
Library Association. II. Title: ALA bulletin.
```

Card 144.   Open entry for periodical on microfilm. [22]

If you are describing separately titled parts of a microform as individual units, relate the part to the whole in the extent of item:

> on reel 1 of 3 microfilm reels
> 2 of 6 microfiches

The fact that the microform is the typical positive, black-and-white reproduction is not recorded, but negative or color reproduction is shown, and illustrations are indicated:

> 1 microfilm reel : negative, ill.
> 1 microfiche : all col. ill.

For aperture cards, microfiche, and microopaques, give height x width in centimeters. For microfilm, give the diameter of the reel if it is other than three inches, and give the film gauge.

Notes. Following the usual notes pertaining to the item, give the reduction ratio, if it is outside the 16x - 30x range, as follows:

> Low reduction--less than 16x
> High reduction--31x - 60x
> Very high reduction--61x - 90x

Ultra high reduction--over 90x (specify ratio)
Reduction ratio varies.

For ultra high reduction, add the specific ratio. Also, when
the equipment to be used depends on the reduction ratio, give
the exact figure. If necessary, indicate the type of reader.
For reproductions of a previously published item, the original
is described briefly (see card 142).

Machine-Readable Data Files

With the advent of the affordable microcomputer, even small
libraries are beginning to acquire collections of floppy diskettes
and cassettes containing programs for data manipulation, instruction, and games. As these collections grow, the need
to catalog them becomes apparent. AACR2 provides a chapter of rules for describing all kinds of machine-readable data
files (MRDFs), including programs and their documentation.
The definition used by AACR2 is "a body of information coded
by methods that require the use of a machine (typically but
not always a computer) for processing." Physically, the
data file may be on magnetic tape, floppy disks, punched
cards, or a variety of other media.

Contrary to the general AACR2 principle that calls
for the physical object in hand to be described, the rules
for machine-readable data files substitute a "file description
area" for the "physical description area." This means that
information needed to determine the "play-back" mode--how
to run or read the data file--is relegated to the note area.
The reason for this departure from the overall AACR2 approach is the ready transmutability of MRDFs from one format to another [23]. This may make sense in the large library or research organization setting where appropriate
equipment is available, but is not very helpful in a situation
where the user has available only a number of microcomputers, each requiring a unique software format. Following
the brief summary of AACR2 rules below, alternative ways
of dealing with this problem will be presented.

Prescribed sources of information. The chief source
of information is the "internal user label," defined as "machine-readable identifier containing alphabetic and/or numeric
characters providing information about the file." [AACR2,
p. 203] If there is no internal label, the information may be
taken from the documentation provided by the creator of the

file, other published descriptions, or other sources (including the container), in that order. The chief source is to be used for all areas except the file description--which takes the place of the physical description--and the note area. For these, any source may be used.

Main entry. A data file may be entered under a personal or corporate author, or under title, applying the same rules as for other formats. If entry is under a name, the name should be that of the person or body responsible for the content of the file, as opposed to the person or body responsible for the formatting.

File description area. Three SMDs are prescribed by AACR2: data file, program file, and object program. Weihs defines these, in order, as the file containing the information, the file containing the instructions to the machine, and the computer language program [24]. The number and type of file are listed, followed by the number of logical records in the data file, or the number of statements and the language for a program. For an object program, the name of the machine for which it is intended follows in pa rentheses. In many cases, printed material (often called documentation) will accompany the MRDF. This is treated in the same way as a teacher's guide for a multimedia or other multipart item through the use of a plus sign and a concise statement about the nature of the accompanying material. Some examples of AACR2 file descriptions follow:

> 1 data file (3,000 logical records) +
> 1 codebook (25 p.)

> 1 object program (IBM 360/40)

> 1 program file (300 statements, COBOL) +
> associated documentation

Note area. The usual clarification about title and other areas are given in the notes. In addition, the program version and/or level, and the kind of equipment needed to use the file are given in the notes. The latter information is expressed in terms of the number and name of the physical medium, quantitative properties, trade name, dimensions, etc. Where these details still do not suffice to specify the equipment needed, a "mode of use" note is added.

Public attitudes toward and exposure to erotic
materials [machine-readable data file] /
Institute for Survey Research, Temple University, for the U. S. Commission on Obscenity
and Pornography. -- Philadelphia : The Institute, 1970.
1 data file (2486 logical records) + 1 codebook (67 p.).

Title taken from codebook.
Summary: Personal interviews were conducted
with a national sample of 2486 adults on their
experience with and views on pornography.

(continued on next card)

Public attitudes toward and exposure to erotic
materials [machine-readable data file].
(Card 2)

1. Erotica.   2. Censorship--United States.
I. Temple University. Institute for Survey Research.   II. United States Commission on Obscenity and Pornography.   I. Title.

Card 145.   Entry for data file [25].

Card 147 shows a microcomputer program using AACR2
rules. An alternative way of dealing with the description of microcomputer MRDFs has been proposed by David Bullers and
Linda Waddle [27].   They combine elements of the usual
AACR2 physical description area with some of those contained
in the "file description area" for MRDFs to produce the kind
of record illustrated in card 148.   In place of the three SMDs
prescribed by AACR2 for MRDFs, Bullers and Waddle substitute "floppy diskette," which is the physical format.   The
software is further defined by the programming language,

```
Jung, Paul.
    Checkers [machine-readable data file] / by
Paul Jung. -- Bloomington, Minn. : Control
Data Corporation, 1976.
    1 program file (TUTOR).

    Mode of use: PLATO system.




    1. Games.  I. Title.
```

Card 146. Entry for program file [26].

```
Button, Jim.
    PC-file [machine-readable data file] : a
database manager program for the Osborne com-
puter. -- Version 8.5. -- Bellevue, WA : J.
Button, 1983.
    1 program file + 1 manual (17 p.)

    Size of file unknown.
    1 floppy diskette : single sided, double densi-
ty ; 5 1/4 in.
    Mode of use: For Osborne 1, CP/M 2.2, 68K
    Summary: For maintenance of mailing lists,
inventory, personnel files, etc.; production of
mailing labels; use with Mailmerge.

    1. Office management--Data processing.
I. Title.
```

Card 147. Entry for microcomputer program file; physical
          format and machine model described in note.

the brand of machine, the operating system, and size of
memory. This approach has the advantage of compressing
into one statement all the information the potential user needs

in order to determine which machine can be used to run the program or read the data file.

Despite the irregularity of the Bullers-Waddle descriptive model, it comes close to a format that can be recommended for small libraries that own microcomputer software, but no other kinds of MRDFs. What microcomputer users need to know is the exact type of machine on which the software will run and what it will do. They really do not care about the number of records or statements, but may need to know the language in which the program was created, as some machines are wired for only one type of language.

```
651.8    Haffer, Gary E.
Haf          IFO-data base manager program(machine
         readable data file). -- Software Technology
         for Computers, c1979.
             1 floppy diskette : Integer Basic(Apple II),
         DOS 3.2, 48K + guide.

             Organizes data into various formats for
         display as reports, lists, labels, etc.

             1. Office management--Data processing.
         2. Utility program.   I. Title.
```

Card 148.   Microcomputer MRDF cataloged by Buller and
            Waddle. [28]

Another variation on the file/physical description area is illustrated in card 149. Follett may well be the only company that offers catalog card sets with the microcomputer software that it sells, and therefore the cataloging standard it uses may become quite influential. Note that Follett treats the machine specifications much the same way as Bullers and Waddle, but that the SMD "microcomputer programs" is substituted for "floppy diskette." The problem with the Follett card is that we do not know whether we have one diskette containing six programs, or six diskettes containing one program each.

```
371.2   Jerman, Max E.
J           Reading level analysis (machine-
        readable data file) / by Max E. Jerman
        and John F. Kropf. -- Seattle :
        Bertamax, 1982, c1981
            6 microcomputer programs (Apple II,
        DOS 3.2, 48K) + user manual
        (A Micro school program)
            Contains reading formulas for deter-
        mining Dale-Chall, Flesch, Fog, Smog,
        Spache and Wheeler/Smith readability
        levels.
            Applesoft BASIC language.

            1. Reading    I. Kropf, John  F.
        II. Title

        341147 95002  08047C
                                        FOLLETT LIBRARY BOOK COMPANY
```

Card 149.   Follett card for microcomputer software.

```
        Visitrend ıvisiplot [machine-readable data
    file] / program by Mitchell Kapor.    Sunnyvale,
    Calif. (1330 Bordeaux Drive, Sunnyvale, 94086) :
    Personal Software, c 1981.
        1 microcomputer program (Apple II, 48K, DOS
    3.3) ı 1 user's guide (loose-leaf).

        This program is a combined time series analysis
    and graph plotting system.
        Title from user's guide.
        Additional contributors to program: Eric Rosenfeld
    and Debra Spencer.
        System requirements: video monitor (color preferred);
    one or more disk drives; Applesoft ROM.
        Summary: Program calculates and generates tables
    of statistical measures; performs trendline forecasting
    and linear multiple regressions; and develops ancillary
    data series used in analysis and forecasting techniques.
    The VisiPlot portion of the program generates various
    charts including line, bar, pie, area, hi-lo, scatter,
    and combinations of same.
```

Card 150.   Microcomputer MRDF cataloged by Sue Dodd. [30]

If the six programs described in card 149 are contained on one diskette, the following description might resolve
the problem by combining elements of file description with
physical description:

6 program files (Applesoft BASIC) (Apple II, DOS 3.2, 48K) : 1 diskette (single-sided, double-density ; 5 1/4 in.) + user manual. -- (A Micro school program)

In Cataloging Machine-Readable Data Files, Sue Dodd suggests that microcomputer programs are so machine-specific that they resemble object programs, and therefore should be treated as such. Her solution is to give the make and model of the micro, memory size, and operating system in the description area, as in the Follett card, but to relegate other "run environment" or system requirements to a note, as in the following example:

Additional system requirements: 2 disk drives (double density); micro music DAC board; speaker or earphones; video monitor or television with RF modulator. [29]

A complete cataloging record from Dodd's book is shown in card 150. In all essentials, the Follett card follows her suggestions.

In addition to the question of how to indicate the physical medium (e.g., type and number of diskettes), another question remains. What about cataloging microcomputer data files? While there are probably none now in commercial distribution, locally created files may well be accumulated in a given library. For example, glossaries of specialized terms used in connection with a course, statistics related to a particular local study, information and referral files, or subject bibliographies could be maintained on microcomputer diskettes to which library users might want access. The SMD [microcomputer data file] would probably be the most appropriate, and would parallel Dodd's SMD [microcomputer program]. A hypothetical example of a data file to be run on a microcomputer is shown in card 151. Note that information about the machine model and programming language are omitted in this case, because the data file is to be used only in the library on the single machine available to the public. If the library had several different Apples, the machine on which the data file runs would have to be specified, either in the note area or in the file description area.

Regional plans for cooperative cataloging of MRDFs ought to be considered before decisions are made about how to adapt AACR2 rules for microcomputer software. Major

decisions would be whether to use [microcomputer program] or [microcomputer data file] for the SMD, or to stay with [program file] and [data file]; how to treat the number of diskettes and their characteristics; and to what extent to describe the machine in the file/physical description area versus the note area.

Community information directory [machine-read-
    able data file] / compiled by the Reference
    Staff, Yourtown Public Library. -- May ed. --
    1983.
    1 microcomputer data file (1234 logical records)
    : 2 diskettes + user instruction sheet.

    One diskette contains entries by subject;
other diskette is directory of agencies.
    Mode of use: For Library's public access
Apple microcomputer.

Card 151.   Hypothetical entry for a locally created micro-
           computer MRDF.

Kits

A kit is "an item containing two or more categories of material, no one of which is identifiable as the predominant constituent of the item," according to the AACR2 glossary. [p. 567] Most typically, a kit is a packaged collection of several types of media which are designed to be used together but are not interdependent; that is, each item can be used alone, as opposed to a sound filmstrip set where the pictures would have no meaning without the accompanying recording. In some cases, a kit may be deemed to be of greater potential usefulness when broken down into its components, which are then cataloged separately.

   Prescribed sources of information.   The rules which apply to the various components should be followed.   When a collective title appears only on the container, use it as the chief source for title information.

Main entry. Most kits will be entered under title.
When there is an "author" who is clearly responsible for the
creation of the kit as a whole, enter under author.

Physical description. The degree of detail provided
will usually be determined by how many different types of
materials are contained in the kit. If there are only a few,
the physical description may be given for each, using separate
lines (see card 153). If there are a considerable number,
give the extent of the various materials, ending with "in container," if there is one, and its dimensions. When there is
a very large number of different items, one can simply use
the phrase "various pieces."

```
    Perception of color [kit] : observing (a) /
    American Association for the Advancement of
    Science. -- Lexington, Mass. : Ginn, c1974.
       3 cubes, 6 balloons, 142 paper squares, 30
    paper rectangles, 10 paper plates, instruction
    booklet, in box, 43 x 27 x 16 cm. -- (Science:
    a process approach II, module 1)



       1. Color.  I. American Association for the
    Advancement of Science.  II. Series.
```

Card 152. Entry for kit.

Access Points

The rules for access points for nonbook materials are, of
course, the same as those for print materials. Frequently,
however, greater judgment must be exercized in assigning
subject headings and added entries when cataloging nonprint.
In the case of subject headings, there is the question of
whether to incorporate the format in the heading. In the case
case of added entries for personal and corporate names associated with an item, there is the question of which ones
will be useful as access points and which ones will not.

```
Unemployment is a social problem [kit] / pre-
    pared by the United States Department of Labor,
    Manpower Administration, Unemployment Insur-
    ance Service, in cooperation with the National
    Council for the Social Studies. -- Washington,
    D.C. : U.S. Government Printing Office, 1973.
    1 simulation game (various pieces).
    1 game (4 game boards, 8 pads of forms, 6 in-
struction sheets).
    1 filmstrip (62 fr.) : col. ; 35 mm. + script.
    5 transparencies ; col.
    35 student manuals.
    35 charts.
                        (Continued on next card)
```

```
Unemployment is a social problem [kit]. (Card 2)

    1 teacher's guide.
    Intended audience: High school.
    Summary: Clarifies nature of unemployment and
operation of U.S. unemployment insurance pro-
gram.




    1. Unemployed.  2. Insurance, Unemployment.
I. United States. Department of Labor. II. Na-
tional Council for the Social Studies.
```

Card 153.   Components of kit described on separate lines.

Library of Congress cataloging of nonprint materials
frequently provides added entries that are of doubtful usefulness in the small library. For example, filmstrips and other
media that have statements of responsibility which include the
name of the production company (often also the distributor)
receive tracings for the company. It is not very likely that
these names would be searched by users.

Subject headings such as SHORT FILMS or ALCOHOL-
ISM--JUVENILE FILMS or CHILDREN'S FILMS are common

on LC cards, but do little to improve access. Added entries
for the various people involved in the production of an audiovisual item are only rarely useful. Similarly, tracing the
names of all the performers listed in the credits or cast is
of dubious value. The cataloger must know the users of the
collection and what is important to them. For the most part,
subject access should get the top priority.

Sound recordings of music present a somewhat different order of priority. Typically, the user will be interested
in locating music by composer or performer within very
broad categories, such as rock, country-western, opera, or
jazz. A library should consider carefully the interests of
its users before deciding on policy for added entries for performers. Do patrons ask for recordings featuring the Chicago
Symphony or the Boston Pops? Do they wish to compare a
Zubin Mehta interpretation of a Beethoven symphony with one
by Eugene Ormandy? Are they interested in anything and
everything recorded by Yo Yo Ma or Bette Midler? Do they
ask for motion picture sound track recordings, ballet music,
children's songs? The kinds and numbers of access points
provided in the catalog should reflect the interests of the library's users, insofar as time and budget constraints permit. For example, one might limit the number of conductors, orchestras, and soloists for whom added entries are
made to those best known to the average listener. In a
school or academic library, music instructors might be in-
vited to advise on types of headings they and their students
would find helpful. In public libraries, public services librarians should be consulted. In a network or consortium,
a sound recording and/or music interest group could be
formed in order to identify user needs and suggest minimal
standards for access points.

Classification

On the subject of classification, no standardized solution is
likely to be acceptable to all kinds of libraries. There is,
however, a general acceptance of the principle of integrated
collections for multi-media learning centers. Thus a media
center which uses unabridged Dewey and Cutter numbers
for books would use these for audiovisual materials also.
Whether or not all kinds of materials are actually interfiled on
the shelves will depend on the space, type of shelving, and
degree of circulation control available in a given situation.
Even where books, filmstrips, records, slides, etc., are

scattered in different places, there are advantages to classifying them all in a uniform manner. A new library with
adequate space for intershelving may someday replace the
old overcrowded one, and meanwhile the mnemonic factor
of class numbers is not to be discounted. It saves time in
helping the student who needs material on Africa to be able
to go directly to the 916's and 960's in the filmstrip cabinet,
record bin and film rack as well as in the book stacks.
Wherever a computer is available, multimedia subject lists
can be more easily produced when all materials have been
classified.

For libraries not swayed by the preceding arguments,
the decisions on how to organize, whether and how to classify
will depend on the type of access given to the user. Is the
material to be in locked storage and available only through
a staff member, or is it accessible to the patron on a self-
service basis? Where there is no intention of letting the
public browse through a collection, a simple alphabetical (by
main entry) or accession order arrangement can be used, as
long as a good subject index is at hand. Whenever materials
are put out in the open for public browsing, some sort of arrangement by categories will evolve as a result of user preferences, unless the collection is to remain so small that the
patron will not object to searching through every item.

The categories will depend on the medium. For example, records might be grouped as they are in many stores:
opera, folk, spoken, jazz, etc. Slides, however, might be
arranged by artist, country, historical period, etc. These
broad user interest groupings would eventually have to be
broken down more discretely as the collection grew in order
to speed retrieval of specific items.

There is no single, simple solution that will be satisfactory for all types of libraries, nor is it overwhelmingly
important to settle on only one all-purpose arrangement as
long as enough points of access are provided for the user.
If it is necessary to have separate print and nonprint collections with different service points, catalog records should be
duplicated so that they may be filed at the service point as
well as in the central catalog.

Some specific organization/classification problems are
discussed in the sections on individual media in this chapter.
For more background on various approaches to handling different types of media and for sources of cataloging informa-

tion, see the references at the end of this chapter and Appendix C. Shelf lists for nonprint media are discussed in chapter 10. The Booklist, Media Review Digest, The Elementary School Library Collection, and Core Media Collection for Secondary Schools will be found helpful as cataloging aids, since they suggest DDC numbers and subject headings for audiovisual materials.

References

1. Margaret F. Maxwell, Handbook for AACR2: Explaining and Illustrating "Anglo-American Cataloguing Rules, Second Edition" (Chicago: American Library Association, 1980), pp. 121-140.
2. Ibid., p. 121.
3. Jean Weihs et al., Nonbook Materials: The Organization of Integrated Collections (Ottawa, ON: Canadian Library Association, 1979), p. 48.
4. Michael Gorman, The Concise AACR2: Being a Rewritten and Simplified Version of "Anglo-American Cataloguing Rules, Second Edition" (Chicago: American Library Association, 1981), p. 66.
5. Music, Books on Music, and Sound Recordings (Washington, D.C.: Library of Congress, 1953- . Semiannual with annual cumulations; title varies).
6. Schwann-1 Record and Tape Guide (Boston: ABC Schwann Publications, monthly). Schwann-2, which lists mono, simulated stereo, international, non-current pop, religious, spoken and miscellaneous, etc., is published semiannually.
7. Freda P. Berkowitz, Popular Titles and Subtitles of Musical Compositions. 2d ed. (Metuchen, N.J.: Scarecrow Press, 1975).
8. Eugene Fleischer and Helen Goodman, Cataloguing Audiovisual Materials: A Manual Based on the Anglo-American Cataloguing Rules II (New York: Neal-Schuman Publishers, 1980), p. 45.
9. California Library Association, Audio-Visual Chapter, Subject Headings Committee, Public Library Subject Headings for 16mm Motion Pictures. rev. ed. (Sacramento, Calif.: California Library Association, 1974).
10. William Dane, The Picture Collection: Subject Headings. 6th ed. (Hamden, Conn.: Shoe String Press, 1968).
11. Nancy B. Olson, Cataloging of Audiovisual Materials: A Manual Based on AACR2 (Mankato, Minn.: Minnesota Scholarly Press, 1981), p. 45.

12. Maxwell, Handbook for AACR2, p. 188.
13. Fleischer, Cataloguing Audiovisual Materials, pp. 194-197.
14. Peter and Linda Murray, A Dictionary of Art and Artists (Baltimore, Md.: Penguin, 1968), p. 382.
15. Weihs, Nonbook Materials, pp. 91-92, 125-126.
16. Olson, Cataloging of Audiovisual Materials, pp. 68-71.
17. Fleischer, Cataloguing Audiovisual Materials, pp. 336-339.
18. Weihs, Nonbook Materials, p. 60.
19. Ibid., p. 61.
20. Maxwell, Handbook for AACR2, pp. 202-203.
21. Frances Hinton, "AACR2 in the Library of Congress: Examples of Change," paper presented at the American Library Association, Reference and Adult Services Division program, New York, 1 July 1980.
22. Weihs, Nonbook Materials, p. 58.
23. Sue Dodd, Cataloging Machine-Readable Data Files: An Interpretive Manual (Chicago: American Library Association, 1982), p. 46.
24. Weihs, Nonbook Materials, p. 45.
25. Conference on Cataloging and Information Services for Machine-Readable Data Files, March 29-31, 1978, Warrenton, Va. Report (Arlington, Va.: MRDF Conference Secretariat, DUALabs, [1978?], p. 116.
26. Ibid.
27. David L. Bullers and Linda L. Waddle, Processing Computer Software for the School Media Collection (Waterloo, Iowa: D. L. Bullers, 1981)
28. Ibid., p. 5.
29. Dodd, Cataloging Machine-Readable Data Files, p. 123.
30. Ibid., p. 126.

Chapter 10

CONTROL: AUTHORITY FILES, REFERENCES, SHELF LIST

Authority work is the process of deciding the particular form of
a personal or corporate name, title, or subject heading to be
used in the catalog and the recording of that decision. When
these records are arranged in alphabetical order, an authority file is the result. A library's carefully annotated Sears
List of Subject Headings can become its subject authority file.
For names and uniform titles, the small library may use the
public catalog, as long as care is taken to make all the references and corrections that are needed. Larger libraries
usually need to maintain separate files, and special libraries
may also find it convenient to create authority files. Examples of subject authority cards are found at the end of
chapter 7, pages 143-145.

For the small public or school library, it is really
not very practical to maintain name authority files because
of the time and range of reference aids needed to do the job
properly. The example of a name authority record given in
Downing's book illustrates the point.[1] Ten cards are needed
to record all the sources checked for the various forms of
Agatha Christie's name, and to establish the correct dates
of birth and death. Ultimately, the form of the name is determined by a count of citations in the National Union Catalog,
as AACR2 specifies that it should be the one that appears
most frequently in the person's works. The last part of the
authority work illustrated in Downing is reproduced below:

Christie, Agatha, 1890-1976.

nd Encyclopedia Brittanica (Macropedia), II, 1978
    ed., Christie, Dame Agatha (Mary Clarissa)
    (b. Sept. 15, 1890. Torquay, Devon--d. Jan.
    12, 1976, Wallingford, Oxfordshire).

d The Times Sept. 17, 1890, under "Births";

"On the 15th of September, at Ashfield,
Torquay, the wife of Frederick Alvar
Miller, of a daughter.

Substantiation of name on title page:
  BIP: Agatha Christie, 128
        Westmacott, 9
  NUC Statement of Responsibility or
    Authority File:
      Pre '56 Imprints: Agatha Christie, 87
                      Westmacott, 6
      NUC (most recent ed.): Christie, 46
                          Westmacott, 6

  x Westmacott, Mary
  x Mallowan, Agatha Christie
  x Mallowan, Mrs. Max Edgar Lucien
  (AACR II Rules: 22.1A, 22.2A, 22.4A;
    22.5A; 22.12B; 22.18)

In authority work, "n" means that a form of the name was
found in the source cited; "d" that birth and/or death dates
were found. The "x," as always, means "refer from" other
forms of the name not used.

    The Christie example in its entirety, as shown in the
Downing book, illustrates the fact that the predominant form
of name may not be known until the bulk of an author's work
has been published. What does one do with names when they
first appear, and when a name authority file seems desirable,
as is sometimes the case in small special libraries where
original cataloging must be done?

    When the cataloger encounters a name for which no
record exists in the library's authority file, the name must
usually be accepted as it is found in the work at hand. The
person is identified through his or her relationship to the
work, and thus the authority record would include the title.
If the name were to appear again in a somewhat different form,
the variant form should be recorded in the authority record,
and a cross reference made, if necessary.

    The items and form for the records in an authority
file may be described as follows: 1) The heading on the
name authority card is the one adopted for the catalog. 2)
The title is that of the first book by that author cataloged for
that library and serves to identify him. 3) The date is the

copyright date (if no copyright date, the imprint or some
other date) of that book, as found on the back of the title
page, preceded by the word "copyright" and given on the card
as [c1952].   4) The abbreviations are for the bibliographical
and biographical aids in which the librarian looked.   5) An
n to the left of the abbreviation for the name of an aid means
that the author's name was found in that aid; a t means that
the title was found.   6) If the author's dates of birth and
death are included in the heading, a d may be added to indicate that the date or dates were found.   7) If the form of the
name in the aid differs from that given in the heading on this
card, or if the date differs, the variant form is put in parentheses after the abbreviation for the aid.   8) If references
are made from other forms of the name, they are indicated
on the line or lines directly above the hole in the card, preceded by an x, the symbol for a see reference.

If the name is not that of the author of the work, but
is a subsidiary author or the subject, it is given above the
author's name, indented to the right.   To the left of the author's name is given an abbreviation which stands for the relationship of the name in the heading to the work (see card
155).

```
        Rosa, Joseph G., 1932–
          The West of Wild Bill Hickok.
        [c1982]

     nd Contemp. Authors, v. 13
     nt BPR 1982 Cum.
```

Card 154.   Name authority card for person as author.

The name authority file may have a record for every
name used as a heading in the catalog (whether as main,

```
            Hickok, Wild Bill, 1837-1876
subj. Rosa, Joseph G.
        The West of Wild Bill Hickok.
      [c1982]

  nd  Encyc. Brit. 15th ed. (Hickok, James Butler)
        also known as "Wild Bill"
        b. 1837, d. 1876
  nd  Amer. encyc. 1982 ed.
  nd  Academic Am. encyc. 1980
  nd  BPR 1982 cum.

                          x Hickok, James Butler
```

Card 155.   Name authority card for person as added entry.

subject, or added entry) or the file may be limited to only
those names requiring cross references.   If the library is
very small and the catalog is near the desk, the catalog itself may serve as the authority file.   In such a case, references made from other forms of a name than that adopted
must be maintained in a separate record, or entered on the
first main card where the name appears.   When that card is
withdrawn, the tracing of the references must be transferred
to another card, and so on.

The value of an authority file for names depends on:
1) whether or not printed cards are used; 2) whether or not
the names to be entered are so complicated that any one of
a number of different forms might be used; 3) whether there
are one or more references from other forms to be recorded;
4) the distance from the desk of the cataloger to the catalog.

The small library that depends on commercial or cooperative cataloging and does not maintain an authority file
must still, however, keep up to date with changes in forms
of headings and make the necessary cross references on a
day-to-day basis.   Current cataloging supplied by commercial
and cooperative services usually reflects LC interpretation
of AACR2 rules, and should be accepted.   However, cross
reference cards signalling a change in the form of entry are
not supplied automatically.   When a new book by Jean Plaidy
arrives with its cards, there is now no clue on the cards to

indicate that the author is the same person as Victoria Holt,
Philippa Carr, and the four other pseudonyms used by Eleanor
Hibbert. If the library has in its catalog a card for Plaidy
which refers the user to the old authorized entry of Hibbert,
the change should be spotted at the time the cards for the
new book are filed. At that point, the old cross references
should be pulled, and new ones made:

Hibbert, Eleanor

see

Burford, Eleanor
Carr, Phillipa
Ford, Elbur
Holt, Virginia
Kellow, Kathleen
Plaidy, Jean
Tate, Ellalice

If, however, the library does not have any books by Hibbert
writing under the name of Burford or Ford, etc., those
names would be omitted from the reference card. The next
step would be (1) to make references linking the old and new
entries, (2) to correct the old entries, or (3) to interfile the
old and new entries, preceded by a guide card:

Plaidy, Jean (including works previously
entered under Hibbert, Eleanor)

The cataloger would also have to catch changes in names for
which there is no previous reference in the catalog. For example, when Rhodesia became Zimbabwe, the first time an
entry had to be made under the new name, it is likely that
only knowledge of world events would have alerted the cataloger
to a need to establish a newly authorized heading and to make
the appropriate corrections/linkages in the catalog.

If one is likely to look under place or parent body for a
name that is entered directly, references are also required:

United States. Bureau of Indian Affairs.
Missouri River Basin Investigations
Project

see

Missouri River Basin Investigations Project

American Library Association. Association
for Library Service to Children

see

Association for Library Service to Children

Similarily, references from variant titles of works for
which a uniform title has been established should be made:

Dickens, Charles
The personal history of David Copperfield

see

Dickens, Charles
David Copperfield

In general, references need to be made 1) from forms of
personal, corporate, and place names not used in the catalog
to those currently authorized as the correct form; 2) from
varying titles of a work to the uniform title; 3) from subject
headings not used to those that are used. In addition, see
also references from subject headings that are used to others
that are in effect and are closely related can be made for the
public catalog. If a decision is made not to make subject
cross references, the list of subject headings used by the
library must be prominently displayed at the catalog so that
users may consult it. Some examples of references follow:

Beyle, Marie Henri
see
Stendhal

Dodgson, Charles Lutwidge
see
Carroll, Lewis

Shaw, George Bernard
see
Shaw, Bernard

Chaikovskii, Petr Il'ich
see
Tchaikovsky, Peter Ilich

Quakers
see
Society of Friends

Buonarroti, Michel Angelo
see
Michelangelo Buonarotti

Little (Arthur D.) inc.
see
Arthur D. Little, Inc.

London.   National Gallery
see
National Gallery (Great Britain) [LC form]
or
National Gallery (United Kingdom) [AACR2 form]

Chicago.   University
see
University of Chicago

United States.   Office of Education.   Bureau
of Adult and Vocational Education
see
United States.   Bureau of Adult and
Vocational Education

Roland
see
Chanson de Roland

Sir Gawain and the Green Knight
see
Gawain and the Green Knight

The poem of the Cid
see
El Cid Campeador

ADDING MACHINES
see
CALCULATING MACHINES

CALCULATING MACHINES
see also
COMPUTERS
OFFICE EQUIPMENT AND SUPPLIES

The Shelf List

The shelf list is a record of all the cataloged materials in a
library, arranged in the order in which they are shelved.
The shelf list is used--

> To take the inventory to see if any materials are miss-
> ing.
> To show how many copies of a given title the library
> owns.
> To show what kinds of books or other materials are
> in a given class as an aid in classifying.
> To show the librarian who is making out orders how
> much material the library already has in any given
> class.
> To serve in a limited way as a classed catalog.   A
> classed catalog has its entries arranged by classi-
> fication numbers rather than alphabetically as in a
> dictionary catalog, and there is an alphabetical sub-
> ject index.   This classed arrangement brings to-
> gether all the entries on a given subject.
> To give source, date and cost, if no accession record
> is kept.
> To serve as a basis for a bibliography or materials
> list on a specific subject.
> To serve as a record for insurance.

The shelf list card is a unit card; i. e. , it is a duplicate of the main entry card.   When printed card sets are
purchased, one intended as a shelf list card is always included.
If the cards are typed locally, however, notes and contents
may be omitted, leaving more space for the shelf list information.   If an accession book is used, the accession number
is added to this card (see chapter 13 for more on accessioning).   Similarly, bar codes are added in libraries using automated circulation systems.   The price is useful in public libraries in order to know what to charge a borrower who loses
or damages library material.   It may be the actual cost or
the list price; this is also of value in estimating the collection for insurance purposes.   Many libraries also give the
source and date of acquisition on the shelf list entry, but this
practice may be questioned, as the library would use its current dealer when reordering.   An unusual source might be
worth noting, and the date may be wanted if it is not intrinsic
to the accession number (e. g. 82-0001, which indicates the
first acquisition in the year 1982), or if the library does not
use accession numbers.

If no accession book is kept, but an accession number is used, this number is added to the shelf list card, as shown in cards 156 and 157, followed by the name of the source, the date received, and cost. Some libraries consider the accession book unnecessary duplication of other records, but like the convenience of having a unique number which stands for each book, audiorecording, etc., in the library.

```
398
              Grimm, Jakob
                The juniper tree and other tales from Grimm.
              Selected by Lore Segal and Maurice Sendak; tr.
              by Lore Segal; with four tales tr. by Randall
              Jarrell.  Ill. by Maurice Sendak.  Farrar,
              Straus, 1973.
                2 v.   332 p.

73-0733 v. 1   B&T.   5-15-73    $6.50
73-0734 v. 2    "                $6.50
73-0921 v. 1   Doe, Mrs. J.   9-5-73   gift
73-0922 v. 2    "                      gift


              1. Fairy tales   2. Folklore--Germany.
              I. Title
```

Card 156.   Shelf list entry for two-volume work of which the library has two copies, with acquisition data.

If an accession number is used, it begins on the second space from the left edge of the card on the second line below the last line of the description. If there are two or more copies or volumes of a work, the accession numbers are listed on the shelf list cards in numerical order. For multi-volume works, the volume numbers are written opposite their respective accession numbers. Thus all copies and volumes of one work go on the same shelf list card, and there are as many shelf list cards as there are titles in the library, i.e., different works in the library. If accession numbers are not used, copy numbers are listed instead.

If it is felt that a record of the source, date, and cost of an item is needed, the form to be used is shown in cards 156 and 157. Abbreviations which will be clear to the librarian may be used, e.g., B&T for Baker and Taylor. If

a book is a gift, the name of the donor may be given. The number of the month, day, and last two figures of the year are given, separated by hyphens (the year may be omitted if it forms a part of the accession number). The date follows the source, with one space between; then the cost, or if it is a gift, the word gift. Note that one ditto mark is sufficient for both source and date, but that the cost, or the word gift is repeated for each volume or copy.

```
AA
822.3
              His infinite variety; a Shakespeare sampler.
            [Audiorecording]  Narrated by Margaret
            Webster.  Miller-Brody, 1973.
            4 cassettes:  Approx. 30 min. each.

AC73-0011  v. 1  ESEAll 3-12-73  $6.50
AC73-0012  v. 2      "          $6.50
AC73-0013  v. 3      "          $6.50
AC73-0014  v. 4      "          $6.50

              1. Shakespeare, William  2. English drama-
            History and criticism  I. Webster, Margaret
```

Card 157. Shelf list entry for four-volume recording, with source of purchase funds indicated.

Where a record must be kept of disbursement of special funds, such as federal or dedicated trust funds, the name of the fund should precede the cost entry on the shelf list card. An inventory card facilitates accounting for special fund expenditures if an accession book is not kept.

Given the rapid advances in automation and the increasing participation of even quite small libraries in cooperative automated systems, it is advisable to add the LC card number to the shelf list, if the number is readily available, in order to speed eventual conversion to a machine-readable record. The ISBN number ought to be part of the description, in any case.

Shelf list cards for nonfiction are arranged exactly as the books are arranged on the shelves, first numerically by

classification number and then alphabetically by author, except individual biography, which is arranged alphabetically by the subject of the biography. Since the figures in all book numbers are regarded as decimals, B219 would precede B31, e. g. :

973	973	973
B21	B219	B31

for Bancroft's History of the United States of America and Bassett's A Short History of the United States, respectively. If book numbers are not used, the name of the subject of a biography may be added to the top line of the card just as it is on the subject card, as an aid in filing the cards by the subject of the biography.

Shelf list cards for separate collections, such as adult, young adult, juvenile, reference, audiovisual, etc. , are usually filed separately, although a school library which intershelves different materials may also interfile the shelf list cards for all types of media. A location symbol such as J for children's room or R for reference is put at the head of the call number on all cards. Some libraries have one shelf list card for all editions of works of fiction in which case the various editions are shown on the shelf list card following the copy or accession number and acquisition data by adding the name of the publisher, edition, and information about the illustrations. The advantages of separate shelf lists are that they can provide a quick overview, of the juvenile or filmstrip collection, for example, or can serve as an additional finding aid. When taking an inventory of a particular part of a collection, it is much easier to work with a shelf list which contains the cards for that collection only. A disadvantage is that duplicate shelf cards must be made for titles which are in different collections. For example, if the library has a third set of The Juniper Tree (card 156) for reference, another shelf card would be required for filing in the reference collection shelf list. For the public card catalog, however, one set of cards suffices, with each card marked $\frac{R}{398}$ but containing a note: "circulating copy also. "

Where audiovisual materials are not intershelved nor uniformly classified, the shelf lists for the different media must perforce be separate. If material is arranged and identified by accession number, the shelf list cards are also filed by accession number, so that when filmstrip number 203 is missing, one can go to the shelf list to find its title. If the

filmstrips were arranged alphabetically by title, the shelf
list would also be in alphabetical order.

Shelf list cards for serials are the same as for other
materials, except that the year or volume number appears
next to the appropriate accession number or copy number, as
in cards 158 and 159.

```
    R
   310
   W92        The World Almanac.  New York, World-Telegram.

  1102   1950
  3106   1956
  3612   1958
  4523   1959
  5502   1960
  6512   1964
  7000   1966
```

Card 158.   Shelf-list entry for a serial.

```
    R
   310
   W92        The World Almanac.  New York, World-Telegram.

  Pub.  2-9-50    $1.00   1950
    "    2-15-56   $1.25   1956
    "    2-8-58    $1.25   1958
    "    3-1-59    $1.25   1959
    "    2-16-60   $1.25   1960
    "    2-13-64   $1.50   1964
    "    2-8-66    $1.65   1966
```

Card 159.   Shelf-list entry for a serial (alternative method).

For periodicals which are not cataloged, the file of check-in forms for magazines and newspapers can double as a shelf list when all changes in title, frequency, etc. are recorded on the forms.

The shelf list is one of the most important records in the library. Some libraries microfilm theirs, so that if anything should happen to the public card catalog, it can be reconstructed from the shelf list. In a situation where a library is not yet fully cataloged, the fiction shelf list may serve as an author list and the nonfiction shelf list may serve as a subject catalog (since it brings together all the botanies, all of the United States histories, etc.) until such time as the library can be completely cataloged. Before beginning the cataloging of an old library, be sure that there is a correct shelf list to use as a basis for the work. In a new library, if it is not possible to catalog the new books as rapidly as they are being bought, it is as well to accession (if an accession record is to be made), classify, and shelf-list them at once. Later, using the shelf list as a check, catalog the different classes. In a well-organized and well-established library it is best to make the shelf list and catalog cards for each book when it is added to the library.

Reference

1.   Mildred Harlow Downing, Introduction to Cataloging and Classification.   5th ed.   (Jefferson, N.C.:   McFarland, 1981), pp. 208-213.

Chapter 11

PRINTED CATALOG CARDS, CENTRALIZED SERVICES, AND OTHER OPTIONS

A library's catalog can be produced and maintained in a variety of ways. The familiar card catalog is still predominant, and no doubt will continue to serve well the needs of
most small libraries for many years to come. However,
advances in library automation have been rapid in the last
decade, and cooperation among libraries of all types and
sizes has increased substantially. Together, these develop-
ments have created opportunities for even the smallest library
to consider alternatives to the traditional card catalog.

Only in the most unusual circumstances should a library do all its cataloging locally. The vast majority of current material acquired by the typical school or public library
has already been cataloged, usually by the Library of Congress on the basis of Cataloging in Publication (CIP) information provided by publishers. The Library of Congress creates a catalog record in MARC format, and this is distributed
in a number of ways directly to libraries, bibliographic util-
ities such as OCLC, and commercial cataloging services such
as the Catalog Card Corporation of America.

The individual library that does not subscribe to the
Library of Congress' distribution service, may still use the
LC cataloging record through OCLC or a similar cooperative
system, or through purchasing its catalog cards from a
vendor who has relied on the LC data base to create them.
Because the original catalog record is in machine readable
form, it can be manipulated and printed out in different ways.
The familiar catalog card can be produced, to be interfiled
in the library's card catalog. It is also possible to produce
a printed book catalog or a computer output microform (COM)
catalog. Increasingly, no physical manifestation of the catalog is created for the user. Rather, the records are entered
into the library's data base and accessed on a cathode ray

terminal by the patron through a keyboard or through a touch-
sensitive screen.

Librarians need to understand the different options and
to become familiar with the various centralized services available through vendors and nonprofit cooperative networks. Even
if they are able to obtain most of their cataloging from another source, librarians still need to know enough about cataloging to be able to evaluate the quality of purchased cataloging, to select the appropriate options for their library,
and to do the occasional original cataloging that is required
when an item has not been entered into a centralized data
base.

Since 1901, printed catalog cards have been available
at a reasonable cost. Today there are cataloging centers in
state, regional, and county libraries and commercial cataloging companies where libraries can have the bulk of their processing done for them. Through cooperative networks, even
small libraries may benefit from a shared online cataloging
system such as OCLC. The individual library must continue
to compare classification numbers with its shelf list, so that
the classified collection may present a consistent whole over
the years, bring material on like subjects together, and keep
policies uniform. Likewise, catalog entries must be checked
to assure uniform headings for the same person, organization,
or subject.

This chapter discusses in some detail the use of Library of Congress printed catalog cards and some of those
available from other centralized services. The time that it
takes to get these printed cards depends upon the location of
the library and whether the cards are available when the order
is received. When deciding how much of a time lag is acceptable, the library must take into consideration the amount
of time it would take for it to prepare the copy and have the
cards typed locally.

Library of Congress Cards

The Library of Congress prints and sells catalog cards for
books, documents, audiovisual materials, and serials. In
1966 it began printing annotated catalog cards for children's
books. Differences will be found between Library of Congress
cards printed at different times as the result of changes in
cataloging policies, but since the older cards and the most

recently printed ones both describe the material accurately, variations in the details of certain items do not matter. Classification numbers and headings must of course be checked and adjusted in any case.

Cards 160 and 161 show the arrangement and punctuation now prescribed by AACR. Note that different sizes and styles of type are used to emphasize or make less conspicuous the different items. Note also that the LC cards give more detail than is needed for simplified cataloging.

Brock, Para Lee.
  Sahani / by Para Lee Brock ; illustrated by Inez Cavender Roskos. — 1st ed — Atlanta Ga · Peachtree Publishers, c1981
  189 p. : ill. ; 24 cm.
  Summary. An extraordinary horse and his lively owner encounter adventure during their journey from New York to the Great Smokey Mountains.
  ISBN 0-931948-19-3 : $8.95

  [1. Horses Fiction] I. Roskos, Inez, ill. II. Title.
  PZ7.B7823 Sah   1981   [Fic]—dc19   81-10611
                                                          AACR 2   MARC

  Library of Congress   AC

Card 160. Library of Congress printed card.

Details included in card 160 that are omitted in simplified cataloging are the edition statement (as it is the first), the summary, and the price. The details about illustrations and size might also be left out. At the bottom are the tracings for added entries made for the Library of Congress catalog. The brackets enclosing the subject entry mean that the tracing is optional, and its use depends on local practice. If a library does not want to use subject headings for fiction, or does not feel the illustrator is important, the tracings may be crossed out. Below the tracing and to the left of the hole is the LC classification. To the right of the hole is the suggested DDC number, and at the far right is the LC card number, which is to be used when ordering cards. Beneath the card number is "MARC," meaning that the cataloging information is stored in a machine-readable format.

Heavy oil and tar sands recovery and upgrading : international
technology / edited by M.M. Schumacher ; based on research
by Roebuck Associates, Booz-Allen & Hamilton, Inc. — Park
Ridge, N.J. : Noyes Data Corp., 1982.

       p.   cm. — (Energy technology review, ISSN 0270-91551 ; no.
78)

   Includes bibliographies and index.
   ISBN 0-8155-0893-X : $48.00

   1. Petroleum engineering. 2. Oil sands. I. Schumacher, M. M. II. Roebuck Associates. III. Booz, Allen & Hamilton, Inc. IV. Series.

TN871.H38   622'.3382—dc19   82-2229
                                       AACR 2 MARC CIP

Library of Congress

Card 161.   LC card, title main entry, CIP cataloging.

On card 161, note that the pagination and size have been left blank, because LC cataloged the item based on CIP data. The missing numbers can easily be filled in when the library receives the cards and matches them against the item in hand. The main point to remember about LC cards is that the suggested headings are based on LC's subject heading list, not Sears, and that the suggested DDC numbers are derived from the unabridged edition.

The librarian who opts to buy LC printed cards should write to the LC Cataloging Distribution Service [1] and ask for a copy of instructions for ordering printed cards and a supply of the forms to be used for each order. Request a supply of order slips for an estimated three-month period. The directions for making out orders are detailed and clear and should be followed exactly.

It is possible to order materials and LC cards simultaneously if a multicopy form is used which meets both the specifications of LC's Card Division and the requirements of the library's jobber. The copy retained by the library constitutes a record of what materials and cards have been ordered. For information about these forms contact the Order Control Unit.

Other Printed Cards

Since the lamented demise of The H. W. Wilson and Library Journal cards, there is no comparable source of typeset cards with Sears headings and abridged DDC numbers.   Libraries

```
520      Sagan, Carl
S            Cosmos.   Random   c1980
         365p illus ( part col )

         The well-known astronomer presents an
         illustrated guide to the universe and
         to Earth's relationship to it, moving
         from theories of creation to human-
         kind's discovery of the cosmos, to
         general relativity, to space missions,
         and beyond.  Bibliog

         1 Astronomy   I Cosmos (Television pro-
         gram)   II T

   ISBN  0-394-50294-9


00005 *DC            001995      c THE BAKER & TAYLOR CO  1177
```

Card 162.   Baker & Taylor card, traditional format.

```
F        Blume, Judy.
DLU          Superfudge / by Judy Blume. -- 1st
         ed. -- New York : Dutton, c1980.
         166 p. ; 22 cm.

         Peter describes the highs and lows
         of life with his younger brother
         Fudge.
         ISBN 0-525-40522-4


         1.Brothers and sisters--Fiction. 2.
         Family life--Fiction. 3.Humorous sto-
         ries. I.Title.

                                          Fic

                    001 375            LC-MARC
                            C 1980 BRODART
```

Card 163.   Bro-Dart card, fiction symbol.

which order their books from one of the large jobbers may find that they can order cards from them also, or can have the books completely processed by the jobber. While most companies will provide cards for materials which have not been purchased through them, Baker & Taylor is one that

```
T        Busch, Ted.
50           Fundamentals of dimensional metrology /
.B87     Wilkie Brothers Foundation ; Ted Busch. --
1966     3rd ed. -- Albany, N.Y. : Delmar, 1966, c1964.
             vii, 424 p. : ill. ; 26 cm.

             Includes index.


             1. Mensuration.   I. Wilkie Brothers
         Foundation.   II. Title.
```

Card 164.   Original cataloging from Shelfmark.

```
                 The IQ game.

155.234  Taylor, Howard Francis, 1939-
T            The IQ game : a methodological
         inquiry into the heredity-
         environment controversy / Howard F.
         Taylor. -- New Brunswick, N.J. :
         Rutgers University Press, c1980.
             xi, 276 p. : ill. ; 24 cm.

             Bibliography: p. 244-261.
             Includes index.
             ISBN 0-8135-0902-5

             1. Intellect.   2. Nature and
         nurture.   I. Title.
BF431.T2523                   155.2'34
                                       80-13997
                                          MARC
         Library of Congress
         04928 *DC        002027        © THE BAKER & TAYLOR CO.   1244
```

Card 165.   Baker & Taylor card, unabridged DDC, headed.

will not.   Most of these companies produce computer-printed cards which are comparable in quality to locally typed and duplicated cards (see cards 162 through 168).   In a number of cases the library can specify either Sears or LC subject headings, and unabridged or abridged DDC or LC classification.   Cards may be ordered headed, i. e. , with headings

```
F        Blume, Judy.
BLU         Superfudge / by Judy Blume. -- 1st
         ed. -- New York : Dutton, c1980.
            166 p. ; 22 cm.

         McNAUGHTON    11/81          9.25




            1.Brothers and sisters--Fiction. 2.
         Family life--Fiction. 3.Humorous sto-
         ries. 1.Title.


                                              Fic

                         001 375          LC-MARC
                                    © 1960 BRODART
```

Card 166.   Shelf list card from set of which card 161 is the main entry card.

```
             TECHNOLOGY--HISTORY.
T
15
.B76     Burke, James, 1936-
1978        Connections / James Burke. -- 1st
         American ed. -- Boston : Little Brown,
         c1978.
            304 p. : ill. ; 26 cm.

            ISBN 0-316-11681-5 : $17.95



            1.Technology--History. I.Title.


T15.B76 1978                    609

                                      78-21662
         CATALOG CARD CORPORATION OF AMERICA ®    MARC
```

Card 167.   Catalog Card Corporation of America card, based on LC data, headed.

and classification numbers already imprinted, or unheaded,
allowing the library to change the headings and classification.
Most companies base their cataloging on LC information provided on MARC tapes and through CIP, using the National
Union Catalog for older titles.   Some original cataloging is
done, and the LC data may be simplified (compare cards 162
and 163), or may be virtually identical.

```
            DESCRIPTIVE CATALOGING — RULES.


Z694        Anglo-American cataloguing rules / prepared by the
.A5         American Library Association ... [et al.] ; edited by
1978        Michael Gorman and Paul W. Winkler. — 2d ed. — Chicago
            : ALA, 1978.

            xvii, 620 p. ; 26 cm.

            ISBN: 083893210X. 0838932118 pbk.

            1. Descriptive cataloging — Rules. I. Gorman,
         Michael, 1941- II. Winkler, Paul Walter. III. American
         Library Association.




            Z694 .A5 1978           025.3/2        78-13789
            Disk No. ALA001
            MINI MARC                                     informatics
```

Card 168.   Informatics card.

        For a library which wishes to purchase cards but pre-
fers Sears headings and abridged DDC, one of these services
may be the answer.   The chart on pages 290-292 presents
some of the options and the costs of selected card services
for the sake of comparison, and is not meant to be comprehensive and of course prices fluctuate.   A list of companies
which supply catalog cards will be found in Library Journal's
"Buyer's Guide," published annually in the August issue.
Write to each company and request their specifications, order
forms, and latest prices in order to determine which service
most nearly conforms to your library's policies.

        Audiovisual materials.   Printed cards for audiovisual
materials are not as readily obtainable as those for books.
LC cards may be purchased for films, filmstrips, sound recordings, videorecordings, transparencies, slides, and maps,
but availability can be disappointing and long time-lags can
occur.   When ordering from a selection aid which cites LC

	Baker & Taylor	Brodart	Catalog Card Corp	Library of Congress	Infronics	Shelf-mark	Specialized Services	Paterson Free PL
Source of Data								
MARC	x	x	x	x	x			x
CIP	x	x	x				x	x
Original	x	1%	x		x		x	x
Other	copy cataloging		NUC	pre-MARC files	CCLC etc.		NICEM, etc.	NUC
Subject Headings								
LC	9th + supp	latest	9th	x	9th + custom options	latest + custom options		x
Sears	11th	11th	11th				11th	
Classification								
LC	latest + changes & Gale updates	latest	latest	latest + changes	latest + changes	latest		ANSCR for sound recordings
DDC	19th	19th	19th	19th	19th	19th	19th	x (print) 19th "
Abridged DDC	11th	11th	11th				11th	
Book Numbers								
Cutter	x				x + custom options	x + custom	1-3	ANSCR for recordings as requested
Author	3 letters; biographee's full name	up to 9	0-7 (DDC only)					
Printing								
Typeset	x	cards for recordings computer printed	computer printed	xerographic laser				computer printed
Typed					x	x	x	
Annotations								
All	x				x		x	
Some		juvenile	juvenile	juvenile		as requested		AV

	Col 1	Col 2	Col 3	Col 4	Col 5	Col 6	Col 7	Col 8
Headed								
Yes						x		
No		x			x		x	
Either	x		x	x				x
Types of Sets								
Cards only			x			x	x	
Kits only	x							
Either		x		x	x			x
Cards per Set	minimum: 5, max based on tracings	varies with tracings	1 main entry + 1 shelf list + 1 per added entry	8 or 1	1 or as requested	varies, as requested	varies, as needed	varies
Costs								
Cards only (headed)	$.50	$.59	$.55 for Dewey/Sears $.58 for LC/MARC*	$.45 (not headed)	$1.80	varies		$.15 for 1st card; .04 each each add'l
Cards + Kits	$.99 with jacket	recordings**	$.65 for Dewey/Sears $.68 for LC/MARC		$2.00		$1.25 (bulk orders cheaper)	$1.45 for processing print; $1.00-2.75 for AV
Availability								
Only for purchases	x							
Anything in database		x						
Print	x	x	x	x	x	x	x	x
Nonprint	x	x	x (with exceptions)	x	x	x except film & video	x	x
								records, filmstrips, cassettes
Average Fulfillment time	2 weeks	7 days	5 working days	5 working days=MARC	10 days =MARC	1 week	varies	1 week=print 1-4 weeks=AV

	Baker & Taylor	Brodart	Catalog Card Corp	Library of Congress	Inforonics	Shelf-mark	Specialized Services	Paterson Free PL
Titles cataloged per year								
Print	45,000	25,000	120,000	220,000+	?	?	---	3,000
Nonprint		2,700**	200	6,000-		?	?	5,000
Total Number of Titles Available								
Print	MARC/LC= 1.5 million Dewey/Sears = 350,000		2 million		1.3 million			1.3 million
Nonprint	1.5 million total	1.5 million total	5,000	7 million total		unlimited	for specified AV producers	13,500
AACR2								
LC Options	x	x	x	x	x	x		x***
Own options							x	
ISBD Format	x	x	x	x	x	x		x***
Traditional format	x		x				x	

* $.48 for LC/MARC main entry card only

** Brodart cataloging for sound recordings is now available on cards from Professional Media Service Corp., Gardena, CA.

*** But see sample cards.

card numbers, one can at least be certain that the cards are available.

A number of audiovisual producers provide cards with materials purchased from them on request. Examine producers' catalogs as you receive them and make a note of which ones supply cards. Caedmon and Weston Woods are among those who will provide card kits. The Specialized Service and Supply Company is the largest supplier of catalog card sets for AV producers. A list of producers who contract with Specialized Service is given on pages 294-95. Card 169 is a sample of their product.

Professional Media Service Corporation supplies cards for sound recordings, based on Bro-Dart cataloging, whether or not the recordings are ordered through them. Until recently, the company was owned by Bro-Dart. It is possible to buy those recordings distributed by Professional Media fully processed and ready to shelve, with cards ready to file. The classification scheme used is the "Alpha-Numeric System for Classification of Recordings" (ANSCR), but one may order cards without any class numbers.

Advantages of using printed catalog cards. When one considers the cost of blank cards and the time required to do the cataloging and typing, printed cards are not expensive. One study of preparation and cataloging time concluded that it takes three and three-fourths times as long to catalog, classify, and assign subject headings for books if no printed cards are used.[2] Besides, there is no waste of cards or expenditure of time in making and revising typed cards.

The copy for printed catalog cards is prepared by expert catalogers, with all that this implies in regard to author headings, items included on the cards, suggestions as to subject headings, classification numbers, and added entries. LC cards give considerable bibliographic information about the book which may be of great value. Some cards give annotations which are very useful. LC cards are uniform in blackness, attractive, and very legible, but even the computer-printed cards are acceptable. Using printed cards saves time in preparing the entry, in typing and otherwise reproducing the cards, and in revising typewritten cards. One printed card may be compared with the book to see if it matches the particular edition which the library has; then, only the call number and the typewritten headings added to the other cards need to be checked for accuracy. Printed cards are especially

Producers for Whom Specialized Service Catalogs

AIMS
American Educational Films
Paul S. Amidon & Associates
Argus Communications
Audio Visual Project
Avid Corp.
AVNA
Barr Films
Bear Films
Bergwall Productions
BFA Educational Media
Bilingual Educational Services
Bowmar
Brunswick Productions
Butterick
Caedmon
Center for Humanities
Centron Educational Films
Changing Times
Childrens Press
Classroom Materials
Classroom World Productions
Clearvue, Inc.
CMS
Columbia Records (special prod-
    ucts)
Coronet Instructional Media
Crestwood House
Croft, Inc.
Thomas Y. Crowell Co.
Current Affairs
Cypress Publishing Co.
Developmental Learning Materials
DCA Educational Products
Double Sixteen
Educational Activities, Inc.
Educational Design
Educational Dimensions
Educational Enrichment Materials
Educational Filmstrips
Educational Materials Corp. (EMC)
Educational Projections Corp.
Encore
Encyclopaedia Britannica Educa-
    tional Corp.
Eye-Gate
FilmFair Communications
Films, Inc.
Films for the Humanities, Inc.
Filmstrip House, Inc.
Folkways
Globe Filmstrips
Golden Press
Greenhaven
Guidance Associates, Inc.

Harcourt Brace Jovanovich (film-
    strips)
Hawkhill Associates
Hester & Associates
Hubbard Scientific Co.
Hudson Photographic
Human Relations Media Center
Ibis Media
Ideal School Supply
Imperial Educational Resources
Imperial International Learning
Instructional Aids, Inc.
International Teaching Tapes
Jabberwocky
Jackdaws
January Productions
Kenalex Corp.
Kimbo
Thomas S. Klise
Knowledge Aid
Learning Corp. of America
Learning Seed
Learning Tree Filmstrips
Listening Library
Lyceum Productions
Macmillan Films
MarshFilm Enterprises
Math House
McGraw-Hill Films
Mealey Productions
Media Basics
Miller-Brody Productions
Milliken Publishing Co.
Modern Learning Aids
Monday Media
Moreland-Latchford
Multi-Media Productions
A. J. Nystrom
Orange Cherry
Pathescope Educational Films
Pendulum Press
Prentice-Hall Media
Q-ED Productions
Random House
RCA Records (juvenile)
RMI Educational Films/Westwood
Roa
Scholastic
Science Research Assoc. (SRA)
Spectrum
Spoken Arts, Inc.
Stallman Records, Inc.
Sunburst Communications, Inc.
Superscope
SVE

Taylor Associates
Thorne Films
Time-Life Video
Troll Associates
United Learning
Universal Ed. & Visual Arts (UEV)
Urban Media Materials, Inc.
   (UMM)
Viewlex
Viking Press
Visual Education Consultants (VEC)

Visual Education Corporation
Visual Publications
Walt Disney Educational Media
Wards Natural Science Estab.,
   Inc.
Warren Schloat Productions
Westinghouse Learning Corp.
H. Wilson Corp.
Windsong Media
Wollensak

025.3
Ca   Cataloging multimedia materials (kit). SSS Inc.,
               1981.
               5 filmstrips : col + 5 sound cassettes + 25
            copymasters + 1 manual
               Contents: Artefacts and realia (80 fr, 12 min).
            Sound recordings (97 fr, 15 min). Graphic mate-
            rials (102 fr, 17 min). Motion pictures and video-
            recordings (84 fr, 12 min). Music (112 fr, 19 min).
               1 Cataloging–Audio-Visual materials
               2 Classification–Audio-visual materials

sss999999   -cont.

025.3   -2-
Ca   Cataloging multimedia materials (kit)...

            3 Libraries–Technical services 4 Library
            education–Audio-visual aids I 5 title anals.

sss999999

Card 169.   Specialized Service and Supply Co. card.

```
           Elgar, Edward.
EA             Cockaigne overture.
ELGA   Elgar, Edward.
EV         [Enigma variations]  Phonodisc.
B 20       Enigma variations.  Angel S 36120.
           1 disc.

           Philharmonia orchestra; Sir John Barbirolli,
       conductor.
           With: Cockaigne overture.

           1. English music.  2. Variations (Orchestra).
       I.T.  II. Barbirolli, Sir John.  III. Title. (1)
       IV. Comp & T. (1)
```

Card 170. Paterson Free Library, card for sound recording.

```
ZM         CHILDREN'S SONGS
SESAME
S 64           SESAME Street 1, Original Cast.

   Words and music by Jeffrey Moss and Joe Raposo. Disc 12 in. 33
rpm. stereo Sesame Street CTW-22064. 1974.
   Contents: Sesame Street Theme; AB-C-DEF-GHI; I've Got Two; Goin'
for a Ride; What Are Kids Called?; Everybody Wash; One of These
Things; Up and Down; Bein' Green; Somebody Come and Play; I Love
Trash; A Face; J-Jump; People in Your Neighborhood; Rub Your Tummy;
The Number Five; Five People in My Family; Nearly Missed; Rubber
Duckie.

   1. Children's Songs 2. Television Music I. Moss, Jeffrey
II. Raposo, Joe

   Copyright 1982                                  00-1474
   Professional Media Service Corp.
```

Card 171.   Professional Media Service Corp. card; ANSCR
classification.

useful for books which require several subject cards or numerous added entries.   Even when there are not enough cards
in a set for analytical entries, the necessary extra cards may
be ordered and, by adding call number, headings, and paging,
the cards are quickly made into analytical entries.   If a library is willing to accept the access points provided by a

cataloging agency, headed cards may be ordered, usually at
no additional cost.

Typewritten reference cards and short form series
cards have to be made by each library for its own catalog.
If the unit card is used for series entries, printed cards may
be used. The simple form of cataloging for fiction recommended in this manual makes the process of cataloging by
the library as quick or quicker than ordering printed cards
and adapting them. It is recommended, therefore, that typewritten cards be used for adult fiction even though printed
cards are ordered for all non-fiction. On the other hand,
it is best to order printed cards for all juvenile books, as
subject headings for children's fiction and annotations are
very helpful.

The question of whether to use LC or other printed
cards depends largely on the type of library. The library
for adults and the more scholarly library, as well as most
kinds of special libraries, would do well to use LC cards
with their added bibliographic information. The elementary
school may want to find a company that can supply books
already processed and cataloged using abridged DDC and
Sears headings. Libraries which have adult as well as juvenile titles but do not want to use LC subject headings should
consider the commercial companies which offer Sears headings.
It is, of course, possible to use LC cards for adult materials
and other cards for the children's collection, ordering LC
cards for those juvenile titles for which other cards are not
available. A mixture of LC cards, other printed cards, and
typewritten cards in the same catalog does not reduce the
usefulness of the catalog, as long as consistency is maintained
in the use of subject headings. As a general rule, however,
choosing one source of catalog card supply and sticking with
it is more efficient.

Adapting printed cards for use in the catalog. The
librarian compares the cards with the book which they are
to represent in the catalog to see that they agree, and with
the catalog or authority file to see whether or not the form
of heading agrees with what has already been used. If, for
example, the printed card has the author's real name on the
first line but the pseudonym is better known, write it on the
line above the real name--beginning at the first indention.

If the library has entered a few books under another
form of the name, it would be better to change those and

adopt the form used on the printed cards. If, on the other hand, there are many cards in the catalog under the other form, it is more expedient to change the printed card and make a cross-reference if one has not already been made. A line can be drawn through the author heading and the preferred form typed above, beginning with the first indention as usual. For older materials, one must be careful to select the AACR2 form of heading, and to remember that LC cards are likely to follow outdated rules for material cataloged by LC before 1981.

If the publisher given is not the publisher of the edition to be cataloged, or if the date or edition is different, the card must be changed. In the case of incomplete sets, date and volume should be changed with pencil so that the card may show what the library has and yet be easily changed when the other volumes are added. Changes may be made by crossing out or erasing items and typing or writing in the corrections. As few corrections as possible should be made, however, so as not to spoil the appearance and legibility of the cards. It is unnecessary to cross out any item given on the printed card if it applies to the book in question.

After the librarian makes the necessary corrections or additions so that the printed card represents the book accurately, the next step is to add the call number. The suggested DDC number on the printed card must be checked with the library's copy of Dewey, as it may be a number derived from a different edition or may not be in accordance with the library's policy for that particular class. For instance, if the number suggested for a biography is 923 it would not be used by the small school or public library which uses 920 for all collective biography and 92 or B for all individual biography.

The next step is to examine the tracings. Does the library need all of the added entries listed? Are the subject headings the same as those listed in the printed list of subject headings which the library has adopted? Does the amount of material on the subject make necessary the subdivisions of the subject given? If a library has only a few books on a country and is unlikely to ever have many, the name of the country alone may be sufficient for all of the books about it, or the general subdivision HISTORY or DESCRIPTION AND TRAVEL may do rather than the more specific subdivisions such as CZECHOSLOVAK REPUBLIC. HISTORY, 1938-1945 or IRELAND. DESCRIPTION AND TRAVEL. 19th CENTURY.

If all of the added entries given in the tracing on the printed card are not used, underscore the number of each one which is to be used, or cross out the entries not wanted. If the subject headings given on the card are not compatible with the printed subject heading list used by the library, use the heading from the printed list and type it with the tracing on the front of the card. If there is insufficient space at the end of the tracing, type it on the back, and type the word "over" beside the hole on the front of the card. Corrections in the tracing need be made on the main entry and shelf list cards only.

On unheaded cards which are to be used as added entries the call number is added, any necessary alterations are made, and the appropriate headings are added. No change is made in the tracing on the added entry cards if it is understood that only the main entry card is consulted for tracing. To make a printed card into an author analytical entry, estimate in advance the number of lines required for the added heading. If contents or any other extra information has made extension cards necessary, use a full set of cards for the main and all other entries except for title and analytical entries. For title cards use the first card only, drawing a line through "Continued on next card." For analytical entries, use the card which contains the part of the contents for which the entry is made, crossing out "continued" notations as needed (see card 172). Please note that card 172 follows AACR1 rather than AACR2, and that the main entry would now be under title. For contents access, however, the card is still serviceable.

Mansfield, Katherine
    Sun and moon
Jones, Phyllis Maud, comp.
    English short stories, 1888–1937; selected by Phyllis M. Jones. London, Oxford University Press, 1973.
        viii, 403 p. 21 cm. (Oxford paperbacks) £0.95   GB 73–06686
        Previous editions have title: Modern English short stories.
        CONTENTS: Hardy, T. The three strangers. — Harris, F. The Holy man.—Jacobs, W. W. A garden plot.—Wells, H. G. A slip under the microscope.—Bennett, A. The lion's share.—Munro, H. H. The open window.—Munro, H. H. The music on the hill.—Maugham, W. S. The door of opportunity.—Coppard, A. E. Fifty pounds.—Forster, E. M. Other Kingdom.—Wodehouse, P. G. Lord Emsworth and the girl friend.—Lawrence, D. H. The last laugh.—Aumonier, S. Juxtapositions. — Mansfield, K. Sun and moon. — Benson, S. Submarine.—Huxley, A. The Tillotson banquet.—Beachcroft, T. O. She

        ~~(Continued on next card)~~
                      73–180459
        73 [4]

Card 172. LC card adapted for analytical entry.

When cards with headings already printed on them are used, there is less opportunity for making adjustments. Unless one can be fairly certain that the choices reflected by the printed card will be acceptable, it is best to order cards that do not have subject headings printed at the top of the subject cards nor the classification number in its place in the upper left-hand corner of the card.

Whether it is the first set of printed cards to be added to the catalog or the thousandth, any cards added have to be first checked with the catalog to assure uniformity of name headings.

Centralized Services

The card distribution service of the Library of Congress, Baker & Taylor, Bro-Dart, and others are examples of "centralized cataloging," a term also used to describe the provision of cataloging by a headquarters operation for members of a system or library district. Some jobbers and some local central services will not only provide cataloging, but will also process the material so that it arrives ready for shelving, with plastic covers, labels, and pockets in place. The larger the centralized operation, the more economical it is. However, the individual library usually has to accept the classification, subject heading, format, and other decisions made by the central agency in order to realize a cost-benefit.

Some commercial services offer customized cataloging in several formats. For example, Inforonics produces online, computer output microform (COM), or book catalogs, as well as cards. They will, in fact, do complete catalog maintenance on a contract basis to a client's specifications. This kind of service is expensive, but may be a viable option for a small company library that does not wish to hire a full-time professional librarian, or needs to organize an uncataloged collection quickly.

Given the increasing cost of human resources and the relatively stable cost of centralized processing, it is very hard for any nonspecialized library to justify the expense of original cataloging (with the exception of current fiction, perhaps). When estimating cataloging costs, one must remember to include the price of the reference tools needed, card duplicating equipment, card stock, etc.

A major development in recent years has been the creation of shared online cataloging systems which allow participating libraries to use cataloging already entered into a data base and to edit it to suit their own specifications. Even small libraries can participate in a national utility such as OCLC through joining a cooperative network that permits sharing of terminals and membership fees.

OCLC is the major example of cooperative cataloging, where the basic data base of MARC records provided by the Library of Congress is added to by participating libraries who create records for those of their holdings which are not already found in the data base. An example of an OCLC screen display is shown on page 302. Online cataloging through OCLC allows each library to customize its cataloging by calling up a record already entered in the data base and editing it to local specifications. Cards can be produced by OCLC for the edited record and mailed to the library. In addition, the library may obtain a magnetic tape of all the records it has entered. The form in which the catalog can ultimately appear is therefore not limited to cards. The tapes can be used to produce a COM catalog, a printed book catalog, or an online catalog.

The current trend seems to be for libraries of various kinds and sizes in geographical proximity to each other to pool their resources for the acquisition of automated systems. Usually, they begin with a circulation system, but plan to add online catalogs. Over a period of years, as more and more records are added to the central data base, a union catalog of the holdings of the member libraries is created. Thus the patron using the smallest library can see immediately what is available not just locally, but within the surrounding area.

For libraries with very small collections, one alternative to the card catalog is an online catalog created locally by using an inexpensive microcomputer. This option is especially attractive for specialized collections where a great deal of original cataloging is necessary. When a record has to be created locally, it is a great advantage to have to type it only once, but to be able to call it up through any of the access points that the librarian assigns. There are a number of microcomputer programs available commercially that make this possible. While the initial cost of hardware and software may still seem high, the amount of time saved is so great as to justify the expenditure within a fairly short period.

```
Screen 1 of 2
NO HOLDINGS IN RUG - FOR HOLDINGS ENTER dh DEPRESS    DISPLAY RECD SEND
OCLC: 7733280       Rec stat: p Entrd: 810807         Used: 830331
Type: a Bib lvl: m Govt pub:    Lang:    Source:       Illus: j
Repr:    Enc lvl:    Conf pub: 0 Ctry: ens    Dat tp: r M/F/B: 11
Indx: 0 Mod rec:    Festschr: 0 Cont: b
Desc: a Int lvl:    Dates: 1981,

 1 010     81-13789
 2 040     DLC c DLC
 3 020     0399126414 : c $11.95
 4 039 0   2 b 3 c 3 d 3 e 3
 5 050 0   PR6015.I3 b E3 1981
 6 082 0   823/.914 2 19
 7 090     b
 8 049     RUGG
 9 100 10  Plaidy, Jean, d 1906-
10 240 10  Edward Longshanks
11 245 10  Hammer of the Scots / c Jean Plaidy.
12 250     1st American ed.
13 260 0   New York : b Putnam, c 1981, c1979.
14 300     318, [1] p. : b geneal. table ; c 23 cm.
15 490 1   The Plantagenet saga / Jean Plaidy
16 500     London ed. has title: Edward Longshanks.
17 504     Bibliography: p. [319]
```

Cards do not need to be filed or duplicated, records can be quickly corrected, updated, or removed. New acquisitions lists and bibliographies can be printed out, and other customized services for patrons can be performed easily. The disadvantage of this kind of catalog is that the records created on one microcomputer cannot be "read" into a different system. Thus, if the library later decided to join a cooperative network, the records would probably have to be converted.

References

1. Customer Services Section, Cataloging Distribution Service Division, Library of Congress, Washington, D. C. 20541.
2. W. B. Hicks & A. M. Lowrey, "Preparation and Cataloging Time in School Libraries," School Library Association of California. Bulletin 30:7-10 (May, 1959).

Chapter 12

ARRANGEMENT OF ENTRIES IN A CATALOG

Next in importance to describing accurately each item owned by a library and assigning appropriate access points is the arrangement of the entries in the catalog. This is especially so when the catalog is in card, microform, or book format, requiring the user to scan the entries in order to locate the one wanted. Even in online catalogs, it is desirable to display related entries together. Therefore, each entry in a catalog must be filed according to rules that will ensure a consistent arrangement and easy retrieval of records.

A quick look at any telephone directory gives an idea of the kinds of decisions that a set of filing rules must cover. See, for example, how the telephone directory arranges such entries as

> A-A Checker Cab Assn
> AAA Auto Club of Central NJ
> A-1 Limousine Service
> A & A Van Lines
>
> McDonald, A
> MacDonald, M
> Machi, B
> MCA
> M'buto
>
> 1001 Auto Parts
> One Hour Martinizing
> 1-2-3 Quick Print

It is not too difficult to grasp the system used in the telephone directory because it is easy to skim the pages. The rules used in organizing any given card catalog are not so readily discerned, however, simply because one can look at only a few cards at a time.

Because the great majority of small libraries still use card catalogs, the following advice on catalog maintenance offered by Susan Akers has been retained. One of the most important mechanical points is to watch that the trays do not become overcrowded. A good rule is never to fill a catalog tray more than two-thirds full; space is needed to shift cards so that the one being consulted may be handled easily.

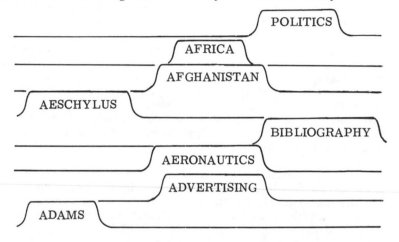

Another important matter is to label the trays so that the reader can easily locate the tray which contains the author, title, or subject for which he is searching. Adequate guide cards, preferably cut in thirds, should indicate the approximate location of the desired card.

A very good method of arranging guide cards in the catalog is to have the authors' surnames on the left, main subject headings in the center, and subdivisions of the subject on the right. This plan enables the caption on the guide card to be short and near enough to the top of the card so that it may be read. So far as possible there should be a guide card for every inch of tightly held cards. A very minor point is to have a blank card in the front of each tray so that the first card will not become soiled.

One of the signs telling how to use the catalog, which may be purchased from a library supply house, may be placed in a poster holder on top of the catalog if it is a low cabinet, or hung beside it. Be sure that the printed directions fit the catalog.

Some large libraries file cards in the catalog once a week; small libraries may file more or less often than this. It is not worthwhile to file a few cards if there will be more tomorrow; if it might be a week or more before there are others, those ready may be filed so that the readers may have the use of these new cards.

Before filing cards, they should be sorted into catalog and shelf-list cards, and counted for the library reports.

After this preliminary sorting the cards are arranged for the catalog alphabetically, according to the rules used in this catalog. The next step is to interfile the cards with those already in the catalog trays, leaving the new cards above the rod. Later, go over these new cards, making sure that they are in their right alphabetical place. Next, pull out the rod and allow the cards to drop into place, locking them in with the rod.

Filing should not be continued for a long period. Since filing cards requires close attention, the eye becomes tired and mistakes are likely to occur. If the same person both files and revises, several hours should elapse between the filing and the revising.

There is no dictionary catalog with all cards filed absolutely alphabetically, word by word or letter by letter. In all catalogs there will be at least a few logical exceptions and in certain areas a chronological or numerical arrangement. Before beginning to file in an unfamiliar catalog, observe what alphabetizing code was used. Whatever code has been used, continue to follow it unless it is unsatisfactory, and be sure that the change will be an improvement before deciding to refile an entire catalog.

Currently there are four sets of filing rules followed by most North American libraries: the 1956 LC rules, the 1968 ALA rules, and the new rules issued by both bodies in 1980. Both the LC and ALA 1980 rules were designed to reflect the fact that computers "read" symbols, not concepts, and therefore tend to follow the "file-as-is" principle. Thus numerals are not treated as though they were words, but precede letters of the alphabet at the beginning of a catalog. Punctuation and nonalphabetic signs and symbols are ignored. As James D. Anderson explains in his "Catalog File Display: Principles and the New Filing Rules,"[1] machine filing has the advantage of being consistent and objective in arranging

symbols in a given order, whereas human interpretation of symbols can vary. He uses the example of "1984" to illustrate concept filing, pointing out that this would file as "nineteen eighty-four" if it refers to a date, but as "one thousand nine hundred and eighty-four" if it refers to the number of recipes in a cookbook.

The new <u>ALA Filing Rules</u> [2] have the advantage of being brief and containing few exceptions or options. They have the disadvantage of splitting subdivisions of a subject heading, and producing some odd looking sequences such as the following:

> $$$ and sense
> Art and beauty
>
> Manual
> *mas star for the poor
> Massachusetts
> % of gain
>
> 5 2/3 minutes
> 5. 2 inches

For an established library that uses a card catalog, converting to the new rules would probably be an impossible task. Consequently, this chapter summarizes the rules presented in the abridged edition of the old ALA rules [3], which are those most often followed by small libraries. A dictionary, rather than a divided catalog, is assumed.

There are two fundamental methods of filing alphabetically; namely, word by word and letter by letter.

Word by word filing:	Letter by letter filing:
Book	Book
Book collecting	Bookbinding
Book of English essays	Book collecting
Book of famous ships	Bookish
Book scorpion	Book of English essays
Bookbinding	Book of famous ships
Bookish	Books
Books	Books and reading
Books and reading	Book scorpion
Books that count	Booksellers and bookselling
Booksellers and bookselling	Books that count

In word by word filing, each word is a unit, and thus Books that count precedes Booksellers and bookselling, since Books precedes Booksellers; while in letter by letter filing no attention is paid to words but each letter is considered. Thus Books that count follows Booksellers because bookst follows bookse. To take another example: Book scorpion precedes Bookbinding in word by word filing as Book precedes Bookb, but in letter by letter filing Bookbinding precedes Book scorpion because bookb precedes books.

Basic Rule

Arrange all entries alphabetically according to the order of the English alphabet.

Arrange word by word, alphabetizing letter by letter within the word. Apply the principle of "nothing before something," considering the space between words as "nothing." When two or more headings begin with the same word, arrange next by the first different word.

Every word in the entry is regarded, including articles, prepositions and conjunctions, but initial articles are disregarded.

> I met a man
> Image books
> Imaginary conversations
> In an unknown land
> In the days of giants

In a dictionary catalog, interfile all types of entries (author, title, subject, series, etc.) and their related references, in one general alphabet.

Abbreviations

Arrange abbreviations as if spelled in full in the language of the entry, except Mrs. and Ms. which are filed as written.

> Dr. Jekyll and Mr. Hyde
> Doctor Luke
> Dr. Norton's wife
> Doctors on horseback
> Documents of American history

Miss Lulu Bett
Missis Flinders
Mister Abbott
Mr. Emmanuel
Mistress Margaret
Mitchell, Margaret
Mrs. Miniver
Ms. O'Hara
Much

St. Denis, Ruth
Saint-Exupéry, Antoine de
Saint Joan
St. Lawrence River
Ste Anne des Monts
Sainte-Beuve, Charles Augustin
Saintsbury, George Edward Bateman

Ampersand

Arrange the ampersand (&) as "and, " "et, " "und, " etc. ,
according to the language in which it is used.

Aucassin and Nicolete, ...
Aucassin & Nicolette: an old French love story....
Aucassin et Nicolette, ...
Aucassin und Nicolette; ...

Analytical Entries

Author: Arrange an author analytic by the title of the analytic. If there are no main entries for the work in the catalog,
file an author analytic in its alphabetical place. Arrange
analytics made in the form of author-title added entries after
main entries for the work, the analytics subarranged by their
main entries.

Huxley, Thomas Henry, 1825-1895.
On a piece of chalk, p. 157-187:
Law, Frederic Houk, 1871-
Science in literature....

Huxley, Thomas Henry, 1825-1895.
Science and education....

Title: Arrange title analytics by the entry for the analytic if different from the main entry for the whole book.

Peabody, Josephine Preston, 1874-1922.
The piper....

Peacock pie, v. 2, p. 95-218:
De la Mare, Walter John, 1873-
Collected poems....

Peacock pie.
De la Mare, Walter John, 1873-
Peacock pie....

Peacocks and pagodas.
Edmonds, Paul.

Subject: Arrange subject analytics by the entry for the analytic if different from the main entry for the whole book.

MASARYK, TOMAS GARRIGUE, PRES. CZECHOSLO-
VAK REPUBLIC, 1850-1937.
Masaryk, Jan Garrigue, 1886-1948, p. 337-355:
Ludwig, Emil, 1881-1948, ed.
The torch of freedom, edited by Emil Ludwig and Henry B. Kranz.

MASARYK, TOMAS GARRIGUE, PRES. CZECHSLO-
VAK REPUBLIC, 1850-1937.
Selver, Paul, 1888-
Masaryk, a biography....

Articles

Disregard an initial article in all languages and file by the word following it. In English the articles are "A," "An," and "The."

A apple pie
Apache
An April after

Laski, Harold Joseph
The last of the Vikings
LATIN AMERICA

All articles occurring within a title or a heading are to be regarded, except those that actually are initial articles in an inverted position or at the beginning of a subdivision.

> Powder River
> Power, Richard Anderson
> POWER (MECHANICS)
> The power of a lie
> Powers, Francis Fountain
>
> STATE, THE
> STATE AND CHURCH
>
> AGRICULTURE--U.S.
> AGRICULTURE--THE WEST
> AGRICULTURE--WYOMING

Author Entry Arrangement

Works by the author: Alphabetize the titles according to the basic rules for alphabetical arrangement.

Interfile all main and added entries under the same author heading in one file. Subarrange alphabetically by the titles of the books.

In both main and added entry headings disregard designations that show the relationship of the heading to one particular work, as "comp.," "ed.," "ill.," "tr.," "joint author," "editor," etc.

> Pennell, Joseph, 1857-1926
>   The adventures of an illustrator.
>
> Pennell, Joseph, 1857-1926, illus.
> Van Rennselaer, Mariana Griswold
>   English cathedrals....
>
> Pennell, Joseph, 1857-1926
>   Etchers and etching....
>
> Pennell, Joseph, 1857-1926, joint author
> Pennell, Elizabeth Robins
>   The life of James McNeill Whistler.
>
> Pennell, Joseph, 1857-1926
>   Our journey to the Hebrides

Arrange different titles that begin with the same words by the title proper, the shorter title before the longer, disregarding any subtitle, alternative title, "by" phrase, etc. that may follow the shorter title.

> Auslander, Joseph
> > The winged horse; the story of the poets and their poetry.
> > The winged horse anthology.

At the beginning of a title the author's name, even in the possessive case, should be disregarded if it is simply an author statement transcribed from the work. However, if the name in the possessive case is the author's pseudonym, or if an author's name is an integral part of the title, do not disregard it in filing. Do not disregard a name other than the author's.

> Barlow, Peter
> > An essay on magnetic attraction
> > [Barlow's] tables of squares, cubes, square roots....
> > A treatise on the strength of timber....

> Shakespeare, William
> > Selections from Shakespeare.
> > The Shakespeare apocrypha.
> > Shakespeare's wit and humor.

Works about the author: Arrange the subject entries for works about the author after all entries for works by the author, in two groups as follows:

1. Subjects without subdivision, subarranged by their main entries, or if an analytic, by the entry for the analytic.

Exception: An author-title subject entry files in the author file in its alphabetical place by the title in the heading, immediately after the author entries for the same title if there are any.

2. Subjects with subdivisions, arranged alphabetically by the subdivisions.

> Shakespeare, William, 1564-1616
> > The winter's tale.

SHAKESPEARE, WILLIAM, 1564-1616
Alexander, Peter
Shakespeare.

SHAKESPEARE, WILLIAM, 1564-1616
Brandes, Georg Morris Cohen
William Shakespeare, a critical study.

 SHAKESPEARE, WILLIAM, 1564-1616--BIBLIOG-
  RAPHY
 SHAKESPEARE, WILLIAM, 1564-1616--CHARAC-
  TERS
 SHAKESPEARE, WILLIAM, 1564-1616, IN FICTION,
  DRAMA, POETRY, ETC.
 SHAKESPEARE, WILLIAM, 1564-1616--NATURAL
  HISTORY

Bible

Entries for Bible, the sacred book, follow entries for the
single surname Bible.

 Arrange Bible entries in straight alphabetical order
word by word, disregarding kind of entry, form of heading,
and punctuation. Under the same author heading subarrange
alphabetically by titles.

 Arrange headings which include a date alphabetically
up to the date, then arrange the same heading with different
dates chronologically by date.

 Arrange different kinds of entries under the same
heading in groups in the following order:
 Author (main and/or added entry), subarranged alphabetically by titles.
 Subject, subarranged alphabetically by main entries.

 Numbered books of the Bible follow in numerical order
the same name used collectively without number.

 Bible, Dana Xenophon
 Bible
 BIBLE. ACTS. see BIBLE. NEW TESTAMENT.
  ACTS
 BIBLE AND SCIENCE
 BIBLE--ANTIQUITIES

  The Bible in art
  Bible. New Testament. Corinthians
  Bible. New Testament. 1 Corinthians
  Bible. New Testament. Matthew
  Bible. Old Testament. Daniel
  Bible. Old Testament. Genesis
  BIBLE STORIES

Compiler See Author entry arrangement.

Compound Proper Names

Arrange names consisting of two or more separate words, with or without a hyphen, as separate words. Alphabetize with regard to all words in the name, including articles, conjunctions, and propositions.

  New Jersey
  A new way of life
  New York
  Newark

Compound Surname Entries

Interfile compound surname entries alphabetically with the group of titles, etc., following entries for the first part of the name alone as a single surname.

  Smith, Woodrow
  Smith College
  Smith Hughes, Jack
  Smith-Masters, Margaret Melville

  Saint among the Hurons
  Saint-Gaudens,
  St. Petersburg
  Saint Vincent
  San Antonio
  Sanborn

Congresses See Numerical and chronological arrangement.

Corporate Name Entries Beginning with a Surname

Arrange a corporate name consisting of a surname followed
by forenames, etc., in its alphabetical place among the personal names in the surname group.

> Rand, Edward Kennard
> Rand, Winifred
> Rand McNally and Company (McNally is the surname
>   of a member of the company)
> Randall, John Herman
> Randall-MacIver, David
>
> Wilson, Forrest
> Wilson (The H. W.) Company
> Wilson, James Calmar
> Wilson, Margery

Arrange a corporate name consisting of a surname
only, followed by a designation, and compound and phrase
names in their alphabetical place in the group of titles, etc.,
following all surname entries under the same name.

> Prentice, William Reed
> The prentice
> Prentice-Hall book about inventions
> Prentice-Hall, inc.
> Prentice-Hall world atlas

Editor   See   Author entry arrangement

Elisions

Arrange elisions, contractions, as written. Do not supply
missing letters. Disregard the apostrophe and treat as one
word any word or contraction of two words that contains an
apostrophe, unless the apostrophe is followed by a space.

> Who owns America?
> Who reads what?
> Who'd shoot a genius?
> Who's who in American art?
> Whose constitution

Figures See Numerals

Forename Entries

Disregard a numeral following a given name except when
necessary to distinguish between given names with the same
designation. Arrange first alphabetically by the designation,
then when there is more than one numeral, numerically by
the numeral.

Arrange all given name entries, both single and compound, after the single surname entries of the same name,
interfiling alphabetically in the group of titles, etc., beginning with the same word. Alphabetize with regard to all
designations and words, articles and prepositions included,
and disregard punctuation.

When an ordinal numeral follows a given name in the
title entry, arrange it as spoken.

Charles, William
Charles Auchester (title)
Charles Edward, the Young Pretender
CHARLES FAMILY
Charles III, King of France
Charles I, King of Great Britain
Charles II, King of Great Britain
Charles the Bold, see Charles, Duke of Burgundy
Charles II and his court (Charles the second)
CHARLES W. MORGAN (SHIP)

Hyphenated Words

Arrange hyphenated words as separate words when the parts
are complete words.

Happy home.
Happy-thought hall.
Happy thoughts.

In the case of compound words that appear in the catalog written both as two separate words (or hyphenated) and
as a single word, interfile all entries, including corporate
names, under the one-word form.

> Campfire adventure stories
> Camp-fire and cotton-field
> Camp Fire Girls
> The Campfire girls flying around the globe
> CAMPFIRE PROGRAMS
> CAMPING

Illustrator   See   Author arrangement.

Initial Articles   See   Articles.

Initials

Arrange initials, single or in combination, as one-letter
words, before longer words beginning with the same initial
letter, wherever they occur in an entry.   Interfile entries
consisting of initials plus words with entries consisting of
initials only.

Arrange initials standing for names of organizations
as initials, not as abbreviations.

Arrange inverted initials standing for authors' names
alphabetically with other initials, disregarding the inversion
and the punctuation.

> A.
> A. A.
> AAAA
> AAA Foundation for Traffic Safety
> AAAS Conference on Science Teaching....
> A., A.J.G.
> AAUN news

Joint Author   See   Author arrangement

Names with a Prefix

A name with a prefix is one that begins with a separately
written particle consisting of an article (e.g., La Crosse),
a preposition (e.g., De Morgan), a combination of a preposition and an article (e.g., Del Mar, Van der Veer), or a

term which originally expressed relationship (e. g., O'Brien), with or without a space, hyphen, or apostrophe between the prefix and the name.

Arrange proper names with a prefix as one word.

Defoe,
De la Roche,
Delaware
Del Mar, Eugene

El Dorado, Ark.
Eldorado, Neb.

Vanderbilt,
Vanderwalker
Vander Zanden

Arrange names beginning with the prefixes M' and Mc as if written Mac.

McHenry
Machinery
MacHugh
Maclaren, Ian
MacLaren, J.
M'Laren, J Wilson
MacLaren, James

Numerical and Chronological Arrangement

A numerical or a chronological arrangement, rather than an alphabetical, should be followed when numbers or dates distinguish between entries, or headings, otherwise identical, with lowest number or earliest date first.

In relation to other entries in the catalog disregard a numeral or date that indicates a sequence. If the number precedes the item it modifies it must be mentally transposed to follow the item (i. e., file U.S. Army. 1st Cavalry as U.S. Army. Cavalry, 1st).

Titles: Numerical designations following or at end of titles that are otherwise identical up to that point.

More, Paul Elmer
    Shelburne essays. 2nd series.

More, Paul Elmer
    Shelburne essays.   Fourth series

Corporate headings:

Dates only:

    Massachusetts.   Constitutional Convention, 1779-1780
    Massachusetts.   Constitutional Convention, 1853

Number only:

    U.S. Circuit Court (1st Circuit)
    U.S. Circuit Court (5th Circuit)

Number and date: Disregard a place name when it follows
a number.

    American Peace Congress, 1st, New York, 1907
    American Peace Congress, 3d, Baltimore, 1911
    American Peace Congress, 4th, St. Louis, 1913

Place and date: If there is no numeral to indicate a sequence,
the heading being followed only by a place and date in that
order, arrange alphabetically by the place, disregarding the
date at the end.

    OLYMPIC GAMES
    Olympic games, Los Angeles, 1932
    Olympic games, Rome, 1960-

For the same heading with and without distinguishing
numerals or dates, arrange as follows: 1. No numerals,
no subheadings; 2. No numerals, interfiling all corporate
and subject subdivisions and longer entries beginning with the
same name. 3. With numerals, but no subheadings. 4.
With numerals, with all its corporate and subject subdivisions.

    Explorer
    EXPLORER (ARTIFICIAL SATELLITE)
    EXPLORER (BALLOON)
    EXPLORER II (BALLOON)
    An explorer comes home

    Ku Klux Klan in American politics
    KU KLUX KLAN (1915-)

United Nations agreements
UNITED NATIONS--BUILDINGS
United Nations Conference on Trade and Employment....
United Nations. Economic Affairs Dept.
UNITED NATIONS--YEARBOOKS
United Nations (1942-1945)

When a series of numerals or dates designates parts of a whole and there are also alphabetical extensions of the inclusive heading, arrange the alphabetical group first.

Chiefs of state: Disregard the name in parentheses that follows the dates.

U.S. President, 1801-1809 (Jefferson)
U.S. President, 1953-1961 (Eisenhower)

Constitutions, charters, etc.:

U.S. CONSTITUTION--AMENDMENTS
U.S. Constitution. 1st-10th amendments
U.S. Constitution. 1st amendment
U.S. CONSTITUTION--SIGNERS

Legislatures:

U.S. CONGRESS--BIOGRAPHY
U.S. Congress. House. Committee on....
U.S. CONGRESS--RULES AND PRACTICE
U.S. Congress. Senate
U.S. 63d Congress, 2d session, 1913-1914. House
U.S. 86th Congress, 1st session, 1959

Military units: Military units with distinctive names are arranged alphabetically by their names. Units beginning with a number are arranged alphabetically by the word following the number, then numerically by the number. Regard the full name of the unit but disregard subdivisions or modifications of a unit except in relation to other headings under the unit with the same number.

U.S. Army. A.E.F., 1917-1920
U.S. Army Air Forces. 8th Air Force
U.S. Army Air Forces. Air Service Command
U.S. ARMY--BIOGRAPHY
U.S. Army. 1st Cavalry
U.S. Army. II Corps
U.S. Army. Corps of Engineers

Numerals

Arrange numerals in the titles of books, corporate names, cross references, etc., as if spelled out in the language of the entry. Spell numerals and dates as they are spoken, placing "and" before the last element in compound numbers in English, except in a decimal fraction where the "and" must be omitted.

> EGYPT
> 1848: chapters of German history.
> Ekblaw, Sidney E.
> ELECTRIC BATTERIES
>
> Nilson, Arthur Reinhold.
> 1940: our finest hour.
> 1939: how the war began.
> 99 stanzas European.
> Norcross, Carl.
>
> On borrowed time.
> ONE-ACT PLAYS
> 100,000,000 allies--if we choose.
> One hundred non-royalty one-act plays
> One man caravan.
> 1001 mechanical facts made easy.
> 1000 questions and answers on T.B.
> O'Neill, Eugene Gladstone.
> OPERA.

Arrange a numeral following a given name in a title as if spelled out in the language of the title, as spoken. In English the numeral is read as an ordinal preceded by "the." See also Forename entries.

> The Henry James reader
> Henry V, King of England, 1387-1422 (Henry King of England, 5)
> Henry VIII, King of England, 1491-1547 (Henry King of England, 8)
>
> Henry VIII   (Henry the Eighth)
> Shakespeare, William
>
> Henry V   (Henry the Fifth)
> Shakespeare, William

Order of Entries

When the same word or combination of words, is used as the heading of different kinds of entry, arrange the entries in two main groups: 1) Single surname entries, arranged alphabetically by forenames. 2) All other entries, arranged alphabetically word by word, disregarding kind of entry, form of heading, and punctuation.

Arrange subject entries under a personal or corporate name immediately after the author entries for the same name.

Interfile title added entries and subject entries that are identical and subarrange alphabetically by their main entries.

> Love, John L.
> LOVE, JOHN L.
> Love, William
>
> Love
> Bowen, Elizabeth
>
> LOVE
> Magoun, F. Alexander
>
> Love and beauty
> LOVE POETRY
> LOVE--QUOTATIONS, MAXIMS, ETC.
> LOVE (THEOLOGY)
> Love your neighbor

Place Arrangement

Entries beginning with a geographical name follow the same name used as a single surname.

Arrange all entries beginning with the same geographical name in one straight alphabetical file, word by word, disregarding punctuation.

Arrange different kinds of entries under the same geographical name heading in groups as follows:

1) Author (main and/or added entry) without subheading, subarranged by titles.

2) Subject without subdivision, and identical title added entries, interfiled and subarranged alphabetically by their main entries.

3) Heading with corporate and/or subject subdivisions interfiled alphabetically with each other and with titles, etc., disregarding punctuation; each corporate author heading followed by its own subject entries.

Arrange headings for the official governmental divisions of a place (i.e., bureaus, committees, departments, etc.) by the first distinctive word of the subheading.

U.S. Dept. of Agriculture
U.S. Bureau of Education

Different places, jurisdictions, and governments of the same name are alphabetized by the geographical or parenthetical designations following the names. Arrangement is first by the complete designation, then under each different heading according to the general rules above.

United States
UNITED STATES
U.S. Adjutant-General's Office
U.S.--ADJUTANT-GENERAL'S OFFICE
U.S. Agricultural Adjustment Administration
The United States among the nations
United States Steel Corporation
U.S.--TERRITORIAL EXPANSION

New York Academy of Medicine
New York and the Seabury investigation
New York (City) Health Dept.
NEW YORK (CITY)--HEALTH DEPT.
New York (City) Police Dept.
NEW YORK (CITY)--POOR
New York (Colony)
New York (County) Court House Board
New York (State)
NEW YORK (STATE)--GEOLOGY
New York Edison Company
New York tribune

Lincoln, William Sever
Lincoln and Ann Rutledge
LINCOLN CO., KY.

Lincoln, Eng.
LINCOLN HIGHWAY
Lincoln, Neb.
Lincoln plays

London, Jack
LONDON--DESCRIPTION
London, Ky.
London, Ont. Council

California as I saw it
California, Mo.
CALIFORNIA, SOUTHERN
California State Chamber of Commerce
California. University. Library
California. University. School of law
California. University. University at Los Angeles

GERMANY--BIBLIOGRAPHY
Germany. Constitution
Germany (Democratic Republic)
GERMANY (DEMOCRATIC REPUBLIC)--ECONOMIC
  CONDITIONS
GERMANY--DESCRIPTION AND TRAVEL
Germany divided
GERMANY, EASTERN
Germany (Territory under Allied occupation, 1945-
  1955)

Possessive Case See Punctuation marks.

Prefixes See Names with a prefix.

Publisher See Corporate name entries.

Punctuation Marks

Disregard punctuation marks that are part of a title or corporate name.

Boys' book of photography
Boys' life with Will Rogers
Boys' Odyssey

Boys of 1812
Boys will be boys

Life
Life--a bowl of rice
"Life after death"
Life, its true genesis
Life! physical and spiritual

References

A reference or explanatory note precedes all other entries
under the same word or words. In relation to other entries
in the catalog consider only the heading on a reference or
explanatory note; disregard the words see and see also, the
heading or headings referred to, and the note.

If a see reference is the same as an actual entry, arrange the see reference first, except that a surname entry
always precedes a reference.

Corea, Lois Fleming
COREA, see KOREA

File a see also reference before the first entry under
the same word or words.

CHILDREN, see also....
CHILDREN
CHILDREN--CARE AND HYGIENE, see also
CHILDREN--CARE AND HYGIENE
CHILDREN--CARE AND HYGIENE--BIBLIOGRAPHY

Subject Arrangement

Subject entries follow the same word used as a single surname.

Arrange entries with the same subject heading alphabetically by their main entries, then by title. Arrange subject analytics by the entry for the analytic if different from
the main entry for the whole book.

BISON, AMERICAN
Allen, Joel Asaph
The American bisons, living and extinct.

>BISON, AMERICAN
>Anderson, George S.
>Roosevelt, Theodore
>American big-game hunting

Arrange a subject, its subdivisions, etc., in groups as follows: 1) Subject without subdivision; 2) Period divisions, arranged chronologically; inclusive periods preceding subordinate periods; 3) Alphabetical extensions of the main subject heading: form, subject, and geographical subdivisions, inverted subject headings, subject followed by a parenthetical term, and phrase subject headings, interfiled word by word in one alphabet with titles and other headings beginning with the same word, disregarding punctuation.

>MASS (MUSIC)
>Mass of the Roman rite
>MASS (PHYSICS)
>MASS--STUDY AND TEACHING

>U.S.--HISTORY--REVOLUTION
>U.S.--HISTORY--1783-1865
>U.S.--HISTORY--1783-1809
>U.S.--HISTORY--WAR OF 1812
>U.S.--HISTORY--CIVIL WAR
>U.S.--HISTORY--BIBLIOGRAPHY
>U.S. history bonus book
>U.S.--HISTORY--SOURCES
>U.S.--IMMIGRATION AND EMIGRATION

Title Entry Arrangement

Title entries are arranged alphabetically, considering each word in turn; the initial article is disregarded, but all other articles and prepositions are to be regarded.

>In an unknown land.
>In and out of the old missions of California.
>In and under Mexico.
>In the Amazon jungle.
>In the days of the giants.
>In the days of the guilds.
>In this our life.
>In tidewater Virginia.
>
>Why Europe fights.
>Why I believe in religion.

Why the chimes rang.
Why the weather.

Translator See Author entry arrangement.

Umlaut

Disregard umlauts and other letter modifications.

Muellen, Abraham
Mullen, Allen
Müllen, Gustav
Mullen, Pat

United States See Place arrangement; Subject arrangement.

Words Spelled in Different Ways

When different entries, including corporate names, begin
with or contain the same word spelled in different ways (e. g.,
Color and Colour) choose one spelling, according to the cri-
teria below, file all entries under that spelling, and refer
from the other spellings.

Generally choose the most commonly accepted current
usage.

When there is a choice between the American and
English spellings, choose the American.

LABOR CONTRACT
Labor in America.
LABOR LAWS AND LEGISLATION
Labour production of the cotton textile industry.
Labor supply.

Words Written in Different Ways

Arrange hyphenated words as separate words when the parts
are complete words.

An epoch in life insurance

Epoch-making papers in United States history
The epoch of reform

Arrange as two words compound words that are written as two separate words. Arrange as one word compound words that are written as one.

In the case of compound words that appear in the catalog written both as two separate words and as a single word, interfile all entries, including corporate names, under the one-word form.

SEA-POWER
Sea power in the machine age
Seapower in the nuclear age
Sea-power in the Pacific
Search

References

1. James D. Anderson, "Catalog File Display," Cataloging & Classification Quarterly 1 (4, 1982): 3-23.
2. ALA Filing Rules. American Library Association, Filing Committee (Chicago: American Library Association, 1980).
3. ALA Rules for Filing Catalog Cards, prepared by the ALA Editorial Committee's Subcommittee on the ALA Rules for Filing Catalog Cards, Pauline A. Seely, Chairman and Editor. 2d ed. abr. (Chicago: American Library Association, 1968).

Chapter 13

RELATED TOPICS AND MISCELLANEOUS INFORMATION

For the librarian of the small library who has not yet found it feasible to participate in a centralized processing and cataloging center, there are a few closely related matters about which some information may be helpful. With a staff of one or possibly two, ordering, accessioning, classifying, cataloging, and preparing materials for circulation are so closely associated that they are thought of almost as one process. This chapter contains some practical hints regarding these processes.

Acquisition

Materials are usually selected by the librarian, but the order may be sent out by a clerk, principal, superintendent, or purchasing office. When the order and the bill are received, the bill is checked with the materials to be sure that the titles and editions received are those which were ordered. Some libraries write the name of the dealer from whom a book is purchased, the date it is received, and the cost in the inner margin of the book on the right-hand page following the title page, writing it parallel to the sewing of the book. This information is useful when one is examining a book with reference to having it rebound, or when checking a book's use over the period in which it has been available for circulation.

Weeding the Collection

Before beginning to classify and catalog an old library, weed the collection, removing material that is worn out, out of date, unsuitable for that particular library, or that has been superseded by a better title. In doing this it is well for the inexperienced librarian to seek the guidance of a trained and experienced librarian, or to check with the best printed se-

lection aids in the field represented in that library. Material that needs mending or rebinding should be put in good physical condition before being cataloged.

Mechanical Processes

After checking the bill for a new book, one should cut the pages when necessary and open the book correctly, i. e., take a few pages at the front and at the back alternately and press them down gently against the covers, until the middle of the book is reached. This makes it easier to open and read the book and minimizes the danger of breaking its back. Sound recordings should be examined to make sure they are not warped or otherwise damaged; filmstrips should be checked to see that they are in their proper containers, and so forth.

The next step is to put the mark of ownership on the item, either by stamping, embossing, or engraving, or--in the case of books--pasting a book plate inside the front cover. For audiovisual material, it is usually more feasible to attach labels to each item, although an electric stylus can be used to mark directly on surfaces not amenable to stamps or embossers.

Accessioning

To accession is to record materials added to the library in the order of acquisition. The accession number is a serial number given to an item as it is added to the library. The lines in an accession record book are numbered consecutively, beginning with one. A brief description of the item follows, and the number on this line is written in the book or on the media label, on the shelflist card, circulation card and pocket. Some libraries do not keep an accession book, but do assign accession numbers. They use a numbering machine and number each item as it is added to the library. The source, date of acquisition, and cost are the only information which the accession book gives that the shelf list ordinarily does not, hence these three items may be added to the shelf-list cards instead of keeping an accession book. Even the date may be omitted if a new series of numbers, prefixed by the year, is initiated each January or at the start of the library's fiscal year (e. g., 83-0001 could be the first book purchased in 1983, while 82-0912 might be the last acquired in 1982, automatically telling the library how many volumes it had purchased in that year).

An accession number is useful in identifying books; e.g., number 1312 means a particular book, even a certain copy or volume. The accession number shows the number of books which have been added to the library, either within a given period or the total number, keeping in mind that some books have been withdrawn from the library. A count of the shelf-list cards before filing, however, enables the librarian to keep any necessary record of the number of titles or individual items added to the library, without the duplication of records involved in keeping an accession book. These statistics usually appear in the monthly or annual reports. Even if the library has always kept an accession record, it may be discontinued at any given date and the accession numbers on older materials ignored or replaced by copy numbers. The two reasons most commonly given for keeping an accession record book are: 1) that a card, i.e., a shelf-list card, may be more easily lost than a book; and 2) that if the library received books from different funds, the accession book is a convenient record of this. Most libraries have abandoned the accession book--and many the accession number as well --feeling that copy numbers are sufficient identification. Before abandoning the accession book, however, it is wise to check its possible requirement by law or established policy.

If an accession record is to be used, the following information is entered under the proper column heading: 1) the date of the bill for the item, or, if there is no bill, the date on which it is being accessioned; 2) the author heading as found on the title page; 3) brief title; 4) the publisher in abbreviated form; 5) date of publication, or copyright if there is no publication date; 6) volume number; 7) the name of the dealer through whom the material was purchased; and 8) the cost to the library. These are the essential items for an accession record. Follow the rules for cataloging in giving the title, capitalizing, etc. If the item is a gift, give the donor's name instead of the dealer's, and enter the word "gift" in the cost column. Use ditto marks where information for successive titles is the same. Give the date of accessioning (month, day, and year) on the top line of each page of the accession book. If a page is not filled during one day, give the new date on the line for the first entry for that day.

The accession number is written in each volume or copy on the first right-hand page after the title page, in the center of the lower margin about one inch from the bottom, or as nearly in this place as possible considering the printing on the page. The accession number should also be written

on one other page, e.g., the page which is stamped with the name of the library. Audiovisual materials which are accessioned must also be marked with the assigned number in such a way that it will neither damage the item nor be in danger of being obliterated. By means of the accession number one can turn at once to the description of the material in the accession record.

Libraries using automated circulation systems usually affix a duplicate of the bar code label to the shelf list. The bar code number becomes a substitute for the accession number.

Cataloging Routine

The first step in the cataloging process is to order the cards if printed cards are used, a step which should coincide with the ordering of the material itself whenever possible. If printed cards are not used, the first step is to classify and assign subject headings. As soon as the classification number is determined, it should be written in pencil on the page following the title page, about one inch from the top of the page and one inch from the hinge of the book. If the number is too close to the top or the hinge, it may be cut off when the book is rebound. Most nonprint materials can be marked with an engraver or permanent marking pen, although some require labels. All pieces in a set should be marked insofar as possible.

The next step is to decide on the form of the heading for the main entry and for other added entries besides subject entries. Check with the name authority file or the catalog to insure consistency in headings and search aids if the name is new to the catalog and there is no CIP data or printed card. If Cutter numbers or author letters are used, they are assigned as soon as the heading for the main entry is determined. The book number is written below the classification number. If there are printed cards, they are checked with the item to be sure that they match; if there are no printed cards, the cataloger prepares a slip from which the cards will be typed.

The third step is to type the main entry card, including the tracing for the added cards; or to add the headings and call number and make any changes which may be necessary on the printed cards. If there are no printed cards,

the added entry cards and shelf-list card are typed or otherwise reproduced and revised. Duplicating machines for making the required additional cards from the unit card save time,
but may be expensive for the small library. If the library
cannot afford a duplicating machine for its exclusive use, possibly it can use one belonging to another department of the
locality or organization which it serves. When cards are
typed, each card has to be revised for accuracy, but mechanically reproduced cards are exactly like the master card
or copy. Consult your state library or state department of
education regarding duplicating machines or commercial card
reproduction centers which may be able to reproduce your
catalog cards correctly, quickly, and less expensively than
you could have them typed in your library. The small library as well as the large library should constantly be on
the alert for new technological methods. As prices of microcomputers and typewriters with memory drop, even very
small libraries may find them to be cost-effective.

    The circulation card and pocket are made at the same
time as the catalog and shelf-list cards. The circulation
card should have the call number in the upper left-hand corner; the accession number, if one is used, in the upper right-
hand corner; the surname of the author or full heading, if a
corporate author, on the line below the call number; and the
title below that. Indent the first letter of the title to the
third space to the right, to make both author and title more
prominent.

    If the library uses an automated circulation system,
a circulation card is not needed, although a pocket for the
date due slip is still desirable.

    When an added copy is acquired by the library, it is
necessary only to remove the shelf-list card from the tray,
add the accession or copy number (and source, date, and
cost of the new copy, if required), or bar code, and refile
the card, since no change is made on the catalog cards. On
the other hand, when another volume is added to the library,
notation of the new volume must be added to the catalog cards
as well as to the shelf-list card. When a new edition is added,
it is necessary to catalog it as a new book, except that as a
rule the same classification number and the same subject
headings will be used.

    After each new order is cataloged, or periodically in
a library buying continuously, the catalog and shelf-list cards

should be sorted, the latter counted and totals recorded. They
are then filed above the rod in the public and shelf-list card
catalogs respectively, the filing is revised, the rod pulled
out, and the cards dropped and locked in the trays.

Marking the spines of books. Call numbers should
appear on the backs of books of nonfiction for greater convenience in locating a given book or returning it to the shelf.
If the library participates in the service of a centralized
processing center, the books may come with the call numbers already on the spines, or labels may be provided for
the library to apply to each book. Otherwise the library
should adopt a simple, inexpensive system for marking books
on the spine.

The call number should be placed at the same distance
from the bottom of all books for the sake of ease in locating
books and the appearance of the shelves. A stiff card with
this distance marked on it should be used as a guide. One
and a half inches from the bottom of the book usually avoids
any printing and is a convenient height.

The most efficient method is to type the call numbers
for a group of books at one time on sheets of self-adhesive
labels, using the largest type face available. The labels are
then peeled from the backing sheet and attached to the book
jackets at the appropriate height, before the jackets are covered with their clear plastic protective covers. When labels
are attached directly to the spine, they should be sprayed
with a clear lacquer or covered with strong transparent tape
to prolong their life. The process of marking uncovered
books by hand is an alternative which may be preferred by
some, and may be outlined as follows:

1. Mark the place to be occupied by the call number,
   noting the exact place where each line begins if
   the call number consists of two lines.
2. Remove the sizing by painting over the spot with
   acetone or book lacquer.
3. Write the call number in white ink or with an
   electric stylus and transfer paper at the place
   marked. For light colored books use black ink
   or dark transfer paper.
4. Cover the lettering with a thin coat of book lacquer. Some libraries prefer to cover the entire
   book with lacquer as it also serves as an insec-
   ticide.

Make the figures of the call number vertical and round rather than angular, so that they may be easily read and so that there may be less variation when the lettering is done by different workers.

Typed self-adhesive labels should be used for nonprint materials whenever possible. Labels in shapes appropriate for audiodiscs, cassettes, filmstrips, etc. are available from library supply houses.

Check list for local, non-automated preparation:

Clerical assistant:
1. Check items received with bill.
2. Write in each book the name of the dealer, date received, and cost. (This step may be omitted.)
3. Cut pages.
4. Open correctly.
5. Stamp with mark of ownership unless book plate is used.
6. Accession. (This process may be omitted.)
7. Order printed cards, if they have not already been ordered.

Librarian:
8. Classify and assign subject headings, making note of them on a slip. If printed cards are available, compare suggested classification number and headings with the shelf list and the library's official classification schedule and list of subject headings.
9. Decide upon the added entries other than subject heading.
10. Determine heading for author and such added entries as editor, translator, illustrator. If printed cards are used, compare forms of names with those in the catalog or name authority file.
11. Note adaptations to be made on printed cards or prepare main entry card copy.

Clerical assistant:
12. Type cards, label, circulation card and pocket.

Librarian:	13.	Revise typed cards, label, etc.
Clerical assistant:	14.	Paste in pocket, date slip, and book plate, if used.
	15.	Attach label or mark spine, cover jacket, insert card in pocket, put out for use.
	16.	Sort cards and count for statistics.
	17.	File cards in shelf-list and catalog trays above rod.
Librarian:	18.	Revise filing and lock cards in trays

Withdrawals

When an item is added to the library it is noted in various records; when it is withdrawn or discarded from the library, those records must be changed. When a book wears out and is to be replaced by a new copy, a note is made on the shelf-list card that the particular copy has been withdrawn, and the addition of the new copy is noted. Since the cards in the public catalog do not show how many copies of a given title are in a library, withdrawing a book does not affect the catalog so long as other copies remain. If, however, there is only one copy of the book and it is not to be replaced, the catalog cards must be taken out of the catalog, and the shelf-list card must also be removed from the shelf list, after having the withdrawl note, the abbreviation "W" and the date, written on it; e.g., W 5-17-80. Some libraries give the cause; e.g., W 5-17-80 Worn out. If one wishes to make a study of the number of books being lost by borrowers, worn out, etc., with reference to a possible change in policy, it is worthwhile noting the cause of withdrawal. This note may be made only as long as it is needed to show the chief cause or causes of withdrawals. It is unnecessary to continue this additional information indefinitely. Instead of using "W" one can draw a line through the accession or copy number to show that a book has been withdrawn.

If a volume of a set is being withdrawn, note should be made, usually in pencil, on the catalog card that the particular volume is lacking. If it is to be replaced as soon as it can be secured, this penciled note can be easily erased when the new copy of the missing volume is added to the library.

Occasionally it will happen that the book being withdrawn is the only one entered under that name, under that
subject, etc. If that is the case, not only should the catalog
cards and the shelf-list card be removed, but the name or
subject cross references to and from these headings and the
corresponding cards in the name and subject authority files
should be withdrawn. If a book is to be replaced as soon as
funds are available or if it is lost but there is the possibility
of its being found, the cards may be withdrawn from the files,
properly labeled, and put aside to be used later.

If there are more copies or volumes in the library,
after making the proper withdrawal note on the shelf-list
card, refile the card in the shelf list.

If the book withdrawn is the only copy or volume, the
shelf-list card for that book, with the withdrawal note on it,
may be filed alphabetically by author in a special file called
a withdrawal file. This file can be a great convenience when
some question comes up as to what has become of a book,
whether or not the library ever had a copy, etc. The cards
do not need to be kept indefinitely, but might well be kept
for several years.

A count of books withdrawn should be made, just as
the count of books added is made. The inventory should show
the number of books in the library at the beginning of the
year for which the report is being made, the number added
during that period, the number withdrawn, and the number
in the library at the end of the year.

All library marks of ownership should be removed or
"Withdrawn by--(name of library)" should be written or stamped
in the book before selling it for old paper or giving it away.
Some libraries are governed by definite laws affecting dis-
posal of books. The first time that a book is withdrawn,
the policy should be carefully worked out, note made of the
procedure to be followed, and a withdrawal file set up.

Where to Catalog

The smallest library should have a place in which to catalog,
even though it is only a desk or a table in a corner. Have
shelves nearby on which the necessary cataloging tools and
aids and the books to be cataloged may be kept. Label these
shelves, so that it will be possible to tell at a glance what

stage of preparation the books are in. Leave any unfinished
work clearly marked so that it may be resumed with a minimum loss of time. A quarter of an hour or half an hour may
be used advantageously to mark ten books on the back, to
order printed cards, or the like. The longer periods may be
used for determining the form of the author's name, classifying and assigning subject headings, or typing the main cards.
The added cards can be typed by any good typist who is given
adequate instruction and supervision at first.

Cataloging Supplies

A few suggestions as to the supplies which will be found necessary in cataloging a collection as described in this manual
may prove useful.

Accession record book. Any of the simplified accession record books which are sold by library supply houses
will be found satisfactory. A loose-leaf accession book,
which may be used on a typewriter, is preferable. Accession books are listed according to the number of lines they
contain. As each volume in the library requires one line,
the number of lines desired depends upon the number of volumes on hand and the approximate number that will be added
in the next two or three years.

Catalog cards. Cards of the same quality may be
used for the shelf list and for the catalog. Medium-weight
cards are best as they are strong enough to stand the wear,
without taking up unnecessary room or adding unnecessary
weight to the card cabinets. The medium weight is similar
to that of the printed cards, and for that reason is much
more satisfactory if the library uses printed cards in addition
to its own. It pays to buy the best catalog cards, and it is
important to use only one kind so that all the cards in the
catalog will be of the same size and thickness and, therefore,
can be handled more quickly in the trays. For fiction, at
least three cards for each book, namely, author, title, and
shelf list, will be necessary. For nonfiction, if many analytical entries are made, an average of five cards for each
book is the minimum number to count on. Catalog cards
come in boxes of 500 or 1,000 and cost less if bought in
these or larger quantities.

Catalog guide cards. Guide cards should be inserted
at intervals of about one inch. Satisfactory plain buff guide

cards, punched for a catalog tray rod, cut in thirds or halves (i. e. , the tab is one-third or one-half the width of the cards) may be purchased in packages of one hundred, five hundred, or one thousand. These cards are available either plain, with labels for typing headings, or printed with headings suitable for various types of libraries.

Sets of shelf-list guide cards for libraries using the Dewey Decimal Classification may also be purchased.

Miscellaneous supplies. If extension cards for the catalog are to be tied to the first card, use heavy linen thread, which may be purchased at any department store.

The special supplies needed for marking call numbers on the spine of books are an electric pencil or an electric stylus and transfer paper, which may be ordered from a library supplier. Transfer paper comes in white, black or dark blue, white for dark colored books, dark for light colored books. A bottle of acetone is needed to remove the sizing from the back of the book before applying the ink; and a bottle of book lacquer to put over the ink when it is dry. Any good pen point, the type depending upon the choice of the person doing the lettering, is satisfactory. Usually a bowl pointed pen is preferred.

A good steel eraser or a razor blade with a bar top with which to erase words, or more especially letters, is a necessity. A good bar pencil and ink eraser is also very useful. Liquid typewriter eraser and Ko-rec-type should also be on hand.

A typewriter is a necessity in any library for the typing of cards, orders, etc. An electric typewriter which has, in addition to a regular platen, a removable platen with a steel grip for holding cards in position is recommended. If possible, invest in the kind of machine which allows the use of different type sizes by changing the element, for while elite type is best for typing cards, the largest possible type size should be used for typing spine labels.

Card catalog cabinets. Although there are many firms making card catalog cabinets, it pays to get the best. Cabinets come in varying sizes from one to sixty trays, and supplier catalogs give an estimate of the number of cards which the cabinets of different sizes will hold. Knowing the number of books in the library and the approximate number of new

books added each year, one can easily determine the size of cabinet needed by counting five cards to a book.

Card catalog cabinets should have standard trays and should be purchased from the same firm so that they will match exactly and so that the trays will be interchangeable when cards are shifted with the expansion of the catalog. Each tray should have a follower-block to hold the cards erect when the tray is only partially filled, and a rod which runs through the holes in the cards and locks them into the tray. It is also very important to have the cards fit the tray exactly so that they will stand straight, drop in easily, and remain in alignment for the rod. Catalog trays should be only two-thirds full if the cards are to be consulted easily.

If the library can afford it, the sectional cabinet is best, as added units are less expensive than the same number of trays in a separate cabinet and the sections fit together and form one cabinet. If as many as eight or nine trays are needed or will be needed relatively soon, it will pay to buy the sectional cabinet, which may be bought in units of five, ten, or fifteen trays. The same base and top will serve for several units.

Automated Systems for Small Libraries

Since the last edition of this book, relatively inexpensive microcomputers have been acquired by many small libraries, and software designed specifically for library applications has been developed at an accelerating rate. It is now perfectly possible for a very small library to maintain an online catalog.[1] While the microcomputer may not yet support online catalogs in a cost effective manner for any but the smallest collections, it can support a number of related operations. Labor and time can be saved in producing catalog cards; book catalogs; serials, audiovisual, and other holdings lists; etc. Indexing of local newspapers, maintenance of subject authority lists for picture files (or other special files), and similar chores can be performed quickly and easily with the aid of a microcomputer.

Most importantly, the microcomputer gives small libraries a local mechanism for preparing input to a larger system for conversion of their holdings records into machine-readable form, which enables them to participate in shared automated systems. The value of membership in an online

cooperative system is enormous, as it gives the user of the smallest participating library access to the joint holdings of all the member libraries.

Reference

1. Betty Costa, "Microcomputer in Colorado--It's Elementary!" Wilson Library Bulletin 55 (May 1981): 676-678, 717.

Most of the following abbreviations are selected from Appendix B of AACR2. Remember that abbreviations should not be substituted for fully spelled out words in the title and statement of responsibility area.

analytic, -s	anal., -s
and all	et al.
approximately	approx.
arranged	arr.
augmented	augm.
black and white	b&w
book	bk.
born	b.
Brother, -s	Bro., -s[1]
bulletin	bull.
centimeter, -s	cm.
circa	ca.
color, colored	col.
Company	Co.
compare	cf.
compiler	comp.[2]
copyright	c
Corporation	Corp.
corrected	corr.
Department	Dept.
diameter	diam.
died	d.
edition. -s	ed.
editor	ed.[2]
enlarged	enl.
et alii	et al.
et cetera	etc.
frame, -s	fr.
frames per second	fps
government	govt.
Government Printing Office	G.P.O.
Her (His) Majesty's Stationery Office	H.M.S.O.
illustration, -s	ill.
illustrator	ill. [2]
inch, -s	in.

inches per second	ips
Incorporated	Inc.[1]
International Standard Bib- liographic Description	ISBD
International Standard Book Number	ISBN
International Standard Serial Number	ISSN
introduction	intro.
Limited	Ltd.[1]
millimeter, -s	mm.
minute, -s	min.
miscellaneous	misc.
monophonic	mono.
no name (of publisher)	s. n.
no place (of publication)	s. l.
number, -s	no.
numbered	numb.
opus	op.
page, -s	p.
part, -s	pt., pts.
photograph, -s	photo., photos.
portrait, -s	port., ports.
preface	pref.
privately printed	priv. print.
pseudonym	pseud.
publishing	pub.
quadraphonic	quad.
reprint	repr.
reproduced	reprod.
revised	rev.
revolutions per minute	rpm
second, -s	sec.
series	ser.
silent	si.
sine loco	s. l.
sine nomine	s. n.
sound	sd.
stereophonic	stereo.
Superintendent of Documents	Supt. of Docs.
supplement	suppl.
title page	t. p.
translator	tr.
volume, -s	v., vol.,[3] vols.,[3]

Geographical names. AACR2 provides a list of abbreviations for place names which may be used as additions to other place names in order to distinguish between those with the same names; as additions to names of corporate bodies, when necessary for identification; as additions to the place of publication or distribution; and in notes. Names not on the list may not be abbreviated.

Term	Abbreviation	Term	Abbreviation
Alabama	Ala.	North Dakota	N. D.
Alberta	Alta.	Northern Terri-	
Arizona	Ariz.	tory	N. T.
Arkansas	Ark.	Northwest Terri-	
Australian Capital		tories	N. W. T.
Territory	A. C. T.	Nova Scotia	N. S.
British Columbia	B. C.	Oklahoma	Okla.
California	Calif.	Ontario	Ont.
Colorado	Colo.	Oregon	Or.
Connecticut	Conn.	Pennsylvania	Pa.
Delaware	Del.	Prince Edward	
District of Co-		Island	P. E. I.
lumbia	D. C.	Puerto Rico	P. R.
Distrito Federal	D. F.	Queensland	Qld.
Florida	Fla.	Rhode Island	R. I.
Georgia	Ga.	Russian Soviet	
Illinois	Ill.	Federated So-	
Indiana	Ind.	cialist Republic	R. S. F. S. R.
Kansas	Kan.	Saskatchewan	Sask.
Kentucky	Ky.	South Australia	S. Aust.
Louisiana	La.	South Carolina	S. C.
Maine	Me.	South Dakota	S. D.
Manitoba	Man.	Tasmania	Tas.
Maryland	Md.	Tennessee	Tenn.
Massachusetts	Mass.	Territory of	
Michigan	Mich.	Hawaii	T. H.
Minnesota	Minn.	Texas	Tex.
Mississippi	Miss.	Union of Soviet	
Missouri	Mo.	Socialist Re-	
Montana	Mont.	publics	U. S. S. R.
Nebraska	Neb.	United Kingdom	U. K.
Nevada	Nev.	United States	U. S.
New Brunswick	N. B.	Vermont	Vt.
New Hampshire	N. H.	Victoria	Vic.
New Jersey	N. J.	Virgin Islands	V. I.
New Mexico	N. M.	Virginia	Va.
New South Wales	N. S. W.	Washington	Wash.
New York	N. Y.	West Virginia	W. Va.
New Zealand	N. Z.	Western Australia	W. A.
Newfoundland	Nfld.	Wisconsin	Wis.
North Carolina	N. C.	Wyoming	Wyo.
		Yukon Territory	Yukon

Publishers. AACR2 rule 1. 4D2 says to give the name of the publisher in the shortest form in which it can be understood and identified internationally. The list below is a selection of publishers, showing both full names and suggested abbreviations.

Abingdon Press	Abingdon
American Book Company	Am. Bk.
American Library Association	A. L. A.

Appleton-Century-Crofts	Appleton
A. S. Barnes & Company	A. S. Barnes
Bobbs-Merrill Company, Inc.	Bobbs
R. R. Bowker Company	Bowker
The British Book Centre, Inc.	British Bk. Centre
Coward, McCann & Geoghegan	Coward-McCann
Thomas Y. Crowell Company	Crowell
Crown Publishers	Crown
The John Day Company	Day
Dodd, Mead & Company, Inc.	Dodd
Doubleday & Company, Inc.	Doubleday
E. P. Dutton & Company, Inc.	Dutton
Farrar, Straus & Giroux, Inc.	Farrar, Straus
Funk & Wagnalls Company, Inc.	Funk
Ginn & Co.	Ginn
Grosset & Dunlap, Inc.	Grosset
Hammond, Inc.	Hammond
Harcourt, Brace, Jovanovich	Harcourt
Harper & Row, Publishers	Harper
D. C. Heath & Company	Heath
Holt, Rinehart, & Winston, Inc.	Holt
Houghton Mifflin Company	Houghton
Alfred A. Knopf, Inc.	Knopf
J. B. Lippincott Company	Lippincott
Little, Brown & Company	Little
Lothrop, Lee & Shepard Company, Inc.	Lothrop
McGraw-Hill Book Company, Inc.	McGraw-Hill
The Macmillan Publishing Company, Inc.	Macmillan
G. & C. Merriam Company	Merriam
William Morrow & Company, Inc., Publishers	Morrow
Thomas Nelson, Inc.	Nelson
W. W. Norton & Company, Inc., Publishers	Norton
Prentice-Hall, Inc.	Prentice-Hall
G. P. Putnam's Sons, Inc.	Putnam
Rand McNally & Company	Rand McNally
Random House, Inc.	Random House
The Scarecrow Press, Inc.	Scarecrow
Scott, Foresman & Company	Scott
Charles Scribner's Sons	Scribner
Simon and Schuster, Inc., Publishers	Simon & Schuster
Superintendent of Documents, Government Printing Office	Supt. of Docs.
Van Nostrand Reinhold Company	Van Nostrand
The Viking Press, Inc.	Viking
Albert Whitman & Company	A. Whitman
John Wiley & Sons, Inc.	Wiley
The H. W. Wilson Company	H. W. Wilson
The World Publishing Company	World Pub.

References

1. Use only in names of firms and other corporate bodies.
2. Use only in a heading as a designation of function.
3. Use at the beginning of a statement and before a roman numeral.

Appendix B

<u>DEFINITIONS OF TECHNICAL TERMS</u>
Revised by Elizabeth G. Mikita

The definitions given below are based on the sources listed in "References" at the end of this appendix; in the main, they are drawn from the <u>A. L. A. Glossary</u> and AACR2. Definitions of audiovisual materials are incorporated in Chapter 9.

ACCESS POINT. A name, term, code, etc., under which a bibliographic record may be searched and identified. <u>See also</u> HEADING

ACCESSION. To record books and other similar material added to a library in the order of acquisition.

ACCESSION NUMBER. The number given to a volume in the order of its acquisition.

ACCESSION RECORD. The business record of books, etc., added to a library in the order of receipt, giving a condensed description of the book and the essential facts in its library history.

ADAPTATION. A rewritten form of a literary work modified for a purpose or use other than that for which the original work was intended, e. g., <u>Lamb's Tales from Shakespeare</u>.

ADDED ENTRY. An entry, additional to the main entry, by which an item is represented in a catalog; a secondary entry. <u>See also</u> MAIN ENTRY.

ADDED TITLE PAGE. A title page preceding or following the title page chosen as the basis for the description of the item. It may be more general, as a series title page, or equally general, as a title page in another language.

ALTERNATIVE TITLE. The second part of a title proper that consists of two parts, each of which is a title; the parts are joined by the word <u>or</u> (or its equivalent in another language), e. g., <u>The tempest, or, The enchanted island.</u>

ANALYTICAL ENTRY. An entry for a work or part of a work that

is contained in a collection, series, issue of a serial, or other bibliographical unit for which another, comprehensive entry has been made. An analytical entry may be under the author, subject or title for a part of a work or of some article contained in a collection (volume of essays, serial, etc.) including a reference to the publication which contains the article or work entered.

ANONYMOUS. Of unknown authorship.

ANONYMOUS CLASSIC. A work of unknown or doubtful authorship, commonly designated by title, which may have appeared in the course of time in many editions, versions, and/or translations.

AREA. A major section of the bibliographic description, comprising data of a particular category or set of categories.

AUTHOR ANALYTICAL ENTRY see ANALYTICAL ENTRY.

AUTHOR ENTRY. An entry of a work in a catalog under its author's name as heading, whether this be a main or an added heading. The author heading may consist of a personal or a corporate name or some substitute for it, e.g., initials, pseudonym, etc.

AUTHOR NUMBER see BOOK NUMBER

AUTHORITY LIST OR FILE. An official list of forms selected as headings in a catalog, giving for author and corporate names and for the forms of entry of anonymous classics the sources used for establishing the forms, together with the variant forms. If the list is a name list, it is sometimes called Name list and Name file.

BIBLIOGRAPHIC RECORD. A catalog entry in card, microtext, machine-readable, or other form carrying full cataloging information for a given item in a library.

BODY OF THE ENTRY. That portion of a catalog record that begins with the title and ends with the publication, distribution, etc. area.

BOOK NUMBER. A combination of letters and figures used to arrange books in the same classification number in alphabetical order.

CALL NUMBER. The combination of a location symbol and/or a media code, the classification number, and the book number (if used) which determines the position of an item on the shelves. See also BOOK NUMBER; LOCATION MARK.

CARD CATALOG. A catalog made on separate cards and kept in trays.

CATALOG. 1. A list of library materials contained in a collection, a library, or a group of libraries, arranged according to some definite plan. 2. In a wider sense, a list of materials prepared for a particular purpose, e.g., an exhibition catalog, a sales catalog.

CATCHWORD TITLE ENTRY see PARTIAL TITLE ENTRY.

CHIEF SOURCE OF INFORMATION. The source of bibliographic data to be given first preference as the source from which a bibliographic description (or portion thereof) is prepared. For example, the title page is the chief source of information for books.

CLASSIFICATION. "The putting together of like things." Book classification, as defined by C. A. Cutter, is "the grouping of books written on the same or similar subjects."

COLLATION see PHYSICAL DESCRIPTION AREA.

COLLECTION. If by one author: Three or more independent works or parts of works published together; if by more than one author: two or more independent works or parts of works published together and not written for the same occasion or for the publication in hand.

COMPILER. One who produces a collection by selecting and putting together matter from the works of various persons or bodies. Also, one who selects and puts together in one publication matter from the works of one person or body. (Cf. EDITOR)

COMPOSITE WORK. An original work consisting of separate and distinct parts, by different authors, which constitute together an integral whole.

COMPOUND SURNAME. A surname consisting of two or more proper names, often connected by a hyphen, conjunction, or preposition.

CONTENTS NOTE. A note in a catalog or a bibliography entry that lists the contents of a work.

CONTINUATION. 1. A supplement (q.v.). 2. A part issued in continuance of a monograph, a serial, or a series.

CONTINUATION CARD see EXTENSION CARD.

CONVENTIONAL TITLE see UNIFORM TITLE.

COPYRIGHT DATE. The date of copyright as given in the book, as a rule on the back of the title leaf.

CORPORATE BODY. An organization or group of persons that is

identified by a particular name and that acts, or may act, as an entity. Typical examples of corporate bodies are associations, institutions, business firms, nonprofit enterprises, governments, government agencies, religious bodies, local churches, and conferences.

COVER TITLE. A title printed on the original cover of an item. See also SPINE TITLE.

CROSS REFERENCE see REFERENCE; "SEE ALSO" REFERENCE; "SEE" REFERENCE.

CUTTER NUMBER see BOOK NUMBER.

DICTIONARY CATALOG. A catalog in which all the entries (author, title, subject, series, etc.) and their related references are arranged together in one general alphabet. The subarrangement frequently varies from the strictly alphabetical.

DISCARD. A book officially withdrawn from a library collection because it is unfit for further use or is no longer needed.

EDITION. 1. In the case of books and booklike materials, all those copies of an item produced from substantially the same type image, whether by direct contact or by photographic methods. 2. In the case of nonbook materials, all the copies of an item produced from one master copy and issued by a particular publishing agency or a group of such agencies. Provided the foregoing conditions are fulfilled, a change of identity of the distributing body or bodies does not constitute a change of edition. See also FACSIMILE REPRODUCTION, REPRINT.

EDITOR. One who prepares for publication an item not his own. The editorial labor may be limited to the preparation of the item for the manufacturer, or it may include supervision of the manufacturing, revision (restitution) or elucidation of the text, and the addition of an introduction, notes, and other critical matter. For certain works it may involve the technical direction of a staff of persons engaged in writing or compiling the text. (Cf. COMPILER.)

ELEMENT. A word, phrase, or group of characters representing a distinct unit of bibliographic information and forming part of an area (q.v.) of the description.

ENTRY. A record of an item in a catalog. See also HEADING.

ENTRY WORD. The word by which the entry is arranged in the catalog, usually the first word (other than an article) of the heading. (Cf. HEADING.)

EXTENSION CARD. A catalog card that continues an entry from a preceding card. Sometimes known as Continuation card [or Second card].

FACSIMILE REPRODUCTION. A reproduction that has as its chief purpose to simulate the physical appearance of the original work as well as to provide an exact replica of the text.

FILING TITLE see UNIFORM TITLE.

"FIRST" INDENTION. The distance from the left edge of a catalog card at which, according to predetermined rules, the author heading begins; also called Author indention.

FORM DIVISION see STANDARD SUBDIVISION.

FORM HEADING. A heading used for a form entry in a catalog, e. g. , Encyclopedias and dictionaries, Periodicals, Short stories. Sometimes known as Form Subject Heading.

GUIDE CARD. A labeled card with a noticeable projection that distinguishes it from other catalog cards. It is inserted in a card catalog to help the user find a desired place or heading in the catalog

HALF TITLE. A brief title of a publication appearing on a leaf preceding the title page.

HANGING INDENTION. The form of indention used when the main entry is under title. The title begins at the first indention while all following lines of the body of the record begin at the second indention.

HEADING. A name, word, or phrase placed at the head of a catalog entry to provide an access point in the catalog.

HOLDINGS. 1. The books, periodicals, and other material in the possession of a library. 2. Specifically, the volumes or parts of a serial in the possession of a library.

ILLUSTRATION. A pictorial or other representation in or belonging to a book or other publication, as issued; usually designed to elucidate the text. In the narrow sense the term stands for illustrations within the text (i. e. , those which form part of the text page).

IMPRINT see PUBLICATION, DISTRIBUTION, ETC. AREA.

IMPRINT DATE. The year of publication or printing as specified on the title page.

INDENTION. The distance from the left edge of a catalog card at which, according to predetermined rules, the various parts of the description and their subsequent lines begin.

INTRODUCTION DATE. The date of a book as given at the beginning or at the end of the introduction.

ISBD. International Standard Bibliographic Description, an internationally accepted format for the representation of descriptive information in bibliographic records.

ISBN. International Standard Book Number, a distinctive and unique number assigned to a book.

ISSN. International Standard Serial Number, a distinctive number assigned to each serial title.

JOINT AUTHOR. A person who collaborates with one or more other persons to produce a work in relation to which the collaborators perform the same function.

LOCATION MARK. A letter, word, group of words, or some distinguishing character added to catalog records, often in conjunction with the call number, to indicate that a book is shelved in a certain place, as in a special collection. Also called Location symbol. See also CALL NUMBER.

MAIN ENTRY. The complete catalog record of an item, presented in the form by which the entity is to be uniformly identified and cited. The main entry may include the tracings of all other headings under which the record is to be represented in the catalog. See also ADDED ENTRY; UNIT RECORD.

MONOGRAPH. A nonserial item, i.e., an item either complete in one part or complete, or intended to be completed, in a finite number of separate parts.

MONOGRAPHIC SERIES see SERIES 1.

NAME AUTHORITY FILE see AUTHORITY LIST OR FILE.

NAME-TITLE ADDED ENTRY. An added entry consisting of the name of a person or corporate body and the title of an item.

NOTATION. A system of symbols, generally letters and figures, used separately or in combination, to represent the division of a classification scheme.

OPEN ENTRY. A catalog entry which provides for the addition of information concerning a work of which the library does not have a complete set, or about which complete information is lacking.

OTHER TITLE INFORMATION. Any title borne by an item other than the title proper or parallel titles; also any phrase appearing in conjunction with the title proper, parallel titles, or other titles, indicative of the character, contents, etc., of its production or publication. The term includes subtitles, avant-titres, etc., but does not include variations on the title proper (e.g., spine titles, sleeve titles, etc.)

PARALLEL TITLE. The title proper in another language or in another script.

PARTIAL TITLE ENTRY. An added entry made for a secondary part of the title as given on the title page, e. g. , a catchword title, subtitle, or alternative title.

PERIODICAL. A serial appearing or intended to appear indefinitely at regular or stated intervals, generally more frequently than annually, each issue of which normally contains separate articles, stories, or other writings. Newspapers disseminating general news, and the proceedings, papers, or other publications of corporate bodies primarily related to their meetings are not included in this term.

PHYSICAL DESCRIPTION AREA. The section of a catalog entry that includes the extent of an item, dimensions, and other physical details. Also called the collation.

PLATE. A leaf containing illustrative matter, with or without explanatory text, that does not form part of either the preliminary or the main sequences of pages or leaves.

PREFACE DATE. The date given at the beginning or end of the preface.

PRELIMINARIES. The title page or title pages of an item together with the verso of each title page, any pages preceding the title page(s), and the cover.

PSEUDONYM. A name assumed by an author to conceal or obscure his identity.

PUBLICATION, DISTRIBUTION, ETC. AREA. The area of a bibliographic record which contains: place of publication, distribution, etc. ; name of publisher, distributor, etc. ; date of publication, distribution, etc. ; and sometimes place of manufacture, name of manufacturer, and date of manufacture. Previously called the imprint.

PUBLISHER. The person, firm, or corporate body undertaking the responsibility for the issue of a book or other printed matter to the public.

REFERENCE. A direction from one heading or entry to another.

REPRINT. 1. A new printing of an item made from the original type image, commonly by photographic methods. The printing may reproduce the original exactly, or it may contain slight variations. 2. A new edition with substantially unchanged text. See also FACSIMILE REPRODUCTION.

SECOND CARD see EXTENSION CARD.

"SECOND" INDENTION. The distance from the left edge of a catalog card at which, according to predetermined rules, the title normally begins; also called Title indention and Paragraph indention.

SECONDARY ENTRY see ADDED ENTRY.

"SEE ALSO" REFERENCE. A direction in a catalog from a term or name under which entries are listed to another term or name under which additional or allied information may be found.

"SEE" REFERENCE. A direction in a catalog from a term or name under which no entries are listed to a term or name under which entries are listed.

SEQUEL. A literary or other imaginative work that is complete in itself but continues an earlier work.

SERIAL. A publication in any medium issued in successive parts bearing numerical or chronological designations and intended to be continued indefinitely. Serials include periodicals; newspapers; annuals (reports, yearbooks, etc.); the journals, memoirs, proceedings, transactions, etc., of societies; and numbered monographic series. See also SERIES 1, PERIODICAL

SERIES. 1. A group of separate items related to one another by the fact that each item bears, in addition to its own title proper, a collective title applying to the group as a whole. The individual items may or may not be numbered. 2. Each of two or more volumes of essays, lectures, articles, or other writings, similar in character and issued in sequence, e. g., Lowell's Among my books, second series. 3. A separately numbered sequence of volumes within a series or serial, e. g., Notes and queries, 1st series, 2nd series, etc.

SERIES ENTRY. In a catalog, an entry, usually brief, of the several works in the library which belong to a series under the name of the series as a heading.

SERIES NOTE. In a catalog or a bibliography, a note stating the name of a series to which a book belongs. The series note ordinarily follows the physical description area.

SHELF LIST. A record of the materials in a library arranged in the order in which they stand on the shelves.

SPINE. That part of the cover or binding which conceals the sewed or bound edge of a book, usually bearing the title, and frequently the author.

SPINE TITLE. The title that appears on the spine of an item. It may differ from the title appearing on the title page of the item.

STANDARD SUBDIVISION. Divisions used in Dewey Decimal Classification that apply to the form a work takes. Form may be physical (as in a periodical or dictionary) or it may be philosophical (such as a philosophy or history of a subject). Formerly called form divisions.

STATEMENT OF RESPONSIBILITY. A statement, transcribed from the item being described, relating to persons responsible for the intellectual or artistic content of the item, to corporate bodies from which the content emanates, or to persons or corporate bodies responsible for the performance of the content of the item.

SUBJECT ANALYTICAL ENTRY see ANALYTICAL ENTRY.

SUBJECT AUTHORITY LIST OR FILE. An official list of subject headings used in a given catalog and the references made to them.

SUBJECT HEADING A word or a group of words indicating a subject under which all material dealing with the same theme is entered in a catalog.

SUBSERIES. A series within a series; that is, a series which always appears in conjunction with another, usually more comprehensive, series of which it forms a section. Its title may or may not be dependent on the title of the main series.

SUBTITLE. A secondary title, often used to expand or limit the title proper.

"THIRD" INDENTION. The distance from the left edge of a catalog card at which, according to predetermined rules, certain parts of the description begin or continue; generally as far to the right of the second indention as the second indention is to the right of the first indention.

TITLE. A word, phrase, character, or group of characters, normally appearing in an item, naming the item or the work contained in it. See also ALTERNATIVE TITLE; COVER TITLE; HALF TITLE; TITLE PROPER; UNIFORM TITLE.

TITLE ANALYTICAL ENTRY see ANALYTICAL ENTRY.

TITLE ENTRY. The record of a work in a catalog or a bibliography under the title, generally beginning with the first word not an article. In a card catalog a title entry may be a main entry or an added entry.

TITLE PAGE. A page at the beginning of an item bearing the title proper and usually, though not necessarily, the statement of responsibility and the data relating to publication. The leaf

bearing the title page is commonly called the title page although properly called the title leaf. See also ADDED TITLE PAGE.

TITLE PROPER. The chief name of an item, including any alternative title but excluding parallel titles and other title informa-

TRACING. 1. The record of the headings under which an item is represented in the catalog. 2. The record of the references that have been made to a name or to the title of an item that is represented in the catalog.

UNIFORM TITLE. 1. The particular title by which a work is to be identified for cataloging purposes. 2. The particular title used to distinguish the heading for a work from the heading for a different work. A conventional collective title used to collocate publications of an author, composer, or corporate body containing several works or extracts, etc., from several works, e.g., complete works, several works in a particular literary or musical form.

UNIT RECORD. The basic catalog record, in the form of a main entry, which when duplicated may be used as a unit for all other entries for that work in the catalog by the addition of the appropriate headings. See also MAIN ENTRY.

VERSO. 1. The left-hand page of a book, usually bearing an even page number. 2. The side of a printed sheet intended to be read second.

WITHDRAWAL. The process of removing from library records all entries for a book no longer in the library.

References

A. L. A. Glossary (Chicago: American Library Association, 1943).

Anglo-American Cataloguing Rules; Second Edition (Chicago: American Library Association, 1978).

Corinne Bacon, Classification. rev. ed. (Chicago: American Library Association, 1925).

C. A. Cutter, Rules for a Dictionary Catalog. 4th ed. rewritten (Washington: Govt. Print. Off., 1904).

Bodhan S. Wynar, Introduction to Cataloging and Classification. 6th ed. (Littleton, Colo.: Libraries Unlimited, 1980).

Appendix C

AIDS IN THE CATALOGING OF A SMALL LIBRARY

General reference tools for the verification of personal, corporate, and geographical names are not included, as it is assumed that every library would have these in its collection, or acquire them (Reference Books for Small and Medium-sized Libraries, 2d ed., American Library Association, 1979, is a good selection aid).

ALA Filing Rules. Filing Committee, Resources and Technical Services Division, American Library Association. Chicago: American Library Association, 1980.
ALA Rules for Filing Catalog Cards. 2d ed. abr. Prepared by the ALA Editorial Committee, Subcommittee on the ALA Rules for Filing Catalog Cards, Pauline A. Seely, Chairman and Editor. Chicago: American Library Association, 1968.
American Book Publishing Record. New York: R. R. Bowker. Monthly, annual cumulations.
Anglo-American Cataloguing Rules. 2d ed. Prepared by the American Library Association, the British Library, the Canadian Committee on Cataloguing, The Library Association, the Library of Congress. Michael Gorman and Paul W. Winkler, eds. Chicago: American Library Association, 1978.
Berman, Sanford. "Do-It Yourself Subject Cataloging: Sources and Tools." Library Journal 107 (April 15, 1982):785-786.
Berman, Sanford. The Joy of Cataloging: Essays, Letters, Reviews, and Other Explosions. Phoenix, Ariz.: Oryx Press, 1981.
The Booklist. Chicago: American Library Association. Semimonthly, once in August.
Brown, Lucy Gregor. Core Media Collection for Secondary Schools. 2d ed. New York: R. R. Bowker, 1979.
Chen, Lois Mai. Cataloging and Classification: an Introduction. New York: McGraw-Hill, 1981.
Children's Catalog. 14th ed. New York: H. W. Wilson, 1981.
Cutter, Charles A. Cutter-Sanborn Three-figure Author Table. Swanson-Swift revision, 1969. Littleton, Colo.: Libraries Unlimited, ca. 1980.
Dewey, Melvil. Abridged Dewey Decimal Classification and Relative Index. Edition 11. Edited under the direction of Benjamin A. Custer. Albany, N.Y.: Forest Press, Division of Lake Placid Education Foundation, 1979.
Dewey, Melvil. Dewey Decimal Classification and Relative Index. Edition 19. Edited under the direction of Benjamin A. Cus-

ter. 3 vols. Albany, N.Y.: Forest Press, Division of
Lake Placid Education Foundation, 1979.

Downing, Mildred Harlow. Introduction to Cataloging and Classification. 5th ed. Jefferson, N.C.: McFarland, 1981.
The Elementary School Library Collection. 13th ed. Edited by Lois
Winkel. Newark, N.J.: The Bro-Dart Foundation, 1982.
Fleischer, Eugene and Goodman, Helen. Cataloging Audiovisual Materials: a Manual Based on the Anglo-American Cataloguing
Rules II. New York: Neal-Schuman, 1980.
Gorman, Michael. The Concise AACR2; Being a Rewritten and Simplified Version of Anglo-American Cataloguing Rules, Second
Edition. Chicago: American Library Association, 1981.
Hill, Donna. The Picture File: A Manual and Curriculum-related
Subject Heading List. 2d ed. Syracuse, N.Y.: Gaylord,
1978.
Junior High School Library Catalog. 4th ed. New York: H.W.
Wilson, 1980.
Maxwell, Margaret F. Handbook for AACR2: Explaining and Illustrating "Anglo-American Cataloguing Rules Second Edition."
Chicago: American Library Association, 1980.
Media Review Digest. Ann Arbor, Mich.: Pierian Press. Annual,
semi-annual supplements.
Miller, Shirley. The Vertical File and Its Satellites: A Handbook
of Acquisition, Processing, and Organization. 2d ed. Littleton, Colo.: Libraries Unlimited, 1979.
Nickel, Mildred. Steps to Service: a Handbook of Procedures for
the School Library Media Center. rev. ed. Chicago: American Library Association, 1983.
Olson, Nancy B. Cataloging of Audiovisual Materials: a Manual
Based on AACR2. Mankato, Minn.: Minnesota Scholarly
Press, 1981.
Osborne, Andrew D. Serial Publications: Their Place and Treatment in Libraries. 3rd ed. Chicago: American Library
Association, 1980.
Public Library Catalog. 7th ed. New York: H.W. Wilson, 1978.
Redfern, Brian L. Organizing Music in Libraries. rev. ed. 2
vols. Hamden, Conn.: Linnet Books, 1978-1979.
Rogers, JoAnn V. Nonprint Cataloging for Multimedia Collections:
a guide based on AACR2. Littleton, Colo.: Libraries Unlimited, 1982.
Schwann-1 Record & Tape Guide. Boston: Schwann. Monthly.
Schwann-2 Record & Tape Guide. Boston: Schwann. Semi-annual.
Sears List of Subject Headings. 12th ed. Edited by Barbara M.
Westby. New York: H.W. Wilson, 1982.
Senior High School Library Catalog. 12th ed. New York: H.W.
Wilson, 1982.
Weihs, Jean; Lewis, Shirley; and MacDonald, Janet. Nonbook Materials: the Organization of Integrated Collections. 2d ed.
Ottowa, Ont.: Canadian Library Association, 1979.
Working List of Subject Headings for Children's Literature. Washington, D.C.: Library of Congress, Cataloging Distribution
Service, 1982.

The Readers' Guide to Periodical Literature and indexes to newspapers and to the literature of specific fields are useful in establishing name headings and suggesting subject headings for new subjects. The Special Libraries Association (235 Park Avenue South, New York, N.Y. 10008) maintains a file of special classification schemes. The Church and Synagogue Library Association (P.O. Box 1130, Bryn Mawr, PA 19010) and the Music Library Association (2017 Walnut Street, Philadelphia, PA 19103) are only two of a number of organizations to which the cataloger of a specialized collection can turn for assistance.

HCL Cataloging Bulletin 142, 169
H. W. Wilson Co. 88, 98, 105, 286
   The Reference Shelf 105
   Standard Catalogs 60, 109, 122, 125, 127, 139, 148, 162, 163
Half title 23, 352
Handbook for AACR2 (Maxwell) 192
Hanging indention 352
Haykin, D. J. 159
Headings 4, 13, 48, 58-59, 86
   definition of term 352
   form of
      corporate names 68-80
      personal names 58-68
      uniform titles 80-85
   see also Subject headings
Hennepin County Public Library see HCL Cataloging Bulletin
Holdings 44, 352
Hyphenated word, arrangement of entries with 316-317, 327-328

ISBD see International Standard Book Description
ISBN see International Standard Book Number
ISSN see International Standard Serial Number
Illustrations 36, 37, 352
Illustrators 4, 87, 88; see also Author entries
Imprint date 15, 352
Imprints 15, 31-32; see also Publication, distribution, etc.
"In" entry 99, 100-101
Indention 19, 352; see also Hanging indention; "First" indention; "Second"
   indention; "Third" indention
Indexes 55, 106, 109, 139
Indexing and abstracting services 138
Inforonics 300
Initials 56, 63, 317
International Meeting of Cataloging Experts (1969) 11
International Standard Book Description (ISBD) 11, 12, 18, 19
   definition of term 353
   descriptive information 22
   physical description of book 36
International Standard Book Number (ISBN) 18, 44-45, 105, 278, 353
International Standard Serial Number (ISSN) 15, 44, 118, 353
International standardization of cataloging practices 10-11
Introduction date 352
Inventory control 7, 173, 279, 337

Jackets 334
Jobbers 161, 200, 285, 287, 300
Joint authors 4, 51-53, 87, 352
Joint pseudonym 63
Junior High School Library Catalog (H. W. Wilson Co.) 122
Juvenile books see Children's materials

Kits 180, 228, 251, 263
   main entry 263
   physical description 263
   sources of information 262